Organization and innovation

ISSUES IN SOCIETY
Series Editor: Tim May

Current and forthcoming titles

Zygmunt Bauman: *Work, Consumerism and the New Poor*
David Byrne: *Social Exclusion*
Graham Crow: *Social Solidarities*
Mitchell Dean: *Governing Societies*
Gerard Delanty: *Citizenship in a Global Age*
Steve Fuller: *The Governance of Science*
Les Johnston: *Late Modernity, Crime and Justice*
David Knights and Darren McCabe: *Organization and Innovation: Guru Schemes and American Dreams*
Nick Lee: *Childhood and Society*
David Lyon: *Surveillance Society*
Linda McKie: *Families, Violence and Social Change*
Graham Scambler: *Health and Social Change*
Graham Scambler: *Sport and Society: History, Power and Culture*
Piet Strydom: *Risk, Environment and Society*

Organization and innovation: guru schemes and American dreams

**DAVID KNIGHTS AND
DARREN MCCABE**

Open University Press

Open University Press
McGraw-Hill Education
McGraw-Hill House
Shoppenhangers Road
Maidenhead
Berkshire
England
SL6 2QL

email: enquiries@openup.co.uk
world wide web: www.openup.co.uk

First published 2003

A catalogue record of this book is available from the British Library

ISBN 0 335 20684 0 (pb)   0 335 20685 9 (hb)

Library of Congress Cataloging-in-Publication Data
CIP data has been applied for

Typeset by RefineCatch Limited, Bungay, Suffolk
Printed in Great Britain by Bell and Bain Ltd, Glasgow

Contents

Series editor's foreword   vii
Acknowledgements   x

Introduction: innovation (in)action   1
  Organization of the book   4

Part one   7

1 Management innovation in historical perspective   9
  Scientific management   13
  Human relations   16
  Neo-human relations   18
  Post-war consensus: collective bargaining   20
  Thatcherism   22
  Conclusion   25

**2 The false promise of the American Dream: organization,
  innovation and change management**   27
  The American Dream   29
  The Great Gatsby   33
  Innovation in context   49
  Business evangelists in a disenchanted world: *Plus ça change,
    plus la même chose*   43

3 A research framework: TQM as an illustrative case   49
  Rational managerialists   50
  A critical control focus   51
  Case study: Carco   53
  A processual approach   57
  Towards an alternative perspective for organizational research   60

Case study: Inco Insurance   64
Summary   71

Part two   75

**4 Manufacturing autonomy: re-engineering and culture
change**   77
Call centre work   79
Case study: Loanco   81
Discussion and summary   94

**5 Tales of the unexpected: strategic management and
innovation**   97
Introduction   97
Strategic planning and innovation   99
The context   103
The case studies   105
Discussion and summary   113

6 Teamworking and resistance   115
Teamworking in retrospect   116
Case study: Intermotors   124
Discussion and summary   139

7 A 'one team' approach to knowledge management   143
Knowledge management in perspective   145
Case study: Loanco revisited   149
Discussion and summary   158

Part three   163

8 Conclusion   165

Notes   178
References   187
Index   201

Series editor's foreword

Collectively, the social sciences develop knowledge that contributes to an understanding of the dynamics of social life in contemporary society. In the process they provide mirrors into which we can gaze in order to understand not only what we as human beings have been and what we are now, but to inform possibilities about what we might become. This is not only about understanding the reasons people give for their actions in terms of the social, political and economic contexts in which they act. It also concerns the hopes, wishes and aspirations that people, in their different cultural ways, hold.

In any society that claims to have democratic aspirations, these hopes and wishes are not for the social scientist to prescribe. Social scientists, however, have a valued role to play in encouraging us to rethink our lives and the social and organizational contexts of their reproduction. After all, in focusing upon what we have been and what we are now, what we might become is inevitably illuminated: the retrospective and prospective become fused.

This international series was devised with this general ethos in mind. It offers a forum in which ideas and topics of interest are interrogated in terms of their importance for understanding key social issues. This is achieved through a connection between style, structure and content that aims to be both illuminating and challenging, as well as representing an original contribution to the subject under discussion.

Social scientific analyses of organization and innovation of the kind presented in this volume reflect the aims of this series to raise critical questions about prescriptive attempts to organise people's lives. They challenge strategic innovations that deny the ability of people to have acted otherwise and thus to imagine and practice different ways of organizing, working and living together.

In the field of management and innovation we find many prescriptions concerning how people should think and act. Ever since the interventions of Taylor's Scientific Management in the early part of the last century, 'one best way' solutions to managerial and workplace problems have characterised the innovation literature. Apart from government regulations, of course, business is comparatively free from democratic constraints. Yet this does not mean that universal, all encompassing solutions are effective independent of the contexts of their application. In societies that treat autonomy and self-determination as synonymous with what it is to be human, autocratically imposed 'one best way' solutions lack legitimacy.

Faced with being facilitated to become something other than one 'is', there is only limitless potential devoid of the clutter of the past. History is an irrelevance for those for whom the future is everything. The individual then has a choice: to move energetically with expectations or get left behind in an era in which the promise of a better future or what David Knights and Darren McCabe here describe as the 'American Dream' plunges us into ever increasing aspirations. 'Innovate', 'create', 'open up possibilities', or become 'stale', 'complacent' and 'unimaginative'. As these choices play out in social life, they take place in situations of what appear like infinite opportunities. Yet this freedom to innovate has its price since to resist the pressure attracts the modern equivalent of the Luddite label of living in the past.

The authors seek to traverse a fine line between a sceptical distancing from the rhetoric of a perfect future and the limits of an impoverished past through providing a systematic analysis of the conditions and consequences of management innovations. Taking us through changes in organizational thought provides them with a strong platform for the interrogation of these ideas in practice. In so doing they draw heavily on the work of Michel Foucault. Prior to Foucault, power was seen as a property of persons or institutions. By contrast, when power is seen to be simply an aspect of social relations, the issues that are part of the exercise of attempts to re-engineer the workplace and the motivations and actions of its employees can be more fully examined.

David Knights and Darren McCabe seek to display the tensions and contradictions that are played out in these practices and how they often result in consequences that are unanticipated and undesirable. The authors show how identity becomes a restless pre-occupation especially where the innovative organisational culture is continually in a disjuncture with the reality that it claims to reflect. The process of permanent innovation is bound to terminate in transgression with rewards being differentially distributed according to the very hierarchies that are denied by the discourses of innovation. In coming to terms which these changes, individuals within organisations then display a number of reactions, ranging from fatalism and apathy to enthusiasm and resistance.

The overall result of this study is an insightful analysis that is not prepared to take the current managerial hype at face value, but instead subject it to critical scrutiny via a series of case studies. Refusing to endorse the faith that so many have in, for example, technological fixes and the gurus who preach salvation for those who have lost their way, the study constantly returns to the disjuncture between the dream of change and everyday reality without allusions to a unitary past or future. In an age when so many relieve themselves of systematic thinking through dialogue and instead fall back on dogma disguised as democracy and opportunity, this book fills an important gap in contemporary understandings of the nature and effect of organisational innovation.

Tim May

Acknowledgements

We wish to thank all those employees and managers whose contribution made this book possible, whose names and identities we have omitted as a condition of research access. We also wish to thank Tim May for his helpful suggestions in the final stages of this manuscript and we would like to thank Jane Pope for her assistance in the final stages of the production of this book.

Introduction: innovation (in)action

This book attempts a sociologically informed, detailed empirical analysis of a diverse range of recent management innovations including business process re-engineering (BPR), culture change, knowledge management (KM), strategic management, teamworking and total quality management (TQM). While it seeks to study innovation in action, it also reflects on some of the conditions and consequences of implementation that can result in what we call innovation *inaction*. No question, many of our case study companies have sought to adopt a range of management innovations, new organizational structures and distinctive methods of managing. However, often these innovations fail to be fully implemented, have effects that are far from those intended, or are abandoned in favour of the most recent management panacea. Also, much remains unaffected by these innovations. For example, we have found that a preoccupation with cost cutting, short-term profits and the reproduction of prevailing relations of power and inequality are undiminished by such interventions. What the field research invariably indicates is that the problems of implementing innovations amount to a lack of radical intent, insufficient action and inadequate commitment on the part of management rather than failure due to employee resistance. Where there was strong evidence of resistance, it tended to be targeted at management due to its inconsistent, contradictory and weak commitment to particular innovative practices.

Running through the book is a thematic focus on the idea of innovation as both a spiritual and pragmatic panacea – something akin to the American Dream. Guru interventions claim to eradicate the painful limits of the past and displace them with a 'progressive', frictionless future that promises new levels of productivity and performance, peace and prosperity, plenitude and pleasure. In our empirical studies, this dream is discrepant with the lives of many of those we have talked to and observed. Nonetheless the proliferation of dreams is evident in the promise of each new generation of management fads and fashions. While management gurus proffer dreams from which everyone supposedly gains, they do so in a capitalist context that is already characterized by immense inequality. Their prescriptions in no way tackle, question or even acknowledge this context. Indeed, their endeavours merely reproduce what they take for granted, directing us up the wooden hill to the land of snooze, where the possibilities of alternative dreams are to be carefully forgotten and locked away along with Teddy and Dolly.

In a Swedish context, business practitioners report that 'our dreams' are the source of creativity, 'inspiration and power' (Holmberg and Strannegård 2002: 40). Indeed the 'common theme [of entrepreneurs] is that of dreaming' and one entrepreneur even suggested that 'If a nation has stopped dreaming it is in trouble' (2002: 44). While for entrepreneurs dreams may be the engine of innovation, creativity and diversity, we suggest in this book that the underlying rationale of such dreaming needs to be exposed and subjected to critical scrutiny, for too much unreflective dreaming can be dangerous. This is especially so when a major purpose or unanticipated effect of it is to produce a soporific population trapped in their own impossible future or worse, the unacceptable present. We want to resist following Goffman (1975:14) in merely 'sneaking in' just to 'watch the way the people snore', for our aim is to try and disrupt the tranquillity so that at least some of us will be shaken from our slumbers. Thus we are concerned less with the misleading promises behind the various dreams that are sold to us than with how they induce a slumber that deprives us of our scepticism. We want to focus on the way that these dreams reinforce the everyday world we inhabit, rendering our taken-for-granted assumptions ever more solid and unquestionable.[1]

We focus on the contemporary American Dream rather than dreaming *per se* because since the rise of US hegemony in the twentieth century, it is the dream of individual material affluence and symbolic success that has driven and underpinned management innovations. While on close reflection we may recognize it to be a myth, the current American Dream nonetheless has the dangerous potential of legitimizing prevailing inequalities under the auspices of everyone being able to rise to the top through their hard work and endeavour. It misleads by promising what it cannot deliver but also diverts attention and energy from other more critical visions that question rather than reproduce the status quo. Although innovations may appear to be mere fashions (Abrahamson 1996), there is a tendency for addiction and, like addicts, we may be swept up in the promise of the next fix. We are so trapped in our headlong dash that we forget that we are on a conveyor belt that churns out products and services that some do not need, many cannot afford and others can only look upon from afar as they are denied access to the conveyor. The numerous cycles of innovation that are presented as the ultimate salvation for a tired and troubled organization are not unlike injections of stimulants that require constant renewal but generate a dependence. We want to question the logic of the 'quick fix' where all social and organizational problems are reduced to their technical form. Instead we encourage critical reflection that may lead to rehabilitation through action. The aim is to counter the message of bland mainstream textbooks that rarely propose a new direction or question the gains from the latest fix.

The book emerged out of nearly a decade of collaboration between the authors in working on Economic and Social Research Council (ESRC) research funded projects[2] where, instead of just interviewing managers and employees, there was also an attempt at observing how innovations were implemented − or not as the case may be. We began by feeling that both supporters and critics respectively provided exaggerated representations of innovation. Much of this exaggeration, we believed, was possible because neither supporters nor critics conducted much empirical research that might have restrained their respective positive and negative images of innovation. We believe that this book might help to counter such excesses. While remaining critical of management interventions that simply reproduce the status quo, we want to urge greater self-reflection in the expectation that this may provide the conditions and impetus for alternative dreams to arise.

Each chapter seeks to analyse management and organization critically by focusing on the dynamic interconnections between management and innovation as it affects people at work, or more particularly, their lived experience. The book's purpose is to explore the idea that innovation is embedded in the reconstitution of positions of privilege and processes of management control. In this sense it is concerned to render the construction and reproduction of management control visible within the processes and practices of managing work organizations. In our view, contemporary management practices privilege that which enables them to 'be in control'. This is not to suggest, however, that management behaviour is uncontested, stable and always and everywhere internally consistent. Indeed, the focus on innovation provides us with a site in which to examine the tensions, contradictions and conflicts surrounding managerial interventions. While such innovations are designed effectively to increase employee effort, productivity and quality of output, we found much evidence of their disruption through unintended consequences when not being openly resisted.

The chapters draw on a series of discrete literatures extending from the gurus of innovation, on the one hand, to the sociology of management and organizations on the other. More specifically, through drawing upon empirical research, the chapters seek to provide a link between the prescriptive hype of unadulterated managerialism and the critical literature that dismisses innovation as a conspiracy to control. We draw on these various literatures to explore concepts and ideas that may elucidate the management of innovation and the lived experience of innovation at work. Drawing on our fieldwork from the financial services and manufacturing sectors, our aim is to 'bring alive' these ideas for the reader. The book examines the way in which power and identity relations contribute to and, in turn, are reconstituted by innovation.

Organization of the book

The book is organized into three parts. The first part sets out our theoretical framework and the contextual background to our concerns with the raft of recent management panaceas. This encompasses Chapters 1 to 3. In the first chapter we locate our discussion of innovation in a wider historical context, considering developments such as Taylorism and human relations. We explore the conditions that have given rise to the popularity of a variety of interventions, ranging from excellence to BPR, that have culminated in the export and adoption of a contemporary version of the American Dream by managers in the UK. We would not, of course, wish to argue that managers would necessarily be aware of, define or understand their actions in this way. Nor are we suggesting that management is an omniscient or unified body (Knights and Murray 1994; Watson 1994; McCabe 2000). We do argue, however, that a reflection and reinforcement of the American Dream has been the emphasis on individualism as extolled by Margaret Thatcher and epitomized by the 'enterprise' culture (Guest 1990; du Gay and Salaman 1992) over the past 20 years. This has provided the necessary, though not sufficient, conditions for the proliferation of a range of management panaceas as advanced largely by American gurus although the success of Japanese management, especially since the 1970s, is intimately bound up with the explosion of interest in concepts such as quality management, culture and teamworking.[3]

Chapter 2 concentrates on the underlying message of the contemporary American Dream and establishes links between the dream and the false promises of current management thinking and practice. Then, in Chapter 3, we seek to elaborate the distinctiveness of our approach towards studying organizations, change management and innovation. We do so by exploring quality management and in particular, TQM. We draw selectively on two case studies to demonstrate empirically how our approach can advance an understanding of the dangers that innovations present for managers and employees, but also the limits to the gurus' projects.

The second part of the book focuses more specifically on our empirical research and includes Chapters 4 to 7. These chapters focus upon different innovations and in total the book draws upon seven case studies. Although each chapter focuses primarily upon one innovation, they do not attempt to treat each innovation as distinct from all the others. This is because the innovations and their assumptions both theoretically and empirically exhibit considerable overlaps. Hence, for some organizations, TQM and BPR both encompass teamworking and all of these can be said to impact on corporate culture. Moreover, such innovations are frequently bound up with corporate strategies such as cost cutting and market differentiation.

Chapter 4 examines a case study of a major building society (Loanco) and its attempts to re-engineer a call and processing centre. This included an attempt by management to change the culture of the centre so as to encourage staff to take on more responsibility and to think of themselves as autonomous agents. The case is an example of the 'productive' exercise of power but we also identify contradictions in management's message of autonomy as it conflicted with traditional hierarchical power relations and conditions of employment insecurity. As we shall see, these contradictions seriously undermined the attempts by management to reconstitute the way in which employees understood and interpreted their world.

Chapter 5 explores the 'strategic' introduction of innovations such as TQM and BPR. Drawing on three case studies, it considers the unintended consequences that arose during the attempts to improve service quality in two banks and an insurance company. It argues that even an 'emergent' approach towards strategy tends to overstate management's ability to behave in a rational way and to exercise power over others.

Chapter 6 examines the case of Intermotors – an automobile manufacturing company. It considers the introduction of teamworking during the 1990s in a context of large-scale redundancies and autocratic management decision making. The case climaxes in a discussion of an industrial dispute that spontaneously erupted following a decision to withhold a profit-related bonus payment. The chapter illuminates our 'relational' understanding of power and reinforces our argument about the unintended consequences that frequently arise from the exercise of power by management.

In Chapter 7 we revisit Loanco and explore the attempt at its head office to introduce what Drucker (1988: 45) refers to as 'an information-based organisation'. At Loanco, this amounted to introducing an email and intranet system so as to encourage staff to share knowledge about work. According to Drucker (1992: 95), 'In the knowledge society, managers must prepare to abandon everything they know', but at Loanco this was far from the case. Indeed, despite couching KM in the language of a 'one-team vision', management continued to be preoccupied with the bottom line, control and cost cutting, and this seriously impaired the success of the initiative.

By way of a conclusion, the third and final part of the book outlines the possibilities that other dreams have to offer and pulls together some of the main findings of our research. It reflects upon the contribution that we believe our work can make towards a critical analysis of organizations but also its limitations. Our relationship with those we research is considered and the very real limits to the impact that it is possible to have as academics. For us, this reflects the power relations that we confront as researchers; the necessarily modest status of our research, but also the resistance that is met when attempts are made to impose our worldview upon others.

PART ONE

Management innovation in historical perspective[1]

In the Introduction, we suggested that the cultural and ideological under-pinning of the proliferation and belief in recent innovations is the 'success ethic' – evident in the American Dream. This is neatly illustrated by the carica-ture of America as the land where 'there are no poor people, just people who have not yet become rich' (Jacques 2002: 26). Although often depicted as the rise from 'rags to riches', we have argued that the American Dream is a myth that legitimizes the existing system of inequality. But the dream thrives in its power to mobilize others to pursue happiness through seeking material and symbolic success. In its most extreme form, this is the cult of celebrity and the 'Hollywoodization' of life, as ironically and dramatically depicted in the David Lynch film, *Mulholland Drive*.

The traditional way of contextualizing any focus of analysis in the social sciences is to trace the historical sequence of the topic under investigation back to its apparent embryonic origins or 'primitive' form. These accounts perceive innovation in terms of technological trajectories from the horse-drawn plough of the agricultural revolution and the steam engine of the Industrial Revolu-tion, through to the current information revolution of micro-electronics. We find such an approach theoretically inconsistent with our analytical designs, but empirically the topic of innovation also does not lend itself to the historicist view of continuity and evolutionary progress from a sequential origin. Of course, it is always possible to detect or construct a sense of continuity between one set of innovations and those that succeed them, but this is often an artifice of writers who believe that the social sciences offer little if they cannot show 'progress'. We believe it is healthy to retain some degree of scepticism toward accounts that present a plausible continuity or progression in the (his)story of innovation. We are therefore not convinced by accounts that point to a 'sequence suggesting an alternation between normative and rational ideologies

Table 1.1   The succession of managerial ideologies since 1870

Ideology	Era of ascent	Tenor
Industrial betterment	1870–1900	Normative
Scientific management	1900–23	Rational
Welfare capitalism/human relations	1923–55	Normative
Systems rationalism	1955–88	Rational
Organizational culture	1980–90	Normative

Source: Adapted from Barley and Kunda (1992).

of control' (Barley and Kunda 1992: 384) linked to 50-year Kondratieff economic cycles[2] (see Table 1.1) or 'pendulum swings' (Abrahamson 1997).

While both management control and technology are important conditions and consequences of reorganization practice, they rarely are the sole determinants as is implied in this kind of analysis. In our view, despite concerted efforts to demonstrate progress or a rational ordering, as each new offering is deemed to resolve or eradicate the problems identified in its predecessor, often management innovations are discontinuous and non-linear in their developments. Alternatively, a range of previous innovations may simply be recombined in a form that gives the appearance of novelty to what is little more than a repackaging of what has gone before. Probably the best example of such repackaging is BPR. Here the novelty is less in the content of the innovation than in the way it is presented as a solution to a set of problems that are, at a particular time, seen as highly significant by practising managers. As Grint and Case (2000: 26) argue, the issue is 'less with whether the *content* of reengineering is radically different *and* demonstrably superior to anything that went before, and rather more with *why* the package is effective in its particular envelope of space and time'. When examining management innovation it is equally as important to study the context of its promotion and practice as its content. In doing so, we are led away from a linear conception of historical evolution and toward an understanding of innovative developments in terms of the conditions that made them possible and, more importantly, plausible and thereby practical in their effects. Consequently, in this chapter we attempt to provide a selective history of innovations that have been groundbreaking in the sense of providing the conditions in which other later innovations have become possible.

It seems to us that management innovations often have paradoxical and unintended effects such as transforming workers into individualized subjects at the same time as attempting to resolve the problems that result from so doing. Such interventions or ways of managing are frequently a response to previous problems where, for instance, the human relations movement emerged to counter the excessive individualism promoted by Taylorism that had begun to undermine collective commitment and responsibility. Moreover, from bureaucracy (Weber 1947) to scientific management (Taylor 1911), and from Fordism through human relations (Mayo 1933), to the most recent quality and re-engineering innovations, the effect of management intervention has often been to stimulate resistance or apathy among workers towards management's goals/aims. Indeed many innovations appear to have faltered in the face of contradictions and tensions that they cannot hope to resolve. What we want to argue, then, is that the conditions that make possible each new innovation are not so much their surface claims as an intensifying strain within capitalist economies between production and consumption, collaboration and competition, and cooperation and conflict.

The strain between production and consumption takes a number of forms. First, there is the simple contradiction within capitalism that productive efficiency can be self-defeating. For it may generate 'excess capacity' or more output than is effectively demanded by consumers who are already satiated or incapable of paying for the goods and services at the prices demanded. One solution to this problem is to increase the variety and range of products and services on offer, and through advertising and sales, stimulate demand. For the affluent, this means that new products are purchased each season or year. For the less affluent, it means increased debt rendered possible through easily accessible credit from financial institutions.

Second, the preoccupation with constraining costs through comparatively low wages in order to maximize profits has the overall effect of restricting effective demand. Mass consumption depends on consumers having sufficient income to buy the goods and services that are produced but the cost preoccupations of business clearly are a constraint on this. As has been intimated, a solution to this problem is the growth of readily accessible credit and an alternative is to engage in cost cutting price wars.[3] At the level of production, however, the most rational solution is to increase productivity through the more effective use of capital (e.g. new technology, new methods of working) and/or work intensification. Costs then rise at a marginally lower rate than output, and consequently wages are sufficient to enable consumers to purchase goods and/or service their debts, thus maintaining increasing levels of consumption.

But here comes a third form of the contradiction between production and consumption – that between an individual short-term and a collective long-term solution to the other two contradictions. What might be good for an individual company might be bad for companies in aggregate and vice versa. It might therefore be beneficial for an individual company to cut costs dramatically by downsizing and shedding labour but if this is carried out by a large number of companies, effective demand will be curtailed dramatically. Conversely, for a company to spend money on advertising might be of benefit to all companies. This is because, except where it relates to the established brands such as Coca-Cola or Benetton, in general advertising rarely establishes a direct link with consumption. Rather, it reinforces an ideology of consumption such that all producers benefit from its continuity and expansion.

This form of the contradiction was exacerbated by changes in twentieth-century capitalism whereby fund managers in the City demanded increased short-term profits and, in their absence, shifted capital funds to other companies, thus bringing down the share price and rendering the abandoned company vulnerable to takeover. This dynamic undermines investment, employment security and the ability of both consumers and producers to adopt a long-term perspective. The scandals during 2002 around the falsifying of financial accounts in Enron and WorldCom to secure or maintain share prices exemplify the intensity of such pressures.[4] Under these conditions, what turns out to be 'bad' for the individual companies may be bad for all as faith in capitalism erodes. These scandals certainly had a more devastating effect on global stock markets than even the 11 September 2001 suicide attacks on the World Trade Center in New York. However, even when scandals remain restricted to a minority of companies, the tensions between collaboration and conflict and between cooperation and competition continue both at the level of the firm *vis-à-vis* other firms and at the internal level of relations within firms. While reform of corporate accounting standards has been a knee-jerk reaction to the scandals, little of this is likely to protect employees (as opposed to shareholders) from the fallout when corporate executives breach the trust that is granted them.[5]

Short of falling foul of the Monopolies and Mergers Commission, collaboration and cooperation between firms has been seen as a strategy that can overcome the disadvantages of competition. Networks and partnerships often take place through the supply chain in place of vertical integration – a classic example being supermarkets who then are able to control the quality and quantity of supply. Inside firms, tensions and contradictions between collaboration and competition may revolve around career interests; for individuals not only compete with one another for jobs, promotion and resources but also compete to demonstrate that they are collaborating (i.e. are you a team player?).

Management innovations are partly designed to tackle or limit the counterproductive tendencies that can result from these tensions. One aspect of the strain is reflected in and reproduced by the launch of corporate culture change programmes where there is a stress on unity and identification with the 'collective' corporate enterprise. Yet managers simultaneously insist on measuring and monitoring individual performance and this reinforces a preoccupation with the pursuit of individual career and ambition that runs counter to a collectivist subjectivity.

Taylorism and the more recent concern to promote individual responsibility and accountability through the discourse of enterprise (du Gay and Salaman 1992; du Gay 1996) are examples of the individualizing tendencies that innovation can promote. Many contemporary interventions attempt to bridge this dilemma by appealing simultaneously to individual and collective values. That is, they combine both individualistic conceptions of economic 'rationality' and more collective 'normative' ideologies of control. This places a contradiction at the heart of innovations such as re-engineering and teamworking that is difficult to reconcile. In recent years, part of the problem has been that each new intervention is often as contradictory as that which went before it. In order to summarize and provide an analytical framework for the chapter, the following summary (see Table 1.2) indicates the diverse assumptions and sanctions of a

Table 1.2   From scientific management to enterprise

Assumptions	Strategy	Sanction/reward	Problems
Economic 'man'[6]	Scientific management	Payment linked to individual output	Economic instrumental self-interest
Social 'man'	Human relations	Social recognition; work groups	Preoccupation with group or team rather than corporate interests; absence of individual motivation
Self-actualizing 'man'	Neo-human relations/ motivation theory	Positive rewards/ success linked to individual performance/ achievements	Psychological or individual self-interest
Collective 'man'	Collective bargaining	Negotiated outcomes/ shared rewards	Reinforced polarized class interests that reproduced instrumental economic self-interest
Enterprise/self-interested 'man'	Anti-unionism; privatization; competition; flexibility; redundancy; downsizing	Individual rewards	Demise of unionism; growing gap rich/poor; individual self-interest

range of historical developments and innovations together with the problems and/or unintended consequences that arose in their wake.

Scientific management

Taylor's basic thesis was that inefficiency in industry resulted from unproductive labour, tolerated by incompetent management. Employees systematically limited their output and pace of work largely because of arbitrary management practices (Taylor 1911). Taylor argued that managerial ignorance about the exact amount of output to be expected results in 'rule of thumb' methods of fixing work rates and rewards, which are then continually contested and negotiated. In those circumstances, labour is quite rational in seeing 'that no job is done faster than it has been in the past' (Taylor 1911: 22). What is necessary, according to Taylor, is to discover the 'one best way' or quickest and most efficient method of performing a given task through what was later to become known as work study. Here the form of work would be 'scientifically' ordered, prescribed in a detailed fashion and linked to rates of pay that employees could no longer contest. Other techniques, such as selecting a 'first-class man' for the type of work and ensuring that incentives guaranteed 'a fair day's pay for a fair day's work' would then need to be employed in order to support the system's potential to improve productivity.

Scientific management was also associated with changes in the organizational structure whereby military-type command hierarchies typical of bureaucracies had to be abandoned and replaced by a functional system. Here 'each workman, instead of coming in direct contact with the management at one point only, namely, through his gang boss, receives his daily orders and help directly from eight different bosses' (Taylor 1911: 99–100). Only half these managers – the gang boss, speed boss, inspector and repair boss – would be in active personal contact with the worker in that the other four, responsible for planning work, were to communicate largely in writing. It was management's task to ensure that employees were adequately trained in the 'scientific principles' of job design and work measurement. Although Taylor has been criticized for his psychological naïveté regarding worker motivation, he seems to have recognized the importance of the labourer's personal commitment to the methods and techniques they employ.

Taylor recognized that in large organizations workers had the power and technical skill to outwit a management that was no longer familiar with the detailed content of labour tasks. If it was to attain control/improve efficiency, management needed to redress the balance by acquiring knowledge that would appropriate the worker's technical superiority, and Taylor's scheme was designed precisely with this objective in mind. Whether or not Taylor was aware of the 'historical importance to capitalism of the re-assertion of control over labour' (Clegg 1979: 14) cannot be easily ascertained. But there is little doubt that managers were often devoid of this vision since they strongly resisted the introduction of his methods into their factories (Rose 1975).

Somewhat paradoxically then, it may be argued that scientific management presupposed the very management controls that it was designed to reassert! Hence it was widely adopted in command economies where authoritarian control was the most dominant feature of the organization. While in practice scientific management often did result in a restoration of managerial prerogative and thereby an intensification of management control, this could be seen to have been a by-product of its objective to secure greater degrees of efficiency and productivity.[7]

A distinctive by-product of scientific management was an individualization of the workforce. This is because it was based upon the belief that individuals could only be motivated to work through direct economic incentives. Whether or not Taylor had absorbed the liberal market ideology of individual self-interest is of less consequence than the fact that his interventions in production were targeted at restrictive practices on the shop-floor, and the collective solidarity that sustained them. Such restrictions involved limiting production output in the belief that not to do so would result in further intensification of work. Taylorism had the effect of reinforcing, if not constructing, individual economic self-interest since Taylor's method of eradicating restrictive practices was to link output directly to individual wage levels. This was done through the introduction of 'piece-work' where a fixed payment for a set task gave the worker an incentive to complete it in a shorter time, thus proceeding to the next task in order to maximize his or her pay.[8]

Furthermore, in so far as the design, conceptualization and organization of tasks was taken out of the employee's hands and appropriated by management, this also reduced the quality of the social work experience and led employees to regard work in a purely instrumental fashion. Thus, the sustained motivation of employees could only be achieved through further financial incentives. This Taylorist legacy is also evident in what has been labelled Fordism or assembly-line production. The divorce between the conception and execution of tasks and the emphasis on financial incentives serves to turn employees' loyalties towards themselves and discontent is then often channelled through trade unions. Although we would question whether employees have ever been universally supportive of their organizations and management, it seems to us that there is little doubt that Taylorism failed to generate such support or loyalty. Consequently, sustained efficiency improvements were not realizable under Taylorism or Fordism because of the problems that unfolded in their wake, including low morale, limited social cohesion, antagonistic industrial relations, costly and complex production flows based around a functional and fragmented form of work, an extensive division of labour and an expensive means of motivating labour (see Beynon 1973; Littler 1986; Sayer 1986).

It could be argued that in certain respects scientific management is more sophisticated than contemporary critics of its mechanistic, economistic and asociological assumptions (Silverman 1970), and its illiberal politics (Rose 1975) allow. There is little question that scientific management subscribed to a general managerial prejudice that assumed workers to be lazy by nature and that it therefore coincides with what McGregor (1960) later termed 'Theory X' or coercive strategies of management control. However, Taylor's understanding, for instance, that low productivity is very often a result of 'systematic soldiering' or what might now be termed work-avoidance strategies is not given the credit it deserves. This is all the more intriguing given that the later Hawthorne experiments were acclaimed for their discovery of 'production norms' or restriction of output on the shop-floor. The Hawthorne studies' explanation of this as a product of worker irrationality is readily criticized in the literature (e.g. Landsberger 1958; Carey 1965) without acknowledging Taylor's prior recognition of the *rational* basis of output restriction or systematic soldiering. Clearly, Taylor's solution to worker restriction of output was overly mechanical. Nonetheless, his thesis was grounded in (largely tacit) assumptions regarding the purely economically instrumental attitudes of labour to work. Such instrumentalism among employees and managers cannot be easily dismissed (Goldthorpe *et al.* 1968; Knights and Collinson 1987) as wholly irrelevant despite a number of critiques that do so (Myers 1924; Roethlisberger and Dickson 1939; Watson 1980).

In this appraisal of Taylor's work, criticism has been restrained in order to draw out some implications of scientific management that have secured only fleeting attention. What has been suggested is that, at best, scientific management provides only temporary relief from restrictive practices or the soldiering that it seeks to ameliorate. At the same time, it stimulates or reinforces an individualistic approach through deploying economic rewards as a technology of control or motivation. Failing to identify the problems of individualization in organizations, scientific management either secured a reception that led to its demise or was accepted only to be in instant need of repair – a task readily assumed by a rapidly expanding human relations school of management. For it was the dehumanized way in which Taylorism was both formulated and executed that left the field wide open to human relation theorists. The latter traded on a conception of labour as dominated by non-logical sentiments and the need for social acceptance and recognition within informal work groups.

Human relations

In so far as scientific management had an effect, and this was more limited in the short term than its reputation in the archives of history intimates, it was to individualize employees around their economic self-interests. It therefore left a fertile territory for an alternative view that perceived industrial work to be social as well as economic. Through various experiments, the Hawthorne researchers reached the conclusion that people sought more than economic reward from work; they also needed to be recognized by their peers. Human relations appeared to be a theory that arrested the individualism and economic instrumentalism of scientific management, for whereas economic individual self-interest would suggest a relative indifference to others, if there is a concern for social recognition some commitment to the group or community is necessary. Both models are essentially neo-behaviourist in viewing human beings primarily as organisms that respond to monetary or social stimuli in relation to their capacity to satisfy a pre-existing set of needs for material sustenance or a sense of belonging. But there is also a sense in which both models are individualistic. For individuals can relate instrumentally to their pursuit of identity as much as they pursue financial rewards. This is because they begin to treat themselves and their own identities as objects to be secured – for instance, as a team player or a good employee, almost in the same way as those who seek only monetary gain.

While Mayo (1933, 1949), who was the theoretical stimulus for the Hawthorne studies, has been berated by a number of critics and especially Landsberger (1958), Carey (1965) and Rose (1975), his deliberations on boredom at work stand out as offering a special insight. In marked contrast to the majority of contemporary commentators on the problems of work in mass production industry, Mayo refused to attribute boredom wholly to the nature of the task (Whitehead 1936: 11). He noted how 'there was no great evidence of that "deadening" effect of machine minding or routine work which literary critics commonly suppose to be the chief problem of a mechanical age' (Mayo 1933: 118). This contrasts sharply with later research that assumes monotonous and routine work to generate boredom and alienation. Many empirical researchers, of course, have documented how employees 'break' the routine and boring nature of their tasks by playing games (e.g. Roy 1952; Burawoy 1979), joking and having fun (Collinson, 1992), or distancing themselves from the formal work routines (e.g. Palm 1970; Willis 1977). But these informal activities are not just a disruption of the routine but ways in which employees can regain some sense of being in control of the work. While routine tasks may contribute to an employee's disinterest at work, they may not be the primary or only source of boredom.

Those analysts (e.g. Walker and Guest 1952; Blauner 1964) who attribute boredom or alienation to the nature of the task divert attention from the way that work is socially organized. Blaming the routine nature of the task for their boredom deflects criticism away from the social organization of production onto the nature of modern technology. The boredom is then easily rationalized away as the price of 'progress', the benefits of which employees themselves enjoy in the form of advances in their material standards of living.

We are not suggesting that Mayo developed arguments in this way for he, no less than the average employee, assumed the prevailing hierarchical structure of social relations in industry to be 'natural' and unquestionable. However, by not attributing boredom entirely to the nature of the task, he leaves the way open for a more radical appreciation of workplace resistance that we seek to advance in later chapters of this book. If we can break away from associating boredom with routine or repetitive tasks, rather than with the wider social organization of work, resistance would not *have* to be seen simply as a negative or unconstructive release of individual frustration in the face of such boredom. Although rarely articulated in this way, it can be regarded as both positive and productive in challenging the prevailing social and hierarchical organization of work.

The Hawthorne research was also radical in anticipating future developments in organizational sociology concerning the problem of 'meaning' in social relations at work. Although the neo-human relations popularizers reduced their insights to the importance of job satisfaction, the Hawthorne researchers saw that 'the responses of workers to what was happening about them were dependent upon the significance these events had for them' (Roethlisberger and Dickson 1939: 15).

The Hawthorne studies were also radical in developing a systems approach (Burrell and Morgan 1979: 130–43). By maintaining a grasp on meaning and interpretation, their use of a systems framework remained more 'open' than subsequent developments where work organizations tended to be viewed as input-output systems that operate almost independently of the human subjects that comprise them (Lawrence and Lorsch 1967). This tendency to 'reify' the system was not at all evident in Hawthorne. Take, for example, their description of work dissatisfaction. It is 'a response to a total situation which includes not only the job but also the worker, with his own peculiar hopes and expectations, in relation to the collective life of the factory and the wider community' (Roethlisberger and Dickson 1939: 573). In contrast to modern adaptations of systems theory, the Hawthorne studies treated it principally as a heuristic device. But this sophisticated analysis of workplace behaviour was occluded by the appropriation of the Hawthorne findings by the neo-human relations school of behavioural science entrepreneurs (Watson 1980).

Neo-human relations

The potential for a more collective, sociologically informed understanding of behaviour at work that Hawthorne represented was quickly hijacked by neo-human relations psychologists steeped in an ideology of individualism. What followed was an approach that focused on the individual as a discrete subject with 'needs' that can be satisfied through a variety of motivating rewards offered by management. Extracting from Hawthorne a view that employees seek social recognition at work, psychologists pursued numerous studies of job satisfaction (Hertzberg *et al.* 1959) largely inspired by Maslow's (1954) hierarchy of needs.

The solution to workplace productivity problems was seen to reside with satisfying the 'needs' of individuals or groups of employees.[9] Instead of viewing the individual employee as someone who passively responds to various stimuli in the work environment, it had now been established that he or she is seeking to belong to, identify with, or achieve recognition in a work group of some kind. In so far as work groups were seen principally as fulfilling employees' affiliation needs, any other purposes or consequences surrounding such group developments, intended or not, were disregarded.

What emerged in the aftermath of Hawthorne was a whole 'industry' concerned to promote 'human relations' skills such as 'expressive' supervision, communication techniques, knowledge of group dynamics, expertise in developing schemes of employee 'participation', etc. Classical interventions (e.g. Taylor 1911; Fayol [1916] 1949; Barnard 1938) to render organizations and management capable of delivering the American Dream of 'progress' and 'prosperity' had been based on principles derived from practitioners' experience. Neo-human relations claimed superiority because of its grounding in science.

Psychologists sought to establish the *causes* of human behaviour through demonstrating connections or correlations between human relations techniques that promote job satisfaction and employee performance (Hertzberg *et al.* 1959). The absence of a simple relationship between job satisfaction and job performance (Vroom 1964: 101–5) in early empirical studies directed psychologists toward the study of motivation. This development did not constitute a break with previous work so much as a broadening of the theoretical assumptions and a narrowing of the empirical focus. It also reinforced the individualistic approach that dominated industrial psychology in that it sought to establish a link between a range of factors and individual performance. This was increasingly being subjected to critique by those (e.g. Landsberger 1958; Carey 1965) that had traditionally interpreted associations in informal work groups as reflecting a conflict of interests (manifested in output restrictions) between employees and management, not a concern for affiliation. If this was so, then human relations efforts to adapt or manipulate work groups toward the pursuit of management goals were destined to fail. Such critiques may have affected significantly the future direction of academic research in the workplace – the neo-human relations movement, however, was too steeped in individualistic conceptions and managerial ideology to be concerned with collectivist notions of class interests and industrial conflict. Indeed, it was their firm belief that conflict was simply an aberration caused by management's lack of human relations skills and their limited understanding of the techniques of leadership, communication and motivation.

We can see that scientific management and the Hawthorne research provided the conditions that made possible a tradition of management innovation based on a neo-behaviourist model. They both relied on a conception of individual needs as the foundation for stimulating given behavioural responses. This is not to argue that there was a sequential transition or continuity between these approaches, nor is it to suggest that they were immediately acceptable to their target audiences. Scientific management experienced considerable resistance from management and unions in the West but had a better reception in the post-revolutionary East (Rose 1975). While some elements of the early human relations work could be seen as a direct critical response to scientific management, this perception was easier to articulate once it had developed its contrasting view of the industrial worker. Moreover, the Hawthorne understanding of worker subjectivity was much more complex than the conceptualizations that flowed from those in the neo-human relations' school whose entrepreneurial vision was to lead to significant commercial exploitation of academic research.

The conditions that made this embryonic management innovation industry possible were not simply the academic research that provided them with a product to sell. A whole range of social and economic conditions in the post-war years rendered industry receptive to these interventions. Economic growth, oligopolistic power and 'tight labour markets' were the conditions in which such interventions gained popularity. In oligopolies, labour is the most costly factor of production but 'tight labour markets', where the demand for labour (especially skilled) exceeds the supply, were exacerbating these costs. If recruiting labour is the problem, then one solution is to achieve more output from the existing employees – in short, increased productivity through labour commitment and motivation (see Barley and Kunda 1992). However, securing the commitment and motivation of employees to the productive demands of the organization became increasingly problematic as antagonism within the workplace grew throughout the post-war period. This industrial conflict was of course fuelled by the tight labour market since, in these circumstances, employees are more willing to risk industrial action in the knowledge that other jobs are available. Also a general 'feelgood' factor diminishes the fear of lost employment/income that results from striking. Ironically, while workplace resistance to management goals (i.e. output restriction) could be seen as stimulating both scientific management and human relations approaches to innovation, it was also instrumental in their demise and displacement by competing innovations. It is not so much that human relations, or for that matter Taylorism, created antagonism within the workplace, but that antagonisms, for which they could offer no solution, remained.

Post-war consensus: collective bargaining

Mainstream accounts of innovation often represent managers as exercising power over others through various interventions. Ramsey's (1977, 1985) account of cycles of employee participation (i.e. joint consultation, collective bargaining, productivity bargaining) arising out of a 'challenge from below' belies such top-down representations, for it was recognized that innovations may derive from the 'bottom-up' pressure of workplace conflict. Thus managers may adopt innovations to curb shop-floor antagonisms – an example being the setting up of the Whitley Consultation Committees in the UK during World War I. In doing so, managers seek to stave off a more fundamental challenge to their authority and power.

In the post-World War II period from 1945 until the mid-1970s, the UK witnessed a burgeoning of collectivism. The trade union movement increasingly proved capable of challenging both management and governments. A specific example of this was the miners' strike during the early 1970s when the then prime minister, Edward Heath, was forced to reduce Britain to a three-day working week to conserve electrical energy supplies. Striking miners were able to close power stations and limit electricity supply and this led to a general election in 1974. Heath had attempted to reform industrial relations during his premiership through the 1971 Industrial Relations Act. Since the 1906 Trade Dispute Act, trade unions had enjoyed immunities from civil liability providing that any industrial action taken was in 'contemplation and furtherance of a trade dispute'. The 1971 Act sought to curtail the ability of unions to take industrial action through restricting union immunities. The Act failed, however, because it defined unions in terms of their leadership not in terms of their assets. Consequently, unions were able to mobilize resistance without fear of fines or asset sequestration. The only route to enforcing the Act was the imprisonment of trade union leaders but this was rarely followed because it inflamed opposition and could attract public sympathy for the victims. During World War II, governments of both main political parties in Britain saw cooperation between unions and management as important to secure a united front in the war effort. After the war, governments by and large continued to support a collective bargaining approach in the regulation of employment relations (Flanders 1969; Bain 1970) largely as a way of institutionalizing or channelling conflict toward constructive rather than disruptive ends (Dubin 1956; Eldridge 1971).

It was not just these conditions, however, that led to the demise of neo-human relations interventions in industry. Apart from the crass simplicity of the 'need theory' assumptions underlying such work, it could be argued that neo-human relations created as many problems as it solved. Many of the problems revolved around the individualizing effects of the psychological interventions it extolled. For they reinforced individual self-interest even though that interest might well be more varied than had been assumed by economists and scientific management theorists. Focusing on the individual's pursuit of personal security, the promotion of conditions of self-esteem, social acceptance or self-actualization was unlikely to encourage the kind of communal or collective sense of interdependence that productive work demands. Moreover, it seemed incapable of resolving the growing antagonisms within the workplace. Consequently, an emphasis on 'good' industrial relations through formalized collective bargaining, for unions, governments and employers alike, seemed attractive. It promised an end to conflict and a communal solidarity that could progress along productive channels.

Obviously, collective bargaining preceded (and ran concurrently, though sporadically, with) both scientific management and human relations. Nonetheless, in the UK it went through a golden era in the 1960s and 1970s as is most evident in the report and recommendations of the Donovan Commission in 1968. The Commission reported that British workplace industrial relations involved wage drift, sectional strikes and restrictive practices which stemmed from there being two systems of industrial relations in conflict with one another. There were, on the one hand, the formal industry-wide negotiations and, on the other, an informal system of plant-level negotiations conducted by hitherto unrecognized shop stewards. These separate agreements were uncoordinated at either the company or plant level.

The conditions of full employment had made it possible for well-organized workforces to challenge management and to negotiate change. Large corporations could readily manage this by passing on leap-frogging wage costs to consumers, but governments were becoming increasingly anxious about the inflationary effects of these developments. The turning point was perhaps the Organization of Petroleum Exporting Countries (OPEC) oil price shock of 1973 that put severe pressure on governments to reduce inflation at a time when organized labour was capable of offering resistance to redundancies and pay cuts. It led the Labour government in 1974 to offer a new social contract (1974–9), where in return for a policy of full employment and public sector investment, unions agreed to wage restraints through incomes policies designed to curb inflation. While successful initially in restraining inflation (Terry 1983), living standards began to fall, especially for public sector workers where wage rises were easier to control through central government spending constraints. Further squeezes on pay in the context of massive inflationary pressures, rising unemployment and demands from the International Monetary Fund (IMF) for cuts in public sector spending culminated eventually in widespread industrial action, or what some sections of the media dubbed 'the Winter of Discontent'. The strikes during this period were as much against the trade union leadership that continued to back the government's policy of income restraint as they were against the government. It was this context that provided the conditions of possibility for the election of Margaret Thatcher in 1979. A section of disaffected Labour supporters, the skilled working classes – many of whom were trade unionists – had suffered falling living standards due to successive incomes policies that constrained pay so as to curb inflation and they switched to voting

Conservative. In view of this, it is important not to over-romanticize the collectivism throughout this period, for many workers remained wedded to an economic instrumental individualism (Goldthorpe *et al*. 1968). Thus, for many employees, unions and Labour were seen as a means to an end and when that end of increased personal wealth was not realized, they quickly shifted position.

In the UK, collective bargaining had become the dominant means of regulating the employment relationship by the late 1970s. It was born out of struggle and strife and yet, as we have already indicated, earlier interventions including Taylorism and human relations also reflected and reproduced tensions in the workplace.

Thatcherism

A cultural theory analysis of Thatcherism draws our attention to the political-ideological dimensions of the emergence of the radical right (Hall 1985: 38). It is argued that Thatcher played on the failings of the past period of social democracy and attributed economic failure to obstacles in the operation of the free market, such as state intervention and trade unions. At the same time, Thatcher emphasized themes such as nationalism, individualism, the Protestant work ethic, thriftiness, and law and order (Hall 1985). It is here that we can begin to see how Thatcherism dovetails with the American Dream, thus providing the conditions that made it possible for the spread of ideas that were hitherto largely alien to the UK, especially in the post-war period. This is because, at this time, Britain had experienced a period in which the collective values associated with trade unionism, the setting up of the National Health Service, the building of council houses, nationalization of mining and steel, and full employment policies, were pre-eminent. All of this needs to be understood in the context of socialist values in the wake of World War II, where returning combatants and those at home who had contributed to the war effort had greater expectations of a land fit for heroes.

A political economy analysis of Thatcherism argues that it has also to be understood in terms of its specific economic and political policies (Jessop *et al*. 1984). Thus unions began to be constrained by anti-union legislation under Thatcher and labour markets were loosened by monetarist controls that sought to cut public sector spending and reduce inflation. The outcome was redundancies and unemployment that officially peaked at 3.1 million in 1986 – a level that had not been seen since the Great Depression of the 1930s. In addition, economic deregulation began to generate levels of competition in the marketplace that made it difficult for employers to rely on simply passing their costs onto the consumer. The economic policies of Thatcher then reflected and reinforced both her government's political and ideological philosophy. At the heart of the ideology was the individual and the importance of promoting entrepreneurial behaviour (du Gay and Salaman 1992). An unconditional faith in competition under 'free market' conditions was the rationale for economic deregulation, legitimized on the basis of ridding British industry of restrictive practices and management inefficiencies, such as 'feather bedding' (i.e. retaining surplus employees to protect against future labour market shortages). The competition agenda also fuelled the privatization of public sector organizations. This coincided with at least the rhetoric of pulling back the boundaries of the state in the belief that reduced public sector spending would reduce inflation/taxation and stimulate more investment. The aim was to encourage responsibility on the part of individuals to provide for themselves rather than be dependent on state support. In the event, the economic policies created such high levels of unemployment that welfare dependency increased rather than declined and could only be funded because of the revenue from North Sea oil and windfalls from privatization. Furthermore, the philosophy of non-intervention was somewhat of a myth because the privatization of state monopolies such as the public utilities required new regulations to prevent them from exploiting their potential to extract monopoly profits. Moreover, there were successive waves of anti-union legislation and, in the context of growing unemployment, it can be argued that the government had not so much withdrawn from, as changed the target of, intervention (Kessler and Bayliss 1992). The aim was to decimate the collective solidarity of employees and the bargaining power of unions. In its place was the elevation of the individual and economic self-interest as a mechanism for securing the best interests of all through a return to a '*laissez faire*' faith in the 'hidden hand' of the market (Smith [1776] 1970; MacInnes 1987: 161). Thatcher in the UK and Reagan in the US, extolled the virtues of neo-liberal market economics and the politics of the New Right became pre-eminent within the western world.

This is the context within which there has been a proliferation of new innovations and interventions by management designed to meet the competitive demands of the age. Global competition increased dramatically, partly as a result of a period of comparative world stability in the West but also because of the growth of multinational and merged corporations seeking out new markets. The dramatic success of the Japanese economy during this period led to an importation of their distinctive management methods and what became known as the Japanization of British industry (see *IRJ* 1988; Oliver and Wilkinson 1988; Elger and Smith 2000). In the first instance, managers engaged in closures, redundancies and restructuring but often left existing industrial relations structures and procedures intact (MacInnes 1987). Subsequently, in what remained of the manufacturing sector, profit growth was facilitated by 'just in time' stock controls that allowed for a pruning of excess costs. Flexibility led to further reductions in the labour force and new measures of accountability shifted responsibility down the line. Japanization, post-Fordism, the flexible firm, flexible specialization (Piore and Sabel 1984) and quality became the new buzzwords in the 1980s as companies endeavoured to become 'lean' (Womack *et al.* 1990).

In the 1990s financial services confronted many of the problems that manufacturing had experienced in the 1980s. It then went through similar cost cutting measures (Cressey and Scott 1992) and more recently there have been moves to compete on the basis of service (McCabe *et al.* 1997). Innovations in corporate culture, quality, teamworking and re-engineering were all designed to improve customer service as well as increase profitability through reducing costs. This preoccupation with controlling or eradicating costs culminated in a 'downsizing' movement that involved reducing the size of the labour force.

The era of Thatcher can be understood to have ushered in a new attempt to exercise power, the chief function of which is to constitute subjects as individuals, to train them into adopting new ways of thinking in line with what has been termed the 'enterprise' culture (du Gay and Salaman 1992). Though disciplinary power is exercised primarily through localized mechanisms such as the factory, office, prison, asylum, hospital and school, it is possible to identify a convergence between the individualizing effects of these institutions and the political, economic and ideological preoccupations of Thatcherism.

'Disciplinary institutions' secrete 'a machinery of control' through observing, measuring, monitoring, comparing, contrasting, normalizing and judging that turns us into individualized beings (Foucault 1977). At the level of the state, there was a congruence between these processes of individualization and Thatcher's concern to dismantle anything that presented a barrier to individualism including the welfare state, nationalized industries, trade unions and council housing. It cannot be argued that Thatcher orchestrated the processes of individualization for, as we have argued throughout this chapter, they have long since taken root as a disciplinary mechanism independent of government. But what we are arguing is that Thatcherism complemented and reinforced the processes of individualization. Indeed, as her anti-union policies reveal, she sought to consolidate and extend individualism into the individualized self-consciousness of the masses.

The individualizing effects of the labour process that take into account 'the activity of men, their skill, the way they set about their tasks, their promptness, their zeal, their behaviour' (Foucault, 1977: 174) were now married to a government that was willing to *use*, or at least turn a blind eye to, unemployment and deindustrialization and their effects on communities. We say *use* because unemployment and the loss of the UK's manufacturing base had a significant impact on the power of trade unions to resist the imposition of change. Manufacturing industry could no longer expect support through government subsidies; instead, it had to stand on its own two feet or go under. Collective traditions that were bound up with the early crafts, trades, and skills were increasingly threatened by an intensification of competition generated by economic deregulation and the promotion of flexibility to meet the perceived demands of customers.

Economic deregulation made the cosy environment of the financial services ultra competitive, leading to widespread redundancies, restructuring and mergers. Branches that served communities were closed and replaced by call centres often far removed from the people they served. Competition and flexibility within 'free market' mechanisms resulted in a fragmentation and fracturing of collectives and a pressure for individual accountability, self-reliance and responsibility. As Margaret Thatcher famously argued, there is no such thing as society – only individuals and groups. Vulnerable and isolated individuals were expected to take responsibility for their own lives through private healthcare and insurance cover, private housing and pensions, and individual pay negotiations through appraisals. Disciplinary power was extended through government and the concern was to reconstitute individuals as 'customers/consumers' who were 'autonomous, self-regulating and self-actualizing individual actors, seeking to maximize the worth of their existence to themselves through personalized acts of choice in a world of goods and services' (du Gay and Salaman 1992: 623).

Conclusion

We are not suggesting a clear line of intentionality on the part of government or management for we believe that Thatcher and neo-liberal managers would have understood their projects as an exercise in freedom and liberation rather than one of power, domination and subjugation. Indeed, as du Gay and Salaman (1992: 622) note, rather than 'a totalitarian attack on diversity and difference . . . the enterprising customer-consumer is imagined as an empowered human being'. Moreover, policies often arose on the hoof rather than as part of some grand scheme conceived in advance of their implementation. These are the dynamics that we believe were at work through the 1980s and 1990s. Of course, there was resistance from unionists, environmentalists, Poll Tax demonstrators, anti-war and anti-globalization protesters and ultimately the electorate resisted through the landslide election of a Labour government in 1997. However, New Labour, in turn, had already imbibed much of Thatcher's libation. Nonetheless, it is important to recognize that the Thatcherite project reflects a will to govern rather than a mechanism of government. For 'we do not live in a governed world so much as in a world traversed by the "will to govern"' (Rose and Miller 1992: 191).

The most intriguing outcome of Thatcherism that we can, as yet, only speculate on is that it may have generated the conditions of its own demise, just as Taylorism and human relations did before it. Thus trade unionism is growing and, in 2002, there was a rash of industrial disputes with the media 'talking up' industrial unrest and the prime minister once more seeking to persuade workers that New Labour was worth supporting. Following New Labour's second election victory, widespread support for public sector investment in education, healthcare and transport has developed. These changes in public consciousness have to be seen in the context of some significant failures of Thatcherism in these areas. It may not be too outrageous to suggest, therefore, that a new collectivism may be the unintended consequence of Thatcherism, a legacy that has arisen in opposition to the individualism of the free market. Whether this might also mean a proliferation in management innovations and guru panaceas that seek to capitalize upon the new collectivist/caring mood is open to speculation. But it is important to remember that such collectivism is often born out of a desire for improved personal living conditions and, as such, an individualistic belief in the success ethic remains largely unchallenged. We turn in the next chapter to an elaboration of the relationship between the American Dream as a tacit promise of success for everyone and the proliferation of prophets of change advocating management innovations in the latter part of the twentieth century.

The false promise of the American Dream: organization, innovation and change management

Gatsby believed in the green light, the orgiastic future that year by year recedes before us. It eluded us then, but that's no matter – tomorrow we will run faster, stretch our arms out farther . . . And one fine morning . . . So we beat on, boats against the current, borne back ceaselessly into the past.

(Fitzgerald [1925] 1986: 182)

The Great Gatsby is renowned as one of the greatest novels to have emerged from contemporary American culture.[1] It captures better than can any academic text the essence of the modern American Dream – a theme that runs through this chapter. The message of the American Dream is that through hard work and endeavour each of us can rise to the very zenith of society no matter how humble or impoverished our origins. This is enshrined in the Declaration of Independence as 'life, liberty and the pursuit of happiness'. In the course of our research in many organizations over nearly a decade,[2] we have frequently been struck by the way that a variety of management interventions bear more of a relationship to dreaming than to 'reality' – dreams that eventually often disappoint rather than discharge their promise.

We acknowledge that dreams about how we would like to see the world are rarely independent of the 'realities' that are experienced, for our aspirations, hopes and visions are inscribed in the very narratives we draw upon to describe reality. But in so far as reality is a social construction (Berger and Luckmann 1966), these narratives have to collectively coincide such that they draw people together rather than separate them. That is to say, reality is only generated and secured when sufficient numbers of people are mobilized to support a given set of narratives about it. The message of the American Dream, as expressed by Fitzgerald, is that if only we 'run faster, stretch our arms out farther' then 'one fine morning' we may reach our destination. It provides a coincidence between 'dreams' and everyday life as it gives us a goal to chase, a project to commit to, a future to believe in and, just as long as it remains a dream, we will continue to strive doggedly towards it despite disappointments, disruptions, displacements or disasters. In our empirical studies, we have witnessed many such incidents yet rarely are they seen as a crisis so much as a stimulant to run faster, stretch out farther and strive more decisively for that 'one fine morning'.

As an ideology that exaggerates the extent of, and the potential for, upward mobility or 'rags to riches' experiences, the American Dream is currently transporting itself across the globe. No better vehicle for legitimizing widespread social inequality behind the myth of universal opportunity are the business schools and their Master of Business Administration (MBA) programmes, management textbooks, consultants and business gurus. For they extol and stimulate a proliferation of discourses such as strategy, excellence, human resource management (HRM),[3] TQM and BPR, the underlying rationale of which is that, regardless of origins, through them everyone can have access to unimaginable individual success and prosperity. In the UK, such discourses are now a central feature of much academic teaching and research, either as a source of analysis, prescription or critique. Yet the overarching relationship to the Dream itself is rarely acknowledged let alone critically examined (cf. Dunn 1990; Guest 1990).

In this book, we argue that the modern manifestation of the American Dream with its emphasis on the self-interested pursuit of wealth by autonomous individuals as an economic panacea is irredeemably flawed, even when applied to the US let alone less prosperous countries. In our studies of UK organizations, its contradictions and limitations became all too clear. This is not simply to decry the American Dream for it reflects, produces and symbolizes hope and purpose for many. We are, however, urging a critical reflection on the individualistic values that the current Dream underpins and reproduces. We live in a world of immense inequality of power, status and wealth. Yet in the guise of a broad range of management innovations, the American Dream promises the majority precisely what it offers the minority an escape from – the conditions of material and symbolic deprivation. As a utopian vision, it makes the striving meaningful but as an expectation that has any chance of being realized it rests upon fallacious assumptions. Yet it lives on, even if not in 'real' lives, then in the escapism of media simulations. Can the fascination with every detail of the lives of celebrities like Madonna, Brad Pitt or David Beckham be understood as 'filling in', at least vicariously, the void left by the failure for most people of the American Dream? And is the popularity of national lotteries and 'reality' TV such as *Big Brother* and *Survivor* in the UK a reflection of the sustained belief in the American Dream, and indeed a way of keeping the dream rolling despite all the evidence that would suggest its abandonment? Except for these routine escapes, the victims of inequality may begin to envy and resent those who appear to wallow in the riches of success rather than in comparative poverty as the American Dream passes them by. As we shall see, however, American

Dream mantras are by no means consistent, immutable or implacable and they can be challenged until such time as other dreams emerge to take their place.

The American Dream

There is, of course, no one single American Dream; it is possible to trace innumerable dreams throughout the comparatively short history of American literature and Parrington ([1947] 1964: 5) argues that 'its greatest charm has been that it was variable, and not bound to a single doctrine'. Nonetheless, what these dreams all share in common is a representation of Utopia.[4] Hence in 1670 Daniel Denton's *A Brief Description of New York* illuminated the possibilities by describing fruits of such abundance that 'the fields and woods are died red' (p. 3, quoted in Parrington [1947] 1964: 5). Parrington reminds us of what Oscar Wilde once said, that 'A map of the world that does not include Utopia is not worth glancing at, for it leaves out the one country at which humanity is always landing. And when humanity lands there, it looks out, and seeing a better country, sets sail' ([1947] 1964: viii).

It is here that comparisons can be drawn between the management guru literature and the American Dream. For both hold out the promise of a better tomorrow. Yet guru dreams involve never 'landing'. Rather, each guru, born on ship, sets a new but almost identical course in the sense that there is no ultimate destination other than to keep on travelling. As we never arrive at a permanent destination, we are required constantly to 'look out' for a 'better country' and are continually setting sail. For 'there are no plateaus any more, only a mountain with no summit' (Hammer and Stanton 1995: 318). This is reminiscent of the American Dream of the frontier where there 'was the sense of escaping beyond the boundaries of society into a world without limits, a world of unbounded potential' (Jacques 1996: 23). The sense in which one is on a 'journey' and never arrives is not surprising given that Utopia literally means 'nowhere' (Carey 1999: xi). Dunn (1990: 21), drawing on a wagon-train metaphor, points out that 'To travel hopefully is the crux of the metaphor. Arrival suggests the end of change, whereas the new . . . is about perpetual change'. The promise, however, is that wherever we are heading/sailing, it is going to be better than where we are now: 'America was always promises. From the first voyage and the first ship there were promises' (Macleish quoted in Parrington [1947] 1964: 1).

Jacques (1996) has traced the roots of the American Dream back to Europe and, in part, to Calvinistic Protestantism and its belief in 'perfectionism'. According to Guest (1990: 390), the American Dream was first formally articulated in the context of the New Deal of the 1930s and it flourished in the post-war period under J.F. Kennedy who re-enacted it as 'a charismatic leader promising the new frontier, including the frontier of space' (Guest 1990: 390). The Dream returned in the guise of Reaganism where the message was simple: 'America is back in business, but back on its own terms. The solution to Japanese competition can be found in America's own backyard, in getting back to basics' (Guest 1990: 390–1). This message is curiously similar to that of the gurus of BPR who argue that it:

> isn't another imported idea from Japan . . . [it] capitalizes on the same characteristics that made Americans such great business innovators: individualism, self reliance, a willingness to accept risk and a propensity for change . . . unlike management philosophies that would have 'us' like 'them', [it] doesn't try to change the behaviour of American workers and managers. Instead, it takes advantage of American talents and unleashes American ingenuity.
>
> (Hammer and Champy 1993: 1–3)

Though a break with Reaganism, the Clinton administration could be seen as a throwback to the American Dream of the type extolled and embodied by JFK. And recently Jacques (1996: 24) reminds us of how a former Clinton cabinet member, Robert Reich (1983) described the post-industrial future as '*the next American frontier*'.

The American Dream, evident in the Horatio Alger stories of the rise from 'rags to riches', is quintessentially an individualistic message that holds out the continual promise of success. For us, it is central to understanding the emergence and popularity of the raft of innovative guru texts that have been exported from America across the globe over the past 20 years (see Dunn 1990; Guest 1990; Clark and Salaman 1998). It might also be viewed as central to understanding the failures and shortcomings of the innovative panaceas. No doubt there are success stories of kids from comparative poverty making it big in the US: film stars like Marilyn Monroe, Kirk Douglas and Tony Curtis; popular singers such as Frank Sinatra, Dean Martin and Madonna; sportsmen such as Mohammad Ali and Babe Ruth; business tycoons such as Andrew Carnegie[5] and John D. Rockefeller;[6] and Molly Brown, who sailed on the maiden voyage of the *Titanic*. But for every success story there are more than a million failures; moreover the majority of the successful already have a head start in being born into privileged circumstances:

> While some millionaires started in poverty, most did not. A study of the origins of 303 textile, railroad and steel executives of the 1870s showed that 90% came from middle- or upper-class families. The Horatio Alger story of 'rags to riches' is true for a few, but mostly a myth, and a useful myth for control.
>
> (Zinn 2002)

The same middle-class background was also pre-eminent in the early frontier wagon trails where families crossed half of America in travelling from Missouri to Oregon or California on the West Coast. Such expeditions would take a whole year and then a further year to await the produce from a land newly planted. Farmers and their families had to be quite wealthy in order to withstand almost two years without income (McLynn 2002: 44).

If we were to reverse the arguments of the American Dream, we would find far more examples of people who remained in comparative 'rags' than those who climbed out of them into 'riches'. Because American society has become wealthier in total, the sense that rags have been all but eliminated is an easy myth to cultivate. But, as most of the literature on inequality argues, poverty is a relative not an absolute concept, established in practice through an assessment of one's life in comparison to those with more wealth. In short, 'relative depriv-ation' (Runciman 1966) is how most people perceive their poverty. At its roots, the American Dream '*means* escape from the limits of zero sum' for 'on the frontier, everyone can have more than their share' (Jacques 1996: 24). But the frontier, as Jacques points out, all too soon ran into the sea. The point being that resources are scarce and ultimately some having 'more than their share' means many more having less. In a society that celebrates only those that 'stand out' or are more successful than the rest, prima donna power and privilege must by definition be limited to the few.

For us, the American Dream is fundamentally flawed in so far as it depends on the celebration of individualistic competition that requires there to be fail-ures with which to contrast the successful. Moreover, while seeking to unite people around the common goal of the pursuit of wealth, this ruthless indi-vidualism can be highly destructive of communities and social integration (Durkheim [1933] 1947), as has recently been lamented in Robert Putnam's (1995, 2000) thesis about the decline of 'social capital' in America as a result of the irreversible growth in individualism. Social capital is the creative and edu-cational potential or material and symbolic resources that derive from the regu-lar social interactions of a collective community (e.g. family, neighbourhood, leisure group, school or workplace).[7] A further flaw is that a culture where everyone supposedly has the opportunity to gain wealth does not look favour-ably on those who do not make the grade. Such individuals are branded failures and feckless outcasts that have not taken advantage of the opportunities on offer. They suffer the 'hidden injuries of class' where the system of inequality gener-ates self-blame for relative failure (Sennett and Cobb 1977). Like eulogies of equal opportunity, the American Dream legitimizes inequality and offers little hope of, or incentive towards, wealth sharing. It reflects and reinforces an individualism that is grounded in a socially abrasive self-interest that, in its celebration of success, is comparatively indifferent to those who slip through the net of material and symbolic power and privilege. Generally speaking then, the American Dream is supportive of an ideology whereby those who seek, or have attained, wealth and success have the legitimate right to dictate to, impose upon or crush those who get in the way.

The America of the American Dream 'was a new continent' (at least for white Europeans)[8] 'where there was neither tradition nor authority to make men conform to any set rules'. Under such conditions the 'new world made men dream' (Parrington [1947] 1964), yet, paradoxically, rules, traditions and authority were very quickly established. These constraints were bound to the Old World of inequality and inequity, but the dream, in various guises, has seemingly prevailed. Moreover, for the early Europeans the dream was to 'escape' from a standardized and hierarchized society. Yet, as the 'largest economic empire on the planet', the US now exports precisely such standardization and hierarchical thinking through products, services and ideas to the rest of the globe (Jacques 1996: 31). There is then a tension within the American Dream between the promise of success and freedom and the 'reality' of inequality and rule-based constraints.

Such tensions are also at the heart of much of the guru-based business literature as it extends the American Dream into the promise of a 'new' world of work juxtaposed against an outdated system that it displaces. As a panacea, innovative forms of work organization and managing clearly appeal to corporations always searching for the ultimate management tool or technique. Culture change, excellence or lean production, quality management, BPR, the learning organization, the knowledge-based company, mass customization etc. all share in common the idea that competitive success can be achieved through an organization that is flexible, flat, team-based, consensual, trust-based and customer and quality focused. Managers are exhorted to abandon the past (e.g. control, hierarchy, bureaucracy and failure) and embrace a 'new' world order even while they reproduce much of what went before (Knights and McCabe 1998a, 1999; McCabe 1999). Moreover, much of what is promised is as vacuous as the mythical stories produced by Horatio Alger. A major concern of senior and divisional managers in a recent survey on management innovation was that 'most tools promise more than they deliver': 68.1 per cent believed this to be the case (Bain & Co. 1994: Table 8). Nonetheless, it seems that America and management must reinvent themselves:

> A numbing focus on cost gives way to an enhancing focus on quality. Hierarchy and three-piece suits give way to first names, shirtsleeves, hoopla, and project-based flexibility. Working according to fat rule books is replaced by everyone's contribution.
>
> (Peters and Waterman 1995: xxv)

> We are watching hierarchy fade away and clear distinctions of title, task, department even corporation blur . . . in these transformed corporations . . . we don't even have words to describe the new relationships, 'supervisors' and 'subordinates' hardly seem accurate, and . . . imply more control and ownership than managers today actually possess.
>
> (Kanter 1989: 85)

> BPR is about beginning again with a clean sheet of paper. It is about rejecting the conventional wisdom and received assumptions of the past.
>
> (Hammer and Champy 1993: 49)

> Transformation of . . . styles of management is not a job of reconstruction, nor is it of revision. It requires a whole new structure, from foundation upward.
>
> (Deming 1986: IX–X)

The Great Gatsby

The story of James Gatz, who transforms himself into Jay Gatsby (the Great Gatsby), is ostensibly a tragic tale of a poor boy that falls for a rich girl (Daisy Fey). But it is also a story about inequality, class, wealth and the pursuit of the American Dream. In 1917, a blossoming romance begins between Gatsby (then a young officer) and Daisy:

> In various unrevealed capacities he had come in contact with such people, but always with indiscernible barbed wire between them . . . He was at present a penniless young man without a past, and at any moment the invisible cloak of his uniform might slip from his shoulders . . . he let her believe that he was a person from much the same stratum as herself.
> (Fitzgerald [1925] 1986: 148–9)

The romance is interrupted by World War I and while Gatsby is away fighting, Daisy, under pressure from her family, makes the correct marriage to the immensely wealthy Tom Buchanan. Five years later, through means that are by no means clear, although Tom attributes it to bootlegging (i.e. selling liquor illegally during the Prohibition years), Gatsby reappears having attained fabulous wealth during America's 'Jazz Age'. From a luxurious mansion he throws equally luxurious parties 'where he dispensed starlight to casual moths' (p. 80) in the hope that 'one day' Daisy Buchanan – the object of his dreams and desires – will float in among the crowd of exotic, beautiful and rich people who flit through his parties. For as her friend (Jordan Baker) later declares, 'Gatsby bought that house so that Daisy would be just across the bay' (p. 79). The first time we see Gatsby is through the eyes of his new next-door neighbour, Nick Carraway, who serendipitously is Daisy's cousin. We see Gatsby, in the early hours of the morning, gazing from the lawns of his house across the bay, at the 'green light', where Daisy lives: 'He stretched out his arms towards the dark water in a curious way, and, far as I was from him, I could have sworn he was trembling. Involuntarily I glanced seaward – and distinguished nothing except a single green light, minute and far away, that might have been the end of a dock' (pp. 21–2).

Gatsby embodies the American Dream and shares with the gurus exhortations the 'following of a grail' (p. 149) or 'an extraordinary gift for hope, a romantic readiness' (p. 2). The gurus hold out the promise that the goal of the American Dream ('the new'; 'success') can be attained, if not through the latest innovation, then through the next one. Managers, like Gatsby, are required to dedicate their lives to the pursuit of a dream. They are continually exhorted to reach out for the dream that is bound up with the pursuit of economic success (corporate and career based) and existential security. Though the dream may subsequently be dashed, as one innovation after another either fails or proves to be highly problematic, managers are persuaded to continue to reach out for the romantic promise that a 'new' organizational form can be attained and with it success. This dashing of a dream is vividly apparent in *The Great Gatsby* by the appearance of Daisy's little daughter during a social gathering at the Buchanan house: 'I don't think he had ever really believed in its existence before' (p. 117). Nonetheless, despite the tangible evidence of cracks in his dream, Gatsby continued to pursue his ideal:

> There must have been moments even that afternoon when Daisy tumbled short of his dreams – not through her own fault, but because of the colossal vitality of his illusion. It had gone beyond her, beyond everything. He had thrown himself into it with a creative passion, adding to it all the time, decking it out with every bright feather that drifted his way. No amount of fire or freshness can challenge what a man will store up in his ghostly heart.
>
> (p. 97)

This is the strength and seductiveness of the American Dream, for it holds out the sustained promise that 'the unattainable' can be reached. According to Guest (1990: 390), 'it always was a dream, an ideal, in part a goal to pursue, in part a counter to cynicism and despair. Like the holy grail it has been a compelling myth'. It carries with it an existential burden of anxiety, for no matter what one achieves or attains, dreams are always beyond us and evade our grasp, but the promise remains that they are just around the corner:

> In a true mass-customization environment, no one knows exactly what the next customer will want, and, therefore, no one knows exactly what product the company will be creating next. No one knows what market-opportunity windows will open, and therefore, no one can create a long-term vision of certain products to service those markets. But everyone does know that the next customer will want something and the next market opportunity is out there somewhere.
>
> (Pine II *et al.* 1993: 118–19)

The American 'frontier' Dream embodies 'the desire for challenge against a powerful unknown adversary' (Guest 1990: 390). It is ultimately a romantic notion that requires a leap of faith and seduces us into imagining a future that is out there 'somewhere' if only we 'run faster', reach further and 'one fine morning' . . . ! It is a spur to action and its promise of wealth is highly appealing in a culture saturated by consumption and material gain. It is productive of subjectivity, hope and action, for 'new concepts set men to thinking, to working out their own plans' (Parrington [1947] 1964: 4). Paradoxically, it provides existential solace, for while we are reaching forward we are able to divert our attention from current anxieties and insecurities. There are, of course, a multiplicity of such anxieties in a society that continually pushes individuals back on themselves and their own devices to achieve the illusive 'holy grail' of success. As we embrace the dream, we are not required to think too much about its contradictions, problems and difficulties or about those who might suffer as a consequence of our success and our pursuit of success (our families, children and partners; peers; competitors; employees; our health; or even the environment).[9] The solace it offers is ultimately an unhappy one for 'contentment is not a permissable goal' (Moore 1969 quoted in Guest 1990: 391). Thus we are never to drink from the well of its accomplishment, for the American Dream is crucially about 'beginnings' in striving for an ideal and ultimately 'Utopias can't be achieved because a utopia achieved is no longer a utopia' (Brown and MacLaran 1996 quoted in Lightfoot and Lilley 2002: 8).

The American Dream is also highly masculine and it shares this in common with the gurus' prescriptions. This is most apparent in the re-engineering literature that 'emphasises competition, control and conquest while simultaneously [and paradoxically] appealing to care, trust, nurturing, creativity and teamwork' (Knights and McCabe 2001: 619). The juxtaposition of humanistic values[10] (care, nurturing, creativity) with competition and the free market is not as paradoxical as it seems at first sight. For these welfare and aesthetic ideals (trust, teamwork) are only means to the instrumental ends of competitive success through control and conquest and the displacement of anything that might constitute a challenge. Thus re-engineering requires a constant drive towards domination: 'Reengineering will not be one-time or short-term . . . its underlying driving force can be summarized in one word: change. Compelling changes [which] . . . create a new world arena of competition' (Hammer and Stanton 1995: 318).

The masculine discourse that these gurus proffer seeks to drive its subjects almost compulsively to engage in a struggle to stay ahead of the competition and it brooks no room for compromise:

> Four or five years ago everyone was on a burning platform. There's a risk now that companies will relax, that they won't see the business case for change. People have to be aware of the physicality of the change, they have to see that they have no choice but to change, or to do something radically different.
>
> (Champy 1995: 28)

Throughout their history – that stretches back, it could be argued, as far as the second decade of the twentieth century – the US gurus have exported their solutions and salvations (Huczynski 1993b). By the latter half of the twentieth century they were truly global and through them the American Dream continues to be transmitted, repackaged and sold by an infantry of consultants and academics backed up by an artillery of books and videos. We never quite know exactly what it is managers are supposed to do or how they are to attain a 'new' organization; or why innovations are frequently problematic or repeatedly fail. For 'like heaven the directions for getting there have been no more specific than the program of entertainment promised upon arrival' (Parrington [1947] 1964: 3).

The gurus simply offer up new recipes or advocate more of the same. So Peters and Waterman (1995) urged us to embrace 'Excellence' by which they meant an abandonment of the 'excesses of the "rational model" and the "business strategy paradigm"' (Crainer 1998: 189) in favour of getting closer to the customer, stimulating productivity through people management and having a propensity to act rather than prevaricate. Yet only two years after the publication of *In Search of Excellence* (first published in 1982), research revealed and wide-scale publicity was given to the fact that 'one quarter of the excellent companies were struggling' (Crainer 1998: 191), and that the others were far from excellent in terms of the bottom line (see also Guest 1992). Rather than simply give up on the one-liners and hyperbole, this failure was in Peters' own words 'a great wake-up call' (quoted in Crainer 1998: 191) and, like the American Dream, an inspiration to strive further. 'There are no excellent companies', Peters later declared (1987: 1) but in order to become excellent, companies would have to learn to 'thrive on chaos' and be able to reinvent themselves continually in response to a fluctuating and fickle marketplace. Flexibility was the new holy grail. Just as the American Dream has been reiterated from JFK to Reaganism, the gurus simply reinvent their innovations in the garb of the American Dream and move on with the same or, in some cases, a reformulated message. Like Gatsby, who embodies the American Dream, the gurus' message and the managers they portray are elusive – 'Somebody told me they thought he killed a man once' or 'it's more that he was a German spy during the war' (Fitzgerald [1925] 1986: 44). In *The Great Gatsby*, we never know what Gatsby does or how he has attained his wealth, and we only learn of his origins towards the end of the book. We learn that James Gatz had already reinvented himself as Jay Gatsby at the age of 17, long before he had met Daisy Fey. He had run away from an impoverished childhood, showing early self-discipline and incredible ambition. Such reinvention is integral to the language of the gurus; viewers of Tom Peters' video *Crazy Ways for Crazy Days* cannot help but be struck by the continual use of revolutionary language. So managers are instructed to 'abandon everything'; 'restructure endlessly'; for 'the only certainty is uncertainty' and there is a need for 'reinvention', 'radicals' and 'anarchists'. Thus managers are exhorted to reconstitute themselves so as to be able to compete in pursuit of the American Dream. Following in the 'flexibility' tradition established by Tom Peters, Hammer and Stanton (1995) describe BPR as a revolutionary programme for ridding corporations of their bureaucratic legacies in order to meet the ever-changing demands of customers for quality and difference. But just as Peters found to his cost (albeit one quickly turned into a profit through self-transformation), re-engineered companies didn't go exactly to plan. Between 60 and 87 per cent of re-engineering projects were unsuccessful (Holland and Kumar 1995 quoted in Jackson 2001: 74). However, unlike Tom Peters, and this perhaps accounts for the fact that they have been a 'one innovation wonder', they tended to advocate more of the same: 'The failures failed because they did it wrong. Success is virtually guaranteed for companies that go about reengineering with will, intelligence and passion' (Hammer and Stanton 1995: 171).

The 'mystery' and appeal that surrounds Gatsby relates to the appeal of the gurus' rhetoric: thus in colourful and opaque language managers are seduced and extolled into thinking that they can and must become heroic through reinventing themselves (Clark and Salaman 1998). The romantic promise of success casts managers in the role of hero – it is they who will change the world and it is on their shoulders that the future prosperity of society rests. Hence 'leaders' in the 'post entrepreneurial corporation' must motivate through 'excitement about mission and a share of the glory and the gains of success' (Kanter 1989: 92). Like Gatsby, they must manufacture a fictional heroic identity – he is a wealthy hero, for as Gatsby tells Nick Caraway, 'I am the son of some wealthy people in the Middle West' (p. 65). He is an intellectual hero: 'Well, he told me once he was an Oxford man' (p. 49); a romantic hero: 'I lived like a young rajah in all the capitals of Europe – Paris, Venice, Rome . . . trying to forget something very sad that had happened to me long ago' (p. 66); a war/ action hero: 'then came the war, old sport. It was a great relief and I tried very hard to die, but I seemed to bear an enchanted life . . . I was promoted to Major, and every Allied government gave me a decoration' (p. 66); a social hero: the popular host of the grandest parties filled with the 'great and the good' and 'If personality is an unbroken series of successful gestures, then there was something gorgeous about him' (p. 2); he is a physical hero: 'an elegant young roughneck' (p. 45); and a moral hero: despite bootlegging, more honourable than Tom Buchanan, his rich competitor from an old, wealthy and established family. For 'Gatsby turned out alright at the end' (p. 2).

Similarly, managers are required to reinvent themselves as heroic visionaries, leaders, buddies, mentors or coaches in the pursuit of success and the 'new' world of work. Like the American Dream, such heroic identities represent and offer an 'idealized and seldom-attained state' (Guest 1990: 391). Or the Dream becomes a 'quest', it represents 'a heroic process of passage through which the questor (seeker), and their world, becomes re-ordered and re-formed' (Jeffcut 1994: quoted in Clark and Salaman 1998: 154):

> Even management's job becomes more fun. Instead of brain games in the sterile ivory tower, it's shaping values and reinforcing through coaching and evangelism in the field – with the worker.
>
> (Peters and Waterman 1995: xxv)

> The leader's primary role is to act as visionary and motivator. By fashioning and articulating a vision of the kind of organization that he or she wants to create, the leader invests everyone in the company with a purpose and a sense of mission . . . From the leader's conviction and enthusiasm, the organization derives the spiritual energy that it needs to embark on a voyage into the unknown.
>
> (Hammer and Champy 1993: 103)

> Leaders who can articulate such an ideology and create the dynamic network that can make it happen will succeed in moving their organizations far beyond continuous improvement to the new competitive arena of mass customization.
>
> (Pine II et al. 1993: 119)

Gatsby and the American Dream as enshrined in the gurus prescriptions are juxtaposed with other less moral characters ('They were careless people, Tom and Daisy – they smashed up things and creatures and then retreated back into their money or their vast carelessness' – p. 180). In this way the American Dream and guru innovations are held up to be pure, for it is only the world that corrupts or 'the foul dust' that floats in its 'wake' (p. 2). Clark and Salaman (1998) have pointed out the moral character of management contained in guru narratives. Indeed, 'the new leader is more than a model of morality: s/he must also manage others' moralities' (1998: 154). In support of this they quote Senge (1990: 9) among others who writes 'Much of the leverage leaders can actually exert lies in helping people achieve more accurate, more insightful, and more empowering views of reality'. Similarly, Kanter (1989: 91) suggests that management is about 'Helping people believe in the importance of their work [for] . . . good leaders can inspire others with the power and excitement of their vision and give people a sense of purpose and pride in their work'. The American Dream, it would seem, is incorruptible and its purity and blind hope, irrespective of contradictions such as persistent inequalities, is part of the attraction.

Gone are the days then of autocrats, dictators or bureaucrats that ordered or coerced people into compliance. Indeed, managers are to embark on a 'journey' that is the American Dream. Yet it has been argued that: 'To ask for these qualities without questioning how their expression is suppressed by industrial practices that have been sedimenting into common sense for a century is naïve and probably futile' (Jacques 1996: 30). It could be argued that our analogy of corporate innovation and the American Dream itself breaks down since the big corporations that can afford to adopt guru innovations are already hugely successful, thus having no connection with 'the rags to riches' element of the ideology. Our argument is that although critical to the ideology of the American Dream, the 'rags to riches' folklore is recognized as a myth that cannot be taken too seriously. The American Dream sustains itself rather on the basis of what is called 'striving for', not necessarily achieving, success or what is called the 'success ethic' (Berger 1963; Luckmann and Berger 1964). Our primary concern is to highlight how the imperative to unite in striving incessantly for more and more innovation and change is a central feature of the guru message to managers and employees. Everyone is required to soak up and unquestioningly enact the individual pursuit of wealth, irrespective of its consequences for others or themselves. Managers are extolled to 'get innovative or get dead' (Peters 1992); to re-engineer 'everything, including ourselves' (Champy 1995: 33) so as to 'profoundly rearrange the way people conceive of themselves, their work, their place in society' (Hammer and Stanton 1995: 321). This transformation of managers and others seeks to procure a 'new loyalty' but seemingly it 'is not to the boss or to the company but to projects that actualize a mission and offer challenge, growth, and credit for results' (Kanter 1989: 92). It seems that we must forget that 'projects' or indeed work occur within a context that is bound up with and reproduces relations of power and inequality.

According to Ishikawa (1985: 44) 'Quality Control is a thought revolution in management' and for Crosby (1979: 6) quality requires 'establishing a cultural revolution – a cultural revolution that would last forever'. Likewise, mass customization is 'not just an extension of continuous improvement' but calls for a 'transformed company' (Pine II *et al.* 1993: 108). Here then is the reinvention, but quite what it means or the problems it confronts are not clear, as we shall explore in the chapters to follow. But for the gurus this is not their concern; they are in the business of selling the American Dream and that dream is bound up with, and secured precisely through, peddling it to others. And once it is passed on, they are no longer responsible for its realization. Numerous guru wannabes, consultants and of course practising managers take on the responsibility for operationalizing the innovations. Clearly these are dream commodities in more ways than one. It is a salesperson's dream to offer products whose effectiveness depends on their application, since if they work, the guru takes the credit. If they should fail, on the other hand, blame falls on the manager who is said to have implemented the innovations imperfectly. The promise that the gurus hold out to managers is paralleled in Fitzgerald's closing articulation of how both the early explorers saw America for the first time and how Gatsby envisaged his future with Daisy. As with all dreams, they are elusive and slip away from us even as they are within our grasp:

> I became aware of the old island that flowered once for Dutch sailors' eyes – a fresh, green breast of the New World. Its vanished trees, the trees that had made way for Gatsby's house, had once pandered in whispers to the last and greatest of all human dreams; for a transitory enchanted moment man must have held his breath in the presence of this continent, compelled into aesthetic contemplation he neither understood nor desired, face to face for the last time in history with his capacity for wonder . . . I thought of Gatsby's wonder when he first picked out the green light at the end of Daisy's dock. He had come a long way to this blue lawn, and his dream must have seemed so close that he could hardly fail to grasp it. He did not know that it was already behind him.
>
> (Fitzgerald [1925] 1986: 182)

Innovation in context

In this section we explore what we mean by innovation. There are a number of broad based definitions of innovation such as it being any novel 'idea, practice or material artefact' (Rogers and Shoemaker 1971: 19) or the 'first commercial application of a new process or product' (Freeman 1982, quoted in Tidd *et al.* 1997: 24). According to Peters and Waterman (1995: 12) the word has a double meaning including 'creative people developing marketable new products and services' and innovative companies 'continually responding to change of any sort in their environment'. One of the problems within the literature is that universal definitions are commonly adopted, which then legislate as to what is to count as innovation independently of the specific conditions of its development and reproduction. Following the view that knowledge is always contingent on the conditions of its genesis and application, we take innovation simply to mean organizational change or the transformation of established practices. In our empirical research, we accepted practitioners' own views about management innovation. Consequently, rather than restrict itself to some ideal that was rarely realized, any organizing practice that an adopting company perceived to be 'novel' or innovatory was included in our study. In this way our definition was able to accommodate the different contexts of innovation in use. We therefore avoided artificially imposing constructions of reality upon our respondents on the basis that if they were convinced their practices were innovative, that was sufficient for us to study them. Likewise, if they defined their interventions as re-engineering, teamworking or KM, we went along with their definitions despite disagreements within the literature as to the meaning and indeed novelty of such initiatives.

The literature is strewn with prescriptive panaceas, and/or rational/technical guides to implementing innovations that displace bureaucratic organization. By rational/technical approaches we refer to the way in which certain authors, and especially the guru literature, treat organizations as problems for which technical solutions (innovations) can be designed. For example, P.B. Crosby (1979) defined quality as 'conformance to requirements' and one of his principal prescriptions was that organizations concentrate on calculating the 'price of non-conformance' (PONC). In a way, that is redolent of the American Dream, Crosby argued that: 'Quality is an achieveable, measurable, profitable entity that can be installed once you have commitment and understanding, and are prepared for hard work' (p. 6). Such approaches, in our view, present a mechanistic stance towards managing organizations (see Knights and McCabe 1997). For it is assumed that once an innovation has been 'installed', organizations respond mechanically – much like a car to pressure from the accelerator. Commands are presumed to be complied with since consensus is treated as a given. Thus there is assumed to be an implicit agreement about whether to innovate, what innovation to pursue and also that everyone will benefit from innovating. This is why Deming (1986) is able to offer a 14-point plan in order to achieve a quality organization or 'constancy of purpose'. Paradoxically, it is also why Peters and Waterman (1995) are able to prescribe 'eight attributes' that characterize excellent companies, such as 'a bias for action' or 'productivity through people', despite avowing a disregard for overly rational approaches towards organization.

In the previous chapter we provided a brief analysis of the historical conditions underlying the contemporary developments in management innovation that are examined in later chapters. In order to distinguish our approach towards innovation further, it is necessary to provide some ideas about how innovation is understood by a limited selection of other authors.[11] Until fairly recently the management innovation literature was primarily occupied by studies of technology and diffusion was the dominant analytical framework. Diffusion was seen to be a product of the cost-benefit potential of any particular innovation (Freeman 1982; Rogers 1995). Analysis was predominantly based on assumptions of economic rationality and, as Newell *et al.* (2001: 7) point out, was capable of explaining the spread of clear-cut innovations that have unambiguous benefits. They were less able to understand the take-up of innovations that are dubious and less likely to offer efficiency benefits (Abrahamson 1991). The fads and fashions approach has broadened the nature of the analysis to include political dimensions (Abrahamson 1991, 1996; Keiser 1997) to account for the selection of certain innovations as opposed to others (Newell *et al.* 2001: 7). This is more in line with our approach but we provide detailed empirical studies of innovation adoptions – something that is quite rare in this field.

There is frequently a blurring of consultancy and academic accounts of innovation as the latter want to demonstrate the practical utility of their work and the former attempt to legitimize their prescriptions, sometimes by reference to academic research (e.g. Davenport 1993; Peters and Waterman 1995). It might also be pointed out that prescription in academic work cannot be separated from the concern to have an impact since if the book has an appeal outside of academic courses, not only are the sales much greater but also potentially highly remunerative consultancy contracts may follow.[12]

Tidd *et al.* (1997) is a good example within the academic literature where, although clearly written with a student audience in mind and offering an analytical framework for studying innovation, the central premise is managerial. That is to say, innovation is to be studied entirely unproblematically as a means of assisting management in their task of growing and making the business more profitable. While the authors resist the 'one best way' formula (p. 15) that more recently has been modified limitedly by a notion of 'best practice' (i.e. a model of organization that becomes a benchmark standard) they make no apologies for being wholly prescriptive. Their first chapter begins by illustrating a few selected examples of successful companies[13] and the remainder of the text is concerned to prescribe guidelines of what companies should do in order to be successful innovators. It does so in terms of a framework or what they describe as a 'blueprint for success' (p. 40) involving sequential phases: scanning, strategy, resourcing, implementation, and learning and 're-innovation'. In presenting their material, however, the authors illustrate many of their prescriptions with reference either to a practical example from industry or a piece of academic research. In this sense, the book can be read as a substitute for reading all the studies and literatures that are quoted since students only need a broad overview of the field and can select a limited range of the material to investigate further when pursuing an assignment in that area.

Although quite comprehensive in covering a wide spectrum of literature as long as it can be supportive of their framework, this book differs in being much less prescriptive and unreflective than most of the guru literature whose target audience is the management practitioner or the lay reader. The concern of such books is to sell millions in airports, railway stations and in promotional presentations to companies by offering simplistic panaceas to a whole range of management *problems* that ironically are themselves treated as unproblematic or commonsensically obvious. In order to avoid complicating the style of presentation, the guru literature refers as little as possible to academic research evidence, displacing it with confident commonplace assertions and generalizations that appear plausible if not examined too closely.

Of course, there are a wide variety of literatures on innovation and not all offer such simplistic prescriptions as we shall see below. In the 1980s, the publication of key texts (Pfeffer 1981; Mintzberg 1983; Pettigrew 1985) challenged the unitarist view that organizations follow a linear trajectory towards greater efficiency and control. The general tenor of this literature (e.g. Pfeffer 1981; Pettigrew 1973) was to acknowledge organizational politics (OP) so as to eradicate its tendency to disrupt the rational goals of organizations (Knights and Murray 1994). Rather than ignore the pursuit of sectional or individual self-interests on the part of both managers and employees, as did much of the previous managerial and guru literature, the objective was to understand OP as a way of limiting its disruptive effects.

Reflecting a similar approach, there has developed a less functionalist literature exploring the place of politics in strategic and change management (Watson 1994), TQM (Wilkinson et al. 1991, 1992; Dawson 1994), employee involvement (Marchington et al. 1993) and in technological change and innovation (Drory and Romm 1990; Scarborough and Corbett 1992). This pluralist or processual literature challenges the gurus' representations of organizations as rational systems. However, it fails to analyse the systematic inequalities within organizations that reflect broader conditions of inequality (e.g. class, race, gender, sexuality) within society. While acknowledging power and the diversity or plurality of interests within organizations, these are seen as things to be managed rather than accepted, or controlled rather than researched.

In sharp contrast to this literature, there is a substantial body of work that is inspired by Marxist theory and labour process analysis (Braverman 1974). Though a diverse collection, this literature places inequality centre stage in its analysis of innovation (Marglin 1974, 1979; Ramsey 1977, 1985; Wilkinson and Willmott 1995; Ackers et al. 1996; Thompson and Warhurst 1998). Innovation therefore reflects the structural antagonism between capital and labour, and can be understood in terms of capital's preoccupation with pumping surplus value from labour power. Thus, capital and its agents (management) are understood to be absorbed with controlling the uncertainties and unpredictability of the labour process. This may lead management to devise new ways of extracting surplus value from labour, for instance, through just-in-time (JIT)/TQM (Delbridge et al. 1992), BPR (Willmott 1994, 1995b; Grey and Mitev 1995) or cultural interventions (Ray 1985; Willmott 1993). For 'the ultimate goal of management under a JIT/TQM regime must be recognised to be Total Management Control' (Delbridge et al. 1992: 105). Alternatively, it may be a response to a challenge from below and, as such, the concern is to share power in order to regain it (Fox and Flanders 1969). Innovation in the form of employee participation is to stave off a more formal challenge to power/authority relations (Ramsey 1977, 1985).

While the above literature is to be applauded for focusing our attention upon the persistent inequalities within society and the structural antagonisms within employment, it also has some limitations. Not least of these is the deterministic representation of management that it offers as the 'agents of capital' rather than subjective beings who may innovate due to individual career interests (Marchington et al. 1993) or indeed as a means to secure control over their lives (Watson 1994). This points to a fundamental weakness in the more traditional labour process literature – its neglect of subjectivity (Thompson 1990) (cf. Knights and Willmott 1989). In contrast to traditional labour process theory, we theorize power as being 'productive' as well as 'repressive' of subjectivity in the workplace (Foucault 1977, 1979). Power is exercised through discursive practices targeted on others in order to secure their power to carry out certain activities. But there are some limits to what can be appropriated by discourse (May 1999) in so far as discourse can never be exhaustive of a subject's potential to act, and therefore does not determine behaviour. De Certeau (1988: xix) linked this to the relationship between strategies and tactics, the former having their own space in which to be enacted whereas the latter involve levels of subjugation in which subjects rely largely on opportunistic moments where gaps, discontinuities or inconsistencies can be exploited. Thus power is not conceived as something that simply limits, denies or refuses the creative potential of labour but instead is understood to be integral to how individuals come to understand themselves as subjects. Moreover, power is not understood to be the 'property' of a capitalist class that pumps surplus value out of a relatively powerless working class who have only their labour power to sell. Instead, power is conceived in 'relational' terms whereby everyone is understood to be capable of exercising power as a condition of their participation in social relations (Smart 1983). As explored in the chapters that follow, an analysis of subjectivity can greatly enhance our understanding of innovation. This is because subjectivity, as constituted through capitalist, gendered and other power relations, is often the target of new management innovations. We will further explore these concepts and ideas in subsequent chapters in relation to specific innovations.

Business evangelists in a disenchanted world: *Plus ça change, plus la même chose*

The analysis of innovation, whether under the auspices of sociological, organizational or management theory, workplace studies, the study of technology or in popular managerialism, proliferates within academia, management consultancy, the media and politics, and more limitedly among management practitioners. As we approached the twenty-first century, the management and organization literature witnessed a veritable boom in demands for, and claims to have discovered, the ultimate innovative panacea. Emulating the pop music charts, the 'Thinkers 50' survey (FT Dynamo.com) provides a list of the top 50 management gurus and still leaves numerous less celebrated or famous management writers on the sidelines. While the narratives that are produced by popular management thinkers have effects disproportionate to the substance of their ideas, it is important not to be entirely dismissive of the guru phenomenon. For it is as much a part of the field of study as the management and organizational practice that it seeks to shock and shape. So much so that a number of social scientists have sought to study management gurus as phenomena in their own right (Huczynski 1993b; Clark and Salaman 1996, 1998; Jackson 1996, 2001).

Our concern in this book is not only to condemn the simplicity, lack of originality, immorality and/or implausibility of guru prescriptions; this we leave to others (Boje and Winsor 1993; Steingard and Fitzgibbons 1993; Willmott 1993, 1994; Grint 1994; Grey and Mitev 1995). Rather it is to examine their frequent failure to deliver what they promise in terms of certain limitations that can rarely be understood in the absence of empirical analysis. But in advance of following this line of thinking, it is interesting to review the guru phenomenon in terms of what might be seen as a religious legacy that is wholly counter to the world of business. It is religious in the sense that it appeals to mysticism or magic (see Clark and Salaman 1996; Fincham 2000) rather than the Enlightenment's emphasis on rationality and order; and as with any religious sect it has its followers, spiritual leaders and heroes or heroines.[14] The paradox, of course, is that one would suppose that the preoccupation with financial rectitude, economic precision and instrumental control of externalities in pursuit of administrative efficiency and/or commercial profit would render business people unsympathetic to spiritual matters. Yet, as we shall see, this is far from being the case.

The success of the gurus is of course to marry these two seemingly incompatible worlds by offering practical solutions to efficiency and/or profitability within a package the spiritual flavour of which can be inspirational to those in need of direction or in search of 'quick fixes' as career moves. Consider, for instance, the popularity of Tom Peters and Robert Waterman's (1995) book *In Search of Excellence* (first published in 1982). Given the routines and highly regulated practices of modern corporations, this may be a welcome supplement that helps to release the tension that Weber (1978) identified when he warned of the incompatibility between issues of ethical substance and the formalism of the 'rule-bound', bureaucratic administration. In so far as the ethical has emotional or irrational content, it must 'reject what reason demands' (Weber 1978: 980). Yet in its idealized form bureaucracy, the legal–rational system of domination becomes indestructible. Consequently, irrespective of vice or virtue, the bureaucracy resists emotion because of its superior system of rational organization (cf. Webster 1978: 987).

Another of Weber's concerns was the associated dehumanizing implications of bureaucracy. In one classic phrase, he commiserated about a stage of cultural development in which there are 'specialists without vision, sensualists without heart' (Weber 1930 quoted in Wrong 1970: 28). Reduced to a 'small cog in a ceaselessly moving mechanism' (Weber 1978: 988), the bureaucrat is devoid of individuality and is virtually impotent to influence the form or content of the activities to which he or she contributes. This results from the bureaucracy's power of organizational control that is an important condition of its rationality. The gurus then bring a breath of spiritual fresh air to the bureaucratic world of business and this must partly account for the favourable reception given to them by practising managers.

But this is only part of the story, for the other big problem for management is that unlike engineering or medicine which are applications of physics or biology, management has no science upon which to base its practice. At the same time, the effects of management practice are highly visible and individual careers are dependent on at least the appearance of success within hierarchical relations (Marchington *et al.* 1993; Watson 1994). This need to be successful, in the context of there being no sure or well defined path to its attainment, generates considerable anxiety among managers and not surprisingly makes them exceedingly vulnerable to charismatic outsiders who seem convinced that they have a solution to their problems (Huczynski 1993b; Jackson 1996). But why did this seemingly become more of an issue in the late twentieth century than previously?

Although by no means exhaustive, a number of conditions that would need to be considered in such an analysis are enumerated here. First is the past success of external consultants and gurus providing a climate in which almost every large company now employs them for various projects, and particularly those concerned with innovation (Huczynski 1993b; Sturdy 1997). Contemporary gurus can not only trade on the legitimacy that these earlier exponents provided but also learn from their mistakes, particularly with respect to self-promotion (see below). Second are the competitive conditions that gave birth to and have been intensified as a result of New Right politics in many western economies, the growth of eastern Tiger economies since the early 1980s, and the concomitant anxieties that these generate. Third, partly as a consequence of these competitive conditions, a merger mania has resulted in the need for major organizational culture transformations. Fourth is the growth and elaboration of marketing and self-promotion that has swept through our society as everything from emotions to entertainment and philosophies to products are commodified (i.e. treated as a commodity to sell in the marketplace) as they claim a piece of consumer action. Fifth is the rather dramatic development in new micro-electronic information and communication technology, including the internet, which provides both a product and a medium of communication for consultants and gurus. Finally is the growth and development of the media that is always looking for stories and news items, providing a convenient vehicle for free advertising for the gurus.

The proliferation and success of management gurus also brings in its train parallel attempts to debunk and deny their substantive value. Should every guru book have written on the cover the warning that reading this 'may seriously damage your wealth'? The empirical research that we draw upon in this book could justify such a warning because rarely have we seen the enormous investment that guru mania has inflicted producing an appropriate return on profits (Cottrell 1992; Hall *et al.* 1993; Stewart 1993). Of course the companies have made profits but there is little evidence to suggest that these were a direct outcome of the particular innovation. The difficulties of establishing a link between a particular intervention and corporate performance have been discussed elsewhere in relation to TQM (Hackman and Wageman 1995). Part of the problem is that, as many of our respondents pointed out, the complexity of organization makes it difficult if not impossible to attribute a particular outcome to a specific cause. While this does not preclude the attempt to identify the causes of specific organizational events, it is not unreasonable to recognize these as political strategies for mobilizing resources and enrolling people toward a particular objective. The outcomes of such political interventions, then, ought to be defined as much as the consequences as a reflection of say, a 'healthy economy' or of a programme of cost cutting. Clearly, cost cutting exercises such as labour depletion enforce productivity increases (see Ezzamel *et al.* 2001) that inevitably have an initial positive effect on the 'bottom line'. However, they can also have highly negative consequences for long-term profitability in limiting the scope for expansion and in removing many of those with a wealth of accumulated tacit knowledge and cultural skill. Because of this, many gurus seek to avoid wrapping their panaceas around one basic cost saving device such as downsizing (see e.g. Hammer and Stanton 1995) because this removes the appeal of their innovation as an ongoing means to profit.

In the words of a senior editor of *The Economist*, the work of management gurus 'is 99 percent bullshit. And everybody knows that' (Micklethwait and Wooldridge 1996: x). Everybody, it would seem, except a very large number of practising managers who are the principal 'consumers' (Huczynski 1993b) that put so many of these books in the best selling charts for non-fiction, and presumably, if they were properly categorized, in the charts for fiction as well. For when it comes down to it, these books are simply stories that promise, like the proverbial fairy godmother, to make things better (Marchington 1995). Some trace the guru craze to F.W. Taylor (Micklethwait and Wooldridge 1996) while others attribute it to the rise of the professional manager in the post-war period (Huczynski 1993b) which has witnessed a divorce between knowledge of work processes in favour of general management techniques that are taught in business schools and on MBA programmes (see Armstrong 2000). One of the necessary conditions for prescriptive solutions to occur regarding what were seen as management problems was presumably the separation of ownership from control that evolved with the Joint Stock Company Act (1844) and the limited liability that facilitated equity shareholdings to be dispersed rather than concentrated. Yet it was not until well into the twentieth century that almost every largish company had assumed a public status wherein management accountability revolved largely around the share price and dividend allocation, in turn dependent on profits. It is in this context that the professional manager as agent of the owner(s) of capital or the shareholder began to become dominant.

Much of the contemporary guru literature professes to be radical and often revolutionary, as is evident from the titles or subtitles (Jacques 1996) of many of the popular treatises on management change. Typical of these titles are Hammer and Champy's *Reengineering the Corporation: A Manifesto For Business Revolution* (1993); Tom Peters' *Liberation Management* (1992); and Deming's *Out of the Crisis* (1986). This often Marxist political language is used more for its shock value than as any meaningful account of these books' content. An important feature of the guru literature that is often neglected can be unlocked by exploring its use of language – especially a language that at first sight might seem so incongruous. Why would a literature that cannot be seen as anything but (albeit) a chastising celebration of the virtues of capitalism borrow from its strongest and most virulent critic? Apart from forcing people to 'sit up' and take notice, such language is presumably used to indicate the seriousness of the problem because if only a revolution can save matters, the situation must be in serious crisis. In order to mobilize resources and enrol supporters for the innovations being proposed, it is necessary to establish that there *is* a crisis. So what better way than to use the language of Marx (who believed that the crisis of capitalism would lead to its overthrow) for purposes of ensuring precisely the opposite – a consolidation of the prevailing inequalities of capitalism through a systematic improvement in its rational efficiency? So the concept of revolution is less about a radical transformation of objectives than a simple tinkering or modification of the means to achieve the existing or prevailing objectives. In the hands of these gurus, revolutionary change becomes the perfect illustration of *plus ça change, plus la même chose* (Karr 1849) or the more we change the more things stay the same.

Ironically, the gurus' justification for advocating change that is little more than keeping things as they are, or reinforcing the stranglehold that capitalist business values and practices have on societies worldwide, is the fact that everything is changing. Their historical grasp of this so-called change to which organizations have to respond by changing in accordance with the gurus' recommendations exists only in so far as it provides a point of past stability against which the dynamic present can be contrasted (Grey 2000a). Clearly gurus as 'future writers' (Toffler 1981) tend to exaggerate current realities by ignoring or bowdlerizing the past but they also refuse to consider the notion of change as an extremely slippery concept and as one that is embedded in the past.

If a change can be detected it is simply the greater nervousness about change that is evident today compared with more than two decades ago. Moreover, it is precisely this anxiety the gurus exploit while at the same time ensuring that there will be more change in order to guarantee a future market for their panaceas. For as Jackson (1996) notes, the gurus simultaneously use fear: 'the choice is survival: it's between redundancies of 50% or 100%' (Hammer 1990: 13) and hope: 'if you learn to do what other managers in your industry thought to be impossible, you will not only thrive, you will literally redefine the industry' (Champy 1995: 122). The question that is in some doubt is that of change itself – can it be seen to be greater now than in the past and what would be the criteria for making such a claim? It might be seen as almost heretical to challenge the idea that we are passing through a historically unprecedented period of change at the beginning of the twenty-first century. For not only does it question the validity of a growing number of writings but more importantly it undercuts a vast army of consultants and gurus by questioning the ground of their managerial solutions and innovative panaceas.

However, the assumptions on which this belief in unprecedented change are based do not stand up to critical scrutiny. Grey (2000a: 3), for example, argues that there are 'flaws, inconsistencies and paradoxes in the discourse of change and change management'. Our selective denial of them is part of a collective myopia that fetishizes the changes of a relatively limited western elite as if they were universal phenomena. Because of the globalization of capitalism, western ethnocentricism probably has more credence today than at other time in history but only in so far as we impose our own social constructions of the privilege given to economic reality on the rest of the world. While Asian children may be supplementing the incomes of peasant parents by illegally working in the sweat-shops of transnational corporations rather than working on the land, their lives are not so much a reflection of change as a reinforcement of world capitalist domination and exploitation. Furthermore, this exploitation of child labour helps to sustain the continuity of competitive capitalism and the privileges it ensures for western populations. Again, *plus ça change, plus la même chose* (Karr 1849).[15]

The absence of much reflexivity in the management literature often means that authors are in denial about the significance of their own interests and values in the production of managerial prescriptions and descriptions. Quite clearly the belief in change is a selective perception of reality that is grounded in the recognition that it can be readily treated as a problem to which organizations have no choice but to respond.[16] Guru prescriptions are simply guidelines or structured means of responding to the unpredictable features of change. Change is thus an important condition and consequence of both the problems and the solutions offered by management consultants and gurus. In the next chapter we seek to articulate a framework through which our empirical analyses are located and illustrate this by discussing quality management or TQM, which is one of the more enduring of the numerous innovations examined in this book.

A research framework: TQM as an illustrative case

This chapter presents a research framework that understands any management innovation, such as TQM, as discursive knowledge that can have certain power effects. It may transform individuals into subjects that secure some sense of their own meaning and identity through participating either as managers or employees in the practices the knowledge embraces. Alternatively, TQM can result in subjects resisting or distancing themselves from, rather than embracing, the discourse. Within the academic literature, TQM discourse can broadly be seen as subscribing to one of three approaches that we describe as *rational managerialist*, *critical control* and *processual*. This chapter critiques each of these approaches so as to offer an alternative way of understanding TQM, and this sets the scene for the variety of innovations discussed in subsequent chapters.

Many contemporary organizations have been persuaded by consultants or gurus to introduce TQM in order to succeed in an increasingly volatile market-place where customer service is seen as *the* pathway to competitive advantage. TQM is central to many companies' attempts to differentiate or distinguish their products and services. TQM is distinctive in so far as it concentrates the mind and body on improving the quality of goods or services. The earliest 'name for these efforts was total quality control' (Steingard and Fitzgibbons 1993: 29)[1] although TQM would now be seen as primarily involved with continuous improvement, teamworking and a customer focus (Dean and Bowen 1994).

Our concern in this chapter is to offer an alternative 'perspective on the nature and meaning, indeed the relevance of quality management to management theory' (Klimoski 1994: 390) to that which is conventionally available (e.g. *Academy of Management Review* 1994). More precisely, drawing on Foucault's (1980, 1982) analysis of power and subjectivity, we contrast our own framework with three other perspectives that are prominent in the literature. Two of these – the rational managerialist and critical control perspectives – would appear diametrically opposed but, in our view, implicitly share a view that in practice, hierarchical control is comparatively unproblematic. The difference is that the managerialists celebrate whereas the critics denounce or lament the effectiveness of management control. After pointing out their exaggeration or unacceptable faith in the control potential of change management programmes such as TQM, we turn to the processual approach. This approach follows a more sophisticated managerialist line of argument than the rational perspective, partly because it fills in some of the messy sociopolitical aspects of organization. However, in our view, it fails to develop or exploit this insight sufficiently. In order to build on these critical evaluations, we turn to Foucault to develop the foundations of an alternative perspective.

Rational managerialists

Implicit in the writings of the gurus of TQM (e.g. Crosby 1979; Deming 1986; Juran 1988) is an 'objectivist' perspective where analysis is conducted as if organizations were purely rational and politically neutral entities. The result is a belief that corporate strategies can be rationally designed and planned so that the quality of an organization's output matches with customers' demands or expectations. Revealing this rationality, Deming (1986) argues that organizations should exhibit constancy of purpose, yet he notes that to achieve this end 'management must give up their sacred cows (e.g. quick profit)' (Spencer 1994). Recognizing that 'variability is inherent to all phenomena' (Anderson *et al.* 1994: 474), Deming nonetheless demonstrates a faith in rational control when he constructs his 14 points[2] in the belief that they provide management with the tools necessary 'to manage this variability'.

In common with all the quality gurus, Deming subscribes to a unitarist conception that assumes a consensus among the members of an organization with respect to its goals and the means to their achievement. Any conflict or diversity regardless of its potential to challenge or disrupt the status quo is disregarded. Ignoring the political tensions of control and resistance that pervade most organizations, Deming assumes that by implementing his 14 points, the organization's goals of reduced waste or uniformity of output can be equated with its employees' goals. According to Crosby (1979) management can plan and achieve 'conformance to requirements' and organizational outcomes will match management's desired intentions and objectives. A similar view was expressed by Ishikawa (1985: 3) who argued that 'by studying quality control, and by applying QC properly, the irrational behaviour of industry and society could be corrected'.

Rational managerialists clearly neglect the central indeterminacy of labour (Marx [1867] 1976) and the dynamics of social interaction which often lead to unplanned for, and unanticipated, consequences (Boudon 1981) in work organizations. This neglect stems from faith in the idea of empowerment as if power can be bestowed on an individual much like a commodity is transferred from one person to another. As we illustrate below, rational managerialists fail to recognize that to exercise power remains the prerogative of all persons who are capable of acting as 'free' agents, not simply in a way that is directed by management. It is our view that for many practitioners empowerment is simply a euphemism for control, and yet since power cannot be possessed in the same way as property, managers are not in a position to 'give' power to employees. 'Empowerment' is thus a rhetorical device to encourage employees to use their power/freedom in ways that are supportive of managerial ends. It does so by an appeal to deeply internalized values of autonomy and responsibility that, as defining features of modern subjectivity, are likely to meet with unexpected outcomes.

Our next group of theorists diverges dramatically from rational managerialist prescriptions in criticizing, rather than celebrating, management control. Nonetheless, they seem to share with the gurus a belief in managerial omnipotence such that there is little question, in this selective example of their work, of management control being anything other than effective.

A critical control focus

One way to look at the critics is to distinguish those that appear to focus on the work intensification aspects from those that concentrate on the self-disciplining effects of quality management programmes. The former perceive TQM as extending surveillance and enforcing ever-increasing workloads on the employee and, thereby, could be seen as the very opposite of empowerment at work. Delbridge et al. (1992), Parker and Slaughter (1993) and McArdle et al. (1995) could readily be placed in this camp. By contrast, a second camp (e.g. Boje and Winsor 1993; Steingard and Fitzgibbons 1993; Tuckman 1994, 1995) understand quality management to inculcate values of quality and customer service so as to result (not necessarily in a directly intentional manner) in collective and individual self-discipline and control. However, whatever the emphasis, all the critics appear convinced that TQM increases the scope and diversity of management control.

Techniques such as increased surveillance and monitoring, heightened accountability, peer pressure through teams and customers, and involvement in waste elimination through continuous improvement, lead to a situation which: 'intensifies work by eliminating "waste" or "slack" . . . Total Quality Control in effect translates into Total Management Control' (Delbridge et al. 1992: 97).[3] Parker and Slaughter (1993) usefully explore the ways in which a concern with management control lies beneath the surface of TQM, such that they refer to it as 'management by stress'. They suggest that, through the rhetoric of the customer, management seek to remove all 'non-management imposed restrictions'. Accordingly, the requirements of each job are linked to internal-external customer needs, but this disguises how managers set specifications and determine hours of work, patterns of work organization, manning levels etc. Unlike the gurus, Parker and Slaughter do not view the concern to 'reduce variability' as a 'neutral' intervention. For it is management that sets the 'standards' of variation and the 'specifications' that attain control over work and employees, leading to highly repetitive and routine tasks, and work intensification. Likewise, in 'documenting' work tasks and standardizing routines, the autonomy of employees is removed, and their indispensability greatly reduced. Another TQM concept, 'waste elimination', is seen by these critics to mean job displacement and further work intensification, since labour is the most expensive factor of production: 'The bottom line is that management reduces the resources and staffing, while demanding increased output through appealing to pride, institutional loyalty and insecurity. Authority and real power move upward while accountability is forced to lower levels' (1993: 53).

Also from a control perspective, Tuckman (1994: 732) has argued that TQM 'takes away individual autonomy and reconstructs worker initiative in a manner that allows management determination'. As has been argued elsewhere (Boje and Winsor 1993), TQM is seen to share in common many of the characteristics of Taylorism (see Chapter 2). Indeed Boje and Winsor (1993: 66) go so far as to suggest that: 'By eliminating the perceived power of management to impose control from above and by deluding workers into thinking that this power now emanates from their own actions, TQM programmes have succeeded in *eliminating the resistance* that has long characterised management/labour relations' (emphasis added)

From the opposite end of the political spectrum to the quality gurus, it may be argued, these authors share a similar belief in the ability of managers to control employees. The difference is that, in contrast to the gurus who believe that TQM will empower and enrich the work experience of employees, these critical theorists are more inclined to perceive TQM as another example of work intensification and worker degradation. Such theorists are in general sympathy with the work of Braverman (1974) and a labour process analysis where the emergence of 'job enlargement, enrichment, or rotation, work groups or teams, consultation or worker "participation"' was seen as a response by management to 'social antagonism' within the workplace. Such innovation, as Braverman saw it, is concerned with 'costs and controls, not the humanization of work' (1974: 36). While post-Braverman, labour process theory has encouraged a departure from such deterministic approaches (Burawoy 1979), there is always a tendency to slide back into 'heavy duty' conceptions of management control (cf. Jermier *et al.* 1994).

Overall, we have several doubts about the prescriptive theories of TQM largely because of their asocial conception of individual employees and their mechanistic assumptions about organizations. But, it is our contention that some of the critics run the risk of following a similar position as the managerialists in assuming that management can impose their techniques unproblematically on employees/staff. By this we mean that both managerialists and critics have a tendency to presume management to be omnipotent, if not omniscient, in their ability to transform rationally planned intentions into realized practical outcomes. Despite the focus of some of these critics on the labour process, many of them pay scarce attention to the power and identity relations that pervade organizations and the possibility that employees may transform, evade or resist strategies and programmes which bear down on them. Despite these misgivings, we have few doubts that TQM and other change strategies have control and work-intensification effects. However, management control cannot be taken for granted since spaces and opportunities for resistance are rarely entirely absent. To illustrate some of the limits to understanding enshrined in rational managerialist and control focused approaches towards TQM, we will now turn to a case study from the manufacturing sector.

Case study: Carco[4]

Carco is a manufacturer of auto-components based in the West Midlands. It recognizes the Transport and General Workers Union (TGWU) which represents the majority of shop-floor employees. This case study utilized a number of methods including formal and informal interviewing techniques, observation and documentary investigation. Primary data was initially gained through formally interviewing a variety of personnel from throughout the organizational hierarchy over a two-month period towards the end of 1991. These included the personnel director, the personnel manager, the TGWU's works convenor, the Manufacturing, Science and Finance Union's (MSF) chief staff representative, five TGWU shop stewards, 15 shop-floor employees and a group interview with seven MSF shop stewards. The interviews were recorded and followed a semi-structured format. In addition, there were many informal conversations with a variety of staff. The company was revisited in June 1993 and in March and July 1997.

Over the past 20 years Carco has gone through a period of substantial organizational restructuring and has introduced a number of innovative work practices. These changes have accompanied massive job losses and the workforce has dwindled from 1200 in 1979 to 600 in 1997. Here the focus will be upon one particular innovation, the total quality approach (TQA), introduced during the late 1980s and early 1990s. In 1988, the managing director (MD) sought advice from a consultant, who provided a one-day seminar for management to improve its understanding of the potential for change. Though entitled 'total quality', the seminar had a great deal to do with JIT. The consultant argued that 'total quality' could be achieved through removing all surplus stocks. In doing so, the company would be able to expose its quality problems and move towards a 'total quality approach'. Hence bottlenecks in the production flow or areas where there were excessive errors or wastage would be revealed. Many members of the board were convinced that this was the way forward. Both the financial and engineering directors could see the cost savings to be gained by reducing stocks.

A different management approach

An alternative approach to that which the consultant recommended was subsequently proposed by the personnel director who considered that a JIT-led road to total quality was inconsistent with how the company should progress. A discussion document was submitted to the board of directors entitled 'A Preferred Future'; the following quote is an extract from that document:

> To become the best at anything, you need to identify where the real advantage can be realized over your competitors. For any manufacturing business to satisfy its market, it utilizes three principal resources: plant, material and people . . . Given the current international trading situation, with a few exceptions of own development, the same plant, equipment and materials can be acquired by our competitors . . . It can be concluded, therefore, that to attain an edge over our competitors may only realistic- ally be secured through the development of our people.

The Personnel Director saw that the way forward was through developing and involving shop-floor workers and the trade unions in problem solving, as opposed to simply shocking the system through removing stocks. He proposed: 'that all employees on an individual and on a representative basis, become involved in the decision-making process in order to encourage and harness the creativity of our work-force'.

Rather than an approach which involves removing stocks, and dealing with the problems that arise, the personnel director was concerned first and foremost with creating the conditions in which participation would thrive. Problems could then be isolated, through employee involvement, and removed. The per- sonnel director recalled: 'I decided to write a paper for the board taking a different approach altogether . . . the engineering director had a big influence on it because he could see the pound notes being brought out of the business through stock reduction and I was out voted'.

The TQA

The MD selected the engineering director to implement the TQA and he presented it to both the unions and employees in the first edition of a company magazine entitled the *Employee Bulletin*. In order to secure employee commit- ment to the proposed changes, the MD outlined in the *Bulletin* the company's financial and market difficulties. During the 1980s management had grouped machines around products (i.e. cellularized) rather than on a functional basis (i.e. grinding, drilling). In view of this, considerable gains had been made in reducing work in progress (WIP) due to the simplified production flow. The TQA involved repositioning machines to ensure the most efficient production flow and concentrating on reducing the amount of in-process stock. To this end, the engineering director set up a pilot cell and began exploring ways to reorganize machines so as to reduce machine set-up times and levels of stock. The engineer- ing director, according to the personnel director: 'understood the mechanics of JIT, but didn't understand the people issues that were involved in it'.

Numerous planning committees were established that effectively excluded the unions. At the end of this, the employees who would be working on the pilot cell were called in, and informed of the changes. The union convenor reflected:

> We used to have hundreds of bins of work waiting to go through the lines, stacked up on the far walls, costing the company a pile of money . . . So this was the idea, but they sat in there [the committee room] with a cell layout, and said 'Well this is the first cell . . . and this is what we'll do'. Now they didn't call any operators, or any shop stewards, or any of the managers, or controllers off the line. They decided what they were going to do . . . 'Course when they came out they said 'Right we'll have some consultation now. This is what we're going to do'. They got the guys in there, and said 'Now this is the layout'. And one of the guys said 'Hang on, you can't work like that'. They [the TQA committee] said 'Well why can't we?' . . . the guy said 'Well because of this . . .'. They said 'Oh, well we will do it'.

The management did not anticipate that the workers would have any suggestions as to how the programme could be better planned. Hence, at the initial meeting of the first cell, management did not invite, nor were they particularly willing to listen to, the employees' suggestions. Management had not expected that shop-floor workers would be concerned about the reorganization, or that they would understand the implications of the changes. Yet employees could immediately see the implications of the changes for their bonus-based pay system that was linked to measured individual output. One example of the confusion and problems that resulted concerned the introduction of an L-shaped layout of machines. This involved reorganizing machines so that an operator would be able to work on two machines that together formed an L shape. The convenor recalled: 'the management committee told the workers what they wanted. They just said "this is how we're having it". The workers said "It's more efficient if you have it back to back". The executives said "We want it like this". The workers said "It's all right you wanting it L-shaped but we have to walk 'x' miles extra, and you're not on bonus"'.

This gave rise to a paradoxical situation. The operators were recommending a more efficient way of working than that offered by management, who were in turn rejecting this more productive suggestion. The union convenor explained this:

> it wasn't his [the engineering director's] idea you see? If it's not invented here [i.e. in the committee room], then it's not going to work . . . the chemistry that existed between the group [the TQA committee] that sat. They were notorious for not wanting anything to do with the unions, or the guys on the shop-floor. They were all fairly bright people. Good engineers I would guess, in their own right, but didn't want anything to do with the shop-floor. 'We'll tell you': that's their attitude.

As management began to reduce stock levels, many of the workers were afraid that the company was closing down, as the training manager explained:

> workers didn't know what was going on . . . workers couldn't see the value of it. Some workers saw its introduction as the precursor to redundancy or closure. As they saw stocks being cut, they thought orders were being lost . . . In the machine shop the large stocks and work-in-progress gave the workers a sense of security, the loss of which led to fears of 'closure'. The problem was that no one informed the workers.

The personnel director reflected upon the TQA:

> it was dragged through many, many, planning committees. No involvement of the unions, and eventually the unions said 'No! Stuff it! This is jobs on the line for our members, all we can see is savings for you, and loss of jobs for our members, and we're having nothing to do with it'. So we had a very difficult time . . . But the engineering director had the loudest voice, if you like, and he took us down the JIT route, on a pilot basis, which alienated the unions . . . The unions were non-cooperative, non-committed to it, and it slowed the programme down so significantly that we, we didn't actually abort it, we carried on tinkering with it, and not really making any progress.

Because of the failure to carry the unions and their members, the TQA was effectively abandoned in the early 1990s despite efforts to continue 'tinkering with it'.

The case helps to illustrate some of the limitations of both the rational managerialist and the critical control focused approaches towards TQM and innovation more broadly. First, as we have seen, management is rarely as homogeneous as implied by these approaches. Rather it is characterized by competitive divisions and factions, power struggles and political machinations (see Knights and Murray 1994; Watson 1994; McCabe 1996). In the case of Carco, we saw conflicting views offered by the personnel director and the MD in terms of how to proceed. The former preferred to involve employees while the latter was primarily concerned to save costs. It was the MD's ability to exercise power over the subordinate personnel director that secured the approach that was eventually adopted.

Second, in view of the politics of management, it cannot be assumed that managers necessarily act in a uniformly rational manner. In the case of Carco the engineering director sought to impose change on others without taking their views into account. At one point this involved rejecting the employees' suggestion of a more efficient way of working because it was perceived as a threat to the superior rationality and status of management and indeed engineering.

Finally, the case reveals that despite the engineering director's intention to impose his will upon others, such an outcome cannot be guaranteed.

Consequently, management was unable to control individual employee re-actions to the TQA. Even though management presented their case for change in a way that precluded worker involvement, the employees insisted on airing their views because of the threat to earnings. Moreover, management were unable to overcome the more organized form of resistance when the unions withdrew their cooperation. Here we see how fragile management power is when a refusal to cooperate is capable of preventing the introduction of a particular management innovation. It also underlines the ability of employees to exercise power over management. In the next section we will explore a proces-sual approach towards TQM that, while resolving some of the limitations of rational managerialist and critical control perspectives, adds a few of its own.

A processual approach

We have found a parallel problem in both the rational managerialist and critical control perspectives on TQM in that there is an explicit or implicit assumption that management control is effective. However, it will be clear from our narrative that we are somewhat more sympathetic to the critics than to the managerialists. In other words, our critique of the managerialists is unambiguous but we are more ambivalent with respect to the critics. This ambivalence extends to the processual approach but for entirely the opposite reasons. Because processual theorists avoid deterministic assumptions that management control is unproblematic, we find their work insightful at the level of everyday implementations of TQM. Having said that, we draw partly on critical modes of analysis to question their tendency to refuse to look outside the organization for understandings of the difficulties that are experienced in implementing TQM and change management strategies. In short, we believe that the processual approach could learn a great deal from the critical approach in recognizing that the frequent failure of TQM programmes is not exclusively a function of communication and implementation problems. They are also related to contradictions in the very design of TQM models, fundamental inequalities in organizations, and perhaps most important of all, the imperatives that capitalist market relations impose on organizations.

Though not always explicitly, in our view, the processual approach[5] draws on a diverse range of theory extending back to Weber's social action/interpretive perspective and Mead's (1934) symbolic interactionism. As advanced by Mintzberg (1983) in the US and Pettigrew (1979, 1985) in the UK, it includes attempts to understand the micro-politics of organizational life and the way in which organizational action is embedded in the past. What is significant about the processual approach is that it does not usually assume linearity and determination or the control of meaning through hierarchical relations. It does not discount hierarchy but recognizes that meanings are constructed, developed and trans-formed through social interactions that involve some element of negotiation. Once it is recognized that social order is negotiated rather than simply imposed from above, politics enters as a process that mediates conflicting interests.

Identity theory

We have three main criticisms of the processual approach. The first concerns its failure to utilize and/or fully develop the insights provided by symbolic interactionism (Mead 1934). One of the principal advantages of the interactionist perspective that was particularly well developed by the Chicago School (e.g. Hughes 1958; Blumer 1969) was the sense in which identity was theorized as a central category of analysis. Processual theorists in general (e.g. Mintzberg 1983; Pettigrew 1985) but those having researched TQM in particular (e.g. Dawson and Webb 1989; Wilkinson *et al.* 1991, 1992; Hunter and Beaumont 1994; Fairhurst 1993; Dawson 1994; Grant *et al.* 1994; Wendt 1994) fail to draw upon this insight into identity in symbolic interactionism, and their analyses are weaker as a result. But there are clearly some limitations in this regard within symbolic interactionism itself. One of these relates to its comparatively close kinship with behaviourism. Although not sharing the crude behavioural determinism whereby the individual responds to stimuli purely in terms of their association with pleasure or pain (Skinner 1953), it can be argued that it is a social version of behaviourism. While the relationship between self and society is wholly interpretive rather than determined by the pattern of past stimulus-response experiences, individuals are driven by a desire for self-confirmation from 'others' in interactions. In short, attachment to particular identities is what drives behaviour.

A second but related problem is how the self is perceived principally as a cognitive machine designed to secure and reproduce itself. As a result, interactionists pay little attention to the body within which the self resides or to the processes of accommodating or managing inconsistent definitions of self. Instead, symbolic interactionists tend to view the self as a unitary and internally coherent and consistent phenomenon whereas there is a large postmodern feminist literature (e.g. Butler 1990; Kondo 1990; Bell 1999) that contradicts this. These feminists are against any universal conceptions of the self, given the different contexts in which it is formed and the multiplicity of identities that may reside within any one individual. From this position the symbolic interactionist conception of the self appears too fixed, cognitive and abstract.

While identity may have been neglected, a number of processual theorists have drawn on interactionist theory to challenge rationalist views of TQM (Wilkinson *et al.* 1991; Fairhurst 1993; Fairhurst and Wendt 1993). Their general argument is that because of the complexity of social interactions, organizations are much less coherent and consistent than such rationality presupposes. What is valuable about processual theory is that it questions the empirical validity of the orthodox assumptions on rationality and control. In their place, processual theory argues that strategies emerge often in a comparatively unstructured fashion and that their effects on an organization are unpredictable because of the consequences of political machinations and unanticipated events.

It has been argued that the model of TQM is full of internal contradictions, particularly in terms of the human dimension. For instance, some commentators have argued that TQM offers employee involvement while excluding employees from strategic level decision making (Dawson and Webb 1989); others point towards the contradiction between employee involvement and TQM's emphasis on clearly laid down instructions (Wilkinson *et al.* 1991, 1992). Many of the tensions facing TQM revolve around the problem of a mechanistic model designed to transform the behaviour of employees in the direction of providing quality products and services to both external and internal customers. However, whereas the quality of material products could often be improved by physical interventions in the work task and its organiza- tion, customer service demands that employees transform both body *and* soul. This means that their very sense of self and identity has to come closer to the task and the relationship with customers than has ever been the case before. Hence, the importance of considering identity when analysing TQM.

Functionalism

Our second criticism of processual theorists is that while they recognize the complexity of organizations they often slip into a functionalism that is not apparent in either Weber or Mead. For wherever they find elements of dis- order or instability they have a strong inclination to promote various social interventions such as improved communication or more broad-ranging HRM techniques in order to repair what they see as the shortcomings of manage- ment. For example, in an account of TQM that has focused on the micro politics of implementing a TQM vision, Fairhurst (1993) has argued that 'microlevel exchanges' are critical in how a TQM vision becomes reality. This is a useful approach since it recognizes that it is not just leaders that manage meaning. Instead, 'middle and lower-level leaders' and 'designated TQ special- ists' are deemed 'responsible for getting the vote out and mobilizing support' (Fairhurst 1993: 335). The important point raised is that middle management must act and communicate in a way that is consistent with the vision presented by senior management, so that new meanings and actions emerge. So, for instance, if there is a lack of clarity in the vision or a perceived conflict between the vision and organizational behaviour then these must be recon- ciled via clear communication and instruction. While there is clearly some substance in attempting 'better' communications, in our view this approach is somewhat limited. This is because it assumes that the TQM 'problem' is simply one of implementation (see also Hunter and Beaumont 1993) rather than possibly one relating to design or something even more fundamental such as the prevailing unequal distribution of scarce material (wealth) and symbolic (status) resources.

Inequality

Our third criticism of the processual approach, therefore, is its neglect of the wider political economy. How, for instance, can organizational members all share the same vision when for some it may mean that they lose their jobs?

Managers may be able to deploy a TQM discourse to deflect attention from the inherent contradictions in workplace relations but the effect on employees is likely to be superficial or short-lived if the innovation is accompanied by redundancy (McCabe *et al.* 1998a) or a more general insecurity. Given the contractual nature of employment, the vagaries of capitalism and the structural inequalities of power, such inconsistencies cannot simply be talked away. The processual approach lacks a political awareness of how organizational practices are a reflection of struggles to create and sustain identities and competition for power and status. These political dimensions of organization are not simply 'contingencies' to be considered and planned for in advance; rather, they are inescapable dynamics of the context, which cannot be anticipated or predicted, nor explained away after the event. It has to be remembered that relations of power, privilege, identity and inequality are reflected in, and reinforced by, organizational life and it would take more than communication or employee involvement to resolve the contradictions of such a system. This is especially the case when it is precisely those (i.e. managers) who could exercise their power to transform organizations whose advantages may well be eroded or threatened by full-blown TQM. Although processual theorists are critical of the orthodox rational approach, and avoid the worst excesses of the critics, they also take for granted much of what is in need of theorizing.

Towards an alternative perspective for organizational research

There is much to learn from these three approaches to TQM that we have examined critically so far. The rational managerialist approach directs us to consider the extent to which employees may embrace rather than reject quality management initiatives. On the other hand, the critics encourage some scepticism and draw our attention to the inequalities outside as well as inside the organization that may impede support for change, especially when that may be accompanied by work intensification and redundancy. The processual approach questions the unitarist assumptions about organizational consensus that are explicitly or implicitly endorsed by the rational managerialist position. Here a diversity and plurality of interests is assumed and change is seen as a product of negotiated interactions in which micro-level political struggle is paramount.

As we have made clear, what we find problematic about the rational and critical approaches is their implicit assumption that decisions about quality made at the top of the organization will be implemented unproblematically. While the processual approach overcomes this deterministic tendency when examining the negotiations surrounding change, it tends to ignore fundamental inequalities as well as the imperatives that market capitalism imposes on organizations. For this reason, it focuses on communications, employee participation or negotiation with employee representatives who are expected to reconcile conflicts, rather than on the power and inequality that often exacerbates them.

We want to address the question as to why rationalists and critics presume that change in relation to quality management is effective. Moreover, recognizing that processual approaches are aware of the difficulties of implementation, we also want to examine critically why they consider that greater attention to people issues offers a solution. In our view, the assumption that change can be imposed effectively, as well as the belief that attention to HRM issues offers a panacea, revolve around the under-theorized conceptions of power and subjectivity within these approaches. Accordingly our focus now turns to how a consideration of power/knowledge relations and subjectivity drawn from Foucault (1979, 1980, 1982) could help us to develop a perspective that might escape these problems. From such a perspective we could view strategies such as TQM as political vehicles that can provide some individuals with a sense of purpose, meaning and reality through participating in or resisting the practices they embrace. For a TQM strategy is a discourse that embodies power relations and knowledge in such a way as to produce particular, albeit not entirely predictable, forms of subjectivity and identity.

While the discourse may be embraced, it may also be resisted. Resistance often takes a non-explicit or subversive form where managers or employees may adopt an indifferent or cynical attitude toward a discourse, merely complying with or even ignoring its imperatives through a form of mental distancing (Goffman 1961; Palm 1970). Alternatively, resistance may occur not over the strategy of quality itself so much as over the failure of management to meet its demands (Knights and McCabe 2000a). Drawing on the ideals embodied in quality, the discourse may be mobilized to challenge management's competence. In this sense, it could be argued that employees here are resisting less in order to escape *from* work (Collinson 1994: 31–40) as to escape *into* it (Sturdy 1992: 136–8). A great deal hinges on identity in seeking to understand both power and resistance and this demands that we conceptualize power, knowledge and subjectivity in a way that is different from the three approaches to quality that we have so far examined. In the subsection that follows we will draw on this form of analysis to discuss the weaknesses that were identified in the three approaches. After this, the final part of the chapter turns to an empirical examination of attempts to improve quality in an insurance company as a way of illustrating our perspective.

Power/knowledge and subjectivity

We follow Foucault (1980) in rejecting conventional or 'juridical' conceptions of power, where it is seen as a property of individuals or groups and negative or constraining in its effects. In the exercise of power, knowledge is drawn upon and reproduced as well as secured as 'truth'. So, for instance, in exercising power to establish the truth of someone's guilt or innocence, knowledge is produced and drawn upon: knowledge of the alleged crime, eyewitness accounts, coroner's reports, police records, video evidence and statements by the accused etc. Power is exercised through such knowledge to prosecute but also to defend an individual. It may ultimately mark someone out and ascribe to them an identity such as that of a criminal, a murderer, a terrorist, a rapist or a thief. Yet the outcome of such an exercise of power cannot be guaranteed because knowledge may equally be used to establish the innocence of an individual. The exercise of power through such knowledge is far from neutral or fixed, either in time or space. Hence, Nelson Mandela was convicted as a terrorist under South African law but is now an international hero recognized as a statesman and applauded for his stoicism as a freedom fighter. Similarly, the law of the land in Ancient Rome, and not so long ago in Britain, was exercised to uphold the rights of slave masters to buy and sell slaves. The law marked slave merchants out as people with legitimate business interests while slaves were depicted as commodities rather than human beings. Spartacus, who led a slave army against his slave masters, is now recognized as a hero who rejected both the power/knowledge relations upon which slavery was based and the identity of a slave that it conferred upon him. Those despised and denigrated in one era as dangerous criminals or revolutionary terrorists can be elevated to the status of romantic heroes or heroines in another. The claim to 'truth' then, and the identities it confers through power/knowledge relations, can always be challenged and the outcome of such relations is uncertain.

From this perspective, power can be understood as positive and productive in creating or sustaining the subjectivity and identity of individuals as well as having negative or constraining effects. In so far as power transforms us as individuals in productive ways it is more difficult to resist. This is because its effects in producing the 'truth' of what it is to be a subject are not easy to trace back to their source. Moreover, we become bound up with the identities and power relations through which we are constituted. For example, it might be relatively easy to locate and understand how and when a person has been marked out as a terrorist following a conviction. It is less easy to establish when and how he or she might have come to understand themselves as intelligent, attractive, happy, depressed, healthy or competent. There is no guarantee that power and the knowledge that it draws on will be internally coherent or that the effects of a diverse range of powers will be consistent one with another (Knights and Vurdubakis 1994; McCabe 2000). Consequently, although the exercise of power may have the effect of defining someone as incompetent or indeed of solving a problem, in doing so it may generate resistance to that identity or solution and/or create other problems in its train, as we saw in the case of Carco.

Both the gurus and critics of quality implicitly subscribe to a propertied view of power, where it is perceived to reside in the hands of an omniscient and omnipotent management or, as in our illustrations, slave masters and supporters of apartheid. Thus it is assumed that management can enrol and mobilize, or coerce and control, their employees' creativity by encouraging, or insisting upon, their involvement in problem solving.

Critical commentators suggest that either management or the TQM discourse 'possesses' the power to transform social relations and/or employee subjectivity, thereby eliminating resistance. Our problem with many of those writing in the labour process tradition is their neglect of subjectivity and identity, which are crucial to understanding continued opportunities for resistance.

Power, from a traditional labour process perspective (Braverman 1974), rests in the hands of capitalists who own or manage the means of production. Employees, who have only their labour power to sell, are viewed as relatively powerless until such time as a revolution transfers ownership of property to the proletariat.

From such an approach, it is difficult to ascertain theoretically how labour might resist and so there is a tendency for heavy-duty conceptions of management control to predominate. Yet, when adopting a 'relational' understanding, it is recognized that there are a multiplicity of power relations exercised in a multiplicity of diverse directions (Knights and McCabe 1999). A relational conception of power seemingly contradicts many of our taken for granted assumptions, where we often experience power as the property of the powerful. As subordinates in hierarchical organizations, power is often experienced as the threat of redundancy, closure, delayering or the absence of recognition, respect and reward. Having said that, power is not the exclusive property of those who are deemed to be powerful (e.g. capitalists, managers), for the effectiveness of power depends in substantial part on those employees who are its target continuing to consent to its demands. We saw in the case of Carco that such power is threatened once employees refuse to consent.

Through collective solidarity, those who are subjected to power can be equally as powerful as those who seek to control them, as the history of trade union activity and other forms of resistance have shown. But as long as unionists or employees refuse to challenge certain norms or traditions such as the respect for authority and governance, resistance will merely chip away at the margins, giving only relative advantages to some subordinates in accordance with supply-demand relationships in the labour market. This is because relative economic and status differentials become self-maintaining as each group either seeks to preserve or improve its relative advantage. Given their market disadvantage, the 'have-nots' can draw on few resources to fight their case. In the absence of alternative sources of material sustenance, employees are tied to the distinctive circumstances and security that their present employment offers them. Such dependence makes employees vulnerable to employers whose power resides in their control over, and ability to withdraw, resources (e.g. pay and promotion) valued by employees. But the power to threaten job or income security is not unlimited since it is subject to certain constraints, values, norms and legislation (e.g. dismissal procedures, redundancy payments, labour market conditions, resistance).

Some transformations in subjectivity have occurred through religious, ethnic, feminist and, more recently, ecological movements. Here there has been a challenge to the hegemony of certain material values, as well as to the power and privilege that reflects and reinforces them. But those challenges so far, at least, have been accommodated with relatively minor modifications to the systems of domination. Examples include the equal opportunities legislation and anti-discrimination laws that legitimize social inequality on the basis of merit, and the provision of organic foods in response to 'Green' protests. They are nevertheless constant reminders of the relational character of power and of how radical thinking that refuses to be subjugated by power can change the direction of society.

Critics, who discuss the totalizing discourse of TQM, suggest that it has the potential to transform subjectivity or the way in which people think. It is as if subjects existed independently of power before the discourse of TQM, only to be corrupted by its power once it is introduced. Such a view ignores how individuals are already constituted through power, and can wield a variety of discourses both prior to and after the introduction of any new discourse. It also ignores how individuals may respond differently to any given discourse by resisting it, rejecting it or distancing themselves from it (Knights and McCabe 2000a).

For us, subjectivity or the way in which we interpret the world is a complex, contradictory, shifting experience that is produced, transformed or reproduced through the social practices within which power is exercised. Thus subjectivity and power are always partial, incomplete and contingent. Subjectivity is constituted through a diverse range of discourses and social interactions – for instance, through hierarchical control and command structures, the family, education and peer groups. All of these institutions and relations impinge on the sense of self in a multiplicity of ways as individuals adopt, reject, assimilate or wrestle with them. Consequently, there is no such thing as an absolute independent identity or autonomous self, which a discourse such as TQM could transform or corrupt in a unidirectional or totalizing fashion. Subjectivity then, needs to be explored in the context of the social or power relations that are its medium and outcome. For when we speak of ourselves as subjects, we do so in the context of our social relations. Having theorized power, knowledge, and subjectivity, we turn in the next and final section of this chapter to some empirical material to illustrate the strengths of our approach.

Case study: Inco Insurance

Inco is a large and long established provider of life and non-life insurance. It sells insurance through sales agents and has over 200 district offices around the country to which sales agents report. The company is highly centralized and all its administration functions are performed at head office, which is organized into two main administrative departments: life and non-life, each employing approximately 400 employees. Inco has a bureaucratic management approach which is characteristically hierarchical, with a strong emphasis upon supervision, work checking, a division of labour, functionalism and a tradition of work study and measurement. In the late 1980s, Inco began to experience pressures from its customers and sales agents for improved quality as a consequence of an expanding product portfolio and competitive pressures due to the recession.

This case study draws upon research which was conducted over a six-month period between July and December 1994. It involved the extensive and intensive interviewing of a range of personnel from throughout the two departments including both departmental heads; all 'officials' (assistant managers) from both departments (eight); supervisors (ten) and staff (50). Staff were interviewed using groups of staff (usually three); the interviews were open-ended discussions as to the nature of work, communication, involvement and staff-management relations. In addition, there was non-participant observation during a number of service circle meetings, and use was made of documentation such as training materials, strategy statements and service circle minutes.

In 1989 supervisors began listing information on the activity of each section (i.e. work outstanding from the previous week, cases received, cases actioned). Each job has target times and a backlog was calculated on this basis. In the early 1990s this information began to be recorded using a PC-based work tracking system and backlogs were quickly reduced to almost zero. Individual measures of work allowed management to highlight problem areas and allocate resources accordingly. The administration managers claimed that control was extensive, with 90 per cent of work covered by targeted (i.e. measured) activity. In the first section of the case study we explore something of the nature of the work and the limitations of management control.

The nature of work

Work study is not universal within the workplace at Inco because not all work tasks can be measured. Complex tasks tend to escape work study but it is significant that these tasks are invariably linked to seniority. Accordingly, supervisors and above are not subject to work study and neither is underwriting, which is a particularly skilled job. Underwriters assess risks for purposes of calculating the premium (price) of policies (i.e. life, motor or home insurance) and the more specialized the area (i.e. large business insurance) the less likely it is that work will be measured. Ultimately, an underwriter has to look at a proposal and decide whether the risk is acceptable, and if so, whether at normal or excess premium rates.[6] Clearly such work is highly varied and has not been subjected to rigid control at Inco. For the junior staff, however, work is quite repetitive and was generally described as 'boring'.

Many staff resented their work being recorded on time sheets. Nonetheless, some felt that time sheets led to greater 'fairness' in terms of work allocation and work effort as everyone had to work equally hard. Some staff preferred the use of time sheets, as it meant being less closely watched by supervisors. But there was a price to be paid in terms of self-regulated time pressures. The surrender section processes work that is associated with the cancellation of insurance policies prior to their end date in the contract. There are 30 staff in the section, 20 of whom are junior grades who either check or complete work that is allocated by batch clerks. Kim, a Grade 1 member of staff on this section remarked: 'You're so concerned about your time that you rush through things; like, you know, I'm half an hour behind on this job, so you've really got to hurry through it . . . No matter what you're doing at all times you're constantly ten minutes, ten minutes'. Here we can see that control is not simply an external set of rules or constraints imposed on employees. Instead, Kim is deeply concerned to meet the demands of her work. She engages in a process of self-regulation, matching her performance against a standardized estimate for the job. This involves a subjective state of alertness that entails clock watching to ensure the maintenance of a set standard. Such a state of consciousness indicates that Kim is not simply responding to the work situation or to rules and regulations. Instead she internalizes the standards by matching herself against the bureaucratic norm or an imagined self. This has been theorized as 'shifting work' (Sturdy 1992) where the anxiety that mounting backlogs of work engender can have the effect of stimulating high levels of self-discipline and productivity without any necessary intervention from managers exercising control. Kim behaves rationally and conforms within the given social setting of Inco and yet she is still Kim – an individual with an identity distinct from the corporation. A less committed or concerned member of staff may have responded differently. Of course, Kim's actions cannot be divorced from the current relations of power and inequality within the workplace. It would seem, therefore, that she has a limited choice but to respond to the demands that her work places upon her.

Within the work regime at Inco there are tensions between the quality and quantity of work output, which management, it seems, are incapable of resolving. An error rate is calculated by Grade 3s to establish the number of errors made each week by every clerk. Yet, there are problems with this as the error rate only covers certain types of work; thus, one individual may be working on checked work (endorsements) and therefore her errors are recorded, while others may be working on unchecked work (assignments) and therefore seem to have no errors. The more experienced staff tend to work on assignments and check their own work. Assignment work generally involves writing letters to customers, and to check this work would require reading each letter. Not only would this be time consuming but also the correctness of a letter (aside from punctuation or grammatical errors) is highly idiosyncratic since there are no absolute rules. Hence, this work is not checked and, as such, does not have an error rate. So, for example, an employee could work all week on assignments without making any mistakes and yet on just two endorsements make one error and generate an error rate of 50 per cent. By contrast, in making mistakes on 20 out of 25 assignments an employee can secure a zero error rate because this work is not checked. Moreover, staff may or may not put their initials on completed work and, therefore, errors are often difficult to trace. We can see then that error rates are far from standardized. Clerks from the quotations section discussed the accuracy of the times set for each job; one of them, Ilene, argued that her performance is something of a mystery to her. Some weeks, when the level of her performance is particularly high, she wonders 'how on earth did I do that?' Here we see staff seeking to make sense of the way in which performance is measured and yet the ambiguity involved renders the situation somewhat opaque. Indeed, the percentage performance was considered by many staff to bear no relation to how hard they worked.

These comments suggest that work measurement is an imprecise technique and this is linked, in part, to the inability of management to accurately control the physical output of labour. This seems to be all the more problematic because of the bureaucratic management style at Inco. In the next section we will look at some specific examples where workers have found space to escape management's control.

Working the batch

Some endorsement clerks revealed that the problems of work measurement are exacerbated by the ability of staff to escape control. Comments from Suzanne (a clerk of 14 years) illustrate both the spaces through which staff can escape but also just how tightly work is controlled. She explained: 'A lot of things with performance are that people cut corners. Some people send a proper memo back, others just a transmission slip. Now that's six and a half minutes, but you might do that because you're behind'. Suzanne's comments refer to staff attaching a transmission slip to a case in order to highlight that it is missing certain information, as opposed to writing a memo which explains what information is missing. Staff are allowed six and a half minutes to write a memo so they can save themselves 'free' time and space by just attaching a slip. But, as Suzanne remarked, this may be necessary simply to avoid backlogs.[7] Suzanne reflected on and rationalized an act of resistance as emanating from work pressures. Within the 'rational' bureaucratic machine, therefore, staff may apply different forms of rationality that are rational in the context of their 'lived experience'.

We can see the importance of the concept of subjectivity as it sheds light on the processes that may stimulate staff resistance. Staff evaluate their circumstances and, on this basis, act in a particular way. Thus Nicola (a clerk of five years) reflected:

> When I do assignments I write on the proposal the address, the roll number and all the details of the bank. Then you come to an assignment, for instance, but the address isn't on. So you've got to waste time digging out the information you need. I mean, if they're not doing the job properly . . . it's because they're rushing, to speed up, they've not got time to write the addresses.

Nicola's remarks reveal that she is on the receiving end of other staff's acts of resistance in that they are not correctly completing details on assignments. However, she is apparently unwilling to take a similar course of action and prefers to complete assignments correctly. In these instances, the pressures of work are serving to generate more work, as staff find 'spaces' to short-circuit management control. In order to escape some of the work pressure, staff simply pass on the extra work to someone else, as is evident from Nicola's complaint.

Nonetheless, staff are preserving some element of their own autonomy and freedom by making decisions as to how to perform the work. This, of course, may contravene how management expects the work to be done. Many staff claimed that they did not take such short cuts in order to 'shift' backlogs.

Intriguingly, by conforming to the specified requirements of the job as defined by management, these staff risk being disciplined for failing to meet productivity targets. But performing 'quality' standards in this way is one means of protecting their self-dignity and maintaining a pride in their work. Hence, Ilene remarked, 'I myself won't send anything out that I don't understand, I've refused to, and I've asked for more training'. One needs to note that Ilene has 14 years of experience – younger staff may be less committed to 'quality' or may be more afraid of getting behind in their work. Sarah, a clerk of five years, from the surrenders section, pointed out that they are 'supposed to be' controlled. Paul, a clerk of two years from surrenders, expanded on this:

> Well you know, there are ways of getting round things, let's put it that way. I mean we shouldn't be like that but they put too much emphasis upon time and things like that, and whereas like, some of the times that they set you, are just completely a joke. So you rush your work and you get more errors so it's just not worth it in the long run. People find ways of getting out of doing things, so, like, whereas they think they've got control you can twist things a little . . . People can get 120 per cent productivity every week but their quality can be really low.

Paul considered management to be 'hypocritical' as they constantly present contradictory messages. On the one hand, staff are told to take their time and do the work correctly, yet on the other, if the performance indicators are down, management confronts staff. Here we can see how staff are forced to interpret the contradictory demands management place upon them and how this often leads to resistance. Times set for a particular job which are unreasonably tight are dismissed as 'a joke'. Paul legitimizes his 'getting round things' on the basis of being given inaccurate job times. He applies his own set of rules to a contradictory situation. The contradiction is that he can meet quota targets and make errors or fail to meet quotas and perform work to a high standard of quality. Either scenario presents dangers and, therefore, Paul prefers to 'twist things' (Mars 1982).[8]

Sarah explained that in the previous week she had 75 per cent productivity with no errors, and the supervisor commented that 'It looks like you're doing three quarters of the work'. Sarah said, 'No, it's not right, it's just that I'm slower doing my work, but I prefer to get everything right'. We can see that Sarah identifies with the work she performs. For her, doing the work correctly provides it with meaning and she would prefer to be disciplined rather than make errors or 'fiddle'. Such actions, as with Ilene above, would not make sense if we simply assume that staff are in conflict with, or occasionally accommodate the demands of, management for pecuniary ends. It is the subjective experience of work interrelated with the identity of individuals that provides a critical insight. Some secure a sense of meaning and identity by meeting quality standards even though failing to reach their output targets, while others sacrifice quality for quantity. Their behaviour cannot simply be 'read off' from where they stand in the division of labour and the hierarchy of status but has to be investigated in the context of their identity concerns and the circumstances of that identity's formation and sustenance.

Many staff were particularly put out as they know that some staff are not pulling their weight and still come out with low error rates and high percentages. Thus, some staff 'put work back' or 'ask for extra time', claiming that there are problems with the work they are doing. Some staff did not know how other staff are able to do this and attributed it to 'knowing the right people'. Other staff do not check the work that they are allocated to check, simply passing it on rather than recalculating the figures. Some claim to have taken more phone call queries than they actually have, or calls of a longer duration. Others claim to have had 'missings', which is where information cannot be found and time has to be spent locating it. The use of work measurement hence does not deliver what it promises in terms of management control for, as we have seen, staff continuously employ their ingenuity to find ways of resisting or at least limiting its impact upon them. For many staff the legitimacy of management is called into question when they present them with contradictory demands. Consequently, many staff feel vindicated in taking actions which management would deem illegitimate. Undoubtedly management would dismiss such behaviour as irrational or recalcitrant, but this ignores the social setting and the power relations which give rise to such behaviour. In the next section we explore the impact of a modern IT-based work tracking system and how recent drives towards 'quality' are concerned to link work to subjective well-being rather than just to an economic reward. Yet, again, staff are able to find ways of protecting themselves from this potential erosion of their autonomy.

Tightening control through technology

During a group discussion with eight processing staff from the motor department, the following comments were made with regard to the changing nature of work.[9]

> *Anne:* They are tightening up, we're more controlled.
> *Jane:* Lot more pressurized.
> *Julie:* They wasn't as strict.
> *Tracey:* Stricter rules for errors.
> *Joan:* At one time you could fix the figure – put seven batches down . . . now they know.
> *Hazel:* Have to do work, can't just slip it into your tray . . . Now you have batch clerks onto you.

Management's control over labour does not simply refer to their physical control over work, but also, and increasingly, to their control over staff subjectivity. It can be seen that there is an awareness of management's increased physical control through IT and that this affects workers' behaviour. Certain fiddles such as falsifying time sheets or putting uncompleted work in the out-tray are considered no longer possible. Staff have to realign their behaviour if they are to avoid the consequences of this increased control. If they continue to fiddle in the old ways, they may be caught and sanctioned. Accordingly, new and imaginative strategies have to be constructed. However, despite feeling that work was becoming 'tighter', staff also felt that management were more relaxed, as they had stopped 'checking all the time' (see Chapter 4). Although on the surface this could be seen as a paradox, management no longer have to use coercive measures because of an increased awareness among the staff of work measurement, error rates, productivity etc. For this has the effect of generating self–control of an internalized nature. To support this, management are now encouraging staff to look at IT-generated figures:

> *Hazel:* Now you can look at statistics, backlogs, production levels. Before that was a 'state secret'.
> *Anne:* You see your own errors on statistics and therefore make sure you don't do it again.
> *Julie:* Because of printouts of errors and percentages you do see where you're going wrong.
> *Jane:* If you've got a problem you can get training to do it correctly.

It seems that by tightening control through IT (computerized work tracking systems), management's hitherto preoccupation with productivity, errors etc. is now being shared by staff. Thus for some staff an awareness of error rates leads them to 'make sure' that they 'don't do it again' as they can see where they are 'going wrong'. In these instances, IT has influenced how staff interpret situations and in turn this influences behaviour. Staff are internalizing aspects of what was once a management concern. Management are encouraging this through allowing staff to see error rates, productivity measures etc. and, in doing so, seek to reconstitute staff subjectivity. In effect, management's problem with error rates and output figures is distributed to staff. Jane's comment above reveals how management now expects work to be done right first time, and should staff not be able to meet such requirements then training is available to ensure conformance. Hence, the problems of management are effectively redistributed such that staff take them on board.

This transformation of labour subjectivity is one objective, if not always the effect, of new management innovations. At Inco it was comparatively successful but pockets of resistance remained. Not all staff become imbued with management's preoccupations. For many, work remained a chore despite an awareness of business and customer needs. According to clerks from the special projects team:

> *Joan:* Some staff are avoiding errors but don't know that it's customer care – some say they're doing it because management are telling you to.
> *Tracey:* They know it's customer care but whether they are bothered about it . . .

It seems that while 'some' workers conform to the dictates of 'customer care' by avoiding errors, simultaneously they are perfectly able to distance themselves from this new ideology. Many staff comply with management's increased demands because of the increased physical control, as opposed to having internalized the culture of the customer (du Gay and Salaman 1992). These staff conform 'because management are telling you to'. Notwithstanding this, there are staff who will continue to fiddle, and others who will refuse to fiddle, not because they have recently internalized the 'customer care' discourse but because 'doing a good job' is bound up with a sense of their own value and self-esteem (i.e. identity). It may be argued that many employees begin their working lives with a great deal of 'goodwill' and are determined to do their best. It is often because of inconsistent and contradictory work demands or experiences that eventually they begin to distance themselves from management concerns, whether in relation to quality, performance or customer service.

Summary

In the first part of this chapter we examined three theoretical approaches to studying TQM – the managerialist, the critical and the processual. In applying two of these to a case study of a motor manufacturer, we found them to be insightful but ultimately to have more weaknesses than strengths. An alternative perspective informed by Foucault's analysis of power and subjectivity was then drawn on to study TQM in an insurance company – Inco. For large numbers of staff at Inco, work is experienced as boring, mundane, monotonous and repetitive largely because they are at the bottom of a coercive and controlling hierarchy. Not surprisingly, where they can find some space to decide for themselves they do so, yet, even then, it is often to overcome an unreasonable requirement or pressure stemming from the formal arrangements. However, their decisions can take the form of diverting or even subverting the goals of the organization, partly because their experiences of work pressure and close supervision have made them highly cynical about the new organizational goals of quality. For these staff, notions of empowerment, 'right first time', customer care or service quality are perceived as empty rhetoric or simply unattainable ideals. Yet, the often inconsistent messages management communicate to staff are interpreted in a variety of ways depending on a wide range of subjective and contextual circumstances.

The case of Inco raises a number of points in relation to both traditional bureaucratic approaches to improving quality and more contemporary moves involving the introduction of TQM. The case reveals that it is not possible for management to secure 'total control' over labour. At Inco, staff were able to escape control by only partly completing documentation, not checking work, recording additional phone calls or claiming time-consuming enquiries. It is intriguing that TQM goes a stage further than work measurement or more bureaucratic forms of management in that it provides a forum (e.g. quality circles) where such 'spaces' can be probed. But this does not imply their eradication and even when it does, new opportunities for resistance are always arising (Knights and McCabe 1997, 2000b). Despite attempts by management to devise universal, coherent strategies, gaps and disjunctions in management practice frequently occur. Employees can readily exploit these spaces where inconsistencies and contradictions prevail. Furthermore, the contradictions within management strategies and practices mean that staff have to interpret their tasks to secure the most effective performance or at least its appearance. These interpretations may lead to acts of resistance which are not always or necessarily a challenge to management (Delbridge 1995), but they cannot be dismissed (Taylor and Bain 1999). Not least this is because employees secure a sense of their own significance and self-worth through acting in accordance with their own 'definitions of a situation' (Thomas 1971). The trick for management is, of course, to secure a coincidence between managerial and staff interpretations. The absence of an overall coherence or unity within management strategies and practices provides space for employees to interpret situations differently. It also enables them to secure alternative identities that facilitate a resistance to the transformation of their subjectivity to meet the corporation's demands.

We have seen that by attempting to tighten control, management stimulated staff resistance simply as a means of managing the pressure or because their practical experience led them to perceive the controls as inconsistent or contradictory. This meant that staff often undermined quality through failing to complete, rushing, or not checking work. Such resistance cannot strictly be seen as a challenge to management or as a means to enhance individual earnings (Mars 1982). It is simply a matter of managing contradictory situations through bypassing the formal rules or requirements of the job to avoid excessive pressure or inconsistent demands. Staff faced dilemmas because they wanted to highlight errors and so conform to management's goals but feared being disciplined if they did so.

Employees often identify with their work sufficiently to correct the mistakes of their bosses. Thus, not all employees are simply concerned 'to get their work done with a minimum of effort' (Bensman and Gerver 1963: 596). At Inco, many staff argued that they wanted to deliver quality (i.e. keep errors low), but were constrained in their ability to do so by productivity targets. Management's solution was to increase control, thus compounding the resistance that can have the effect of undermining quality. In so far as management suffer from a fallacious belief that they can control labour and secure the intended outcomes that they desire, there is a tendency to undermine, as they seek to appropriate the wholly embodied skills and commitments of employees.

The case of Inco indicates a complex web between staff subjectivity and staff responses to innovations. While staff can find spaces to avoid management's control, this is by no means how all staff respond. Sometimes, and despite managerial incoherence and inconsistency, staff subjectivity coincided with the goals of the organization for profitable performance. Some staff engaged in fiddles and thereby distanced themselves from their work experience. Some acted out management's designs because they lacked the imagination or will to escape, but these staff were often indifferent to the outcome. In effect, they protected themselves from the indignity of their subordination by pretending indifference to the experience. Although distancing themselves from management, others displayed commitment through meeting the demands of customers for quality, irrespective of the barriers created by management control and work intensification. Doing so was consistent with their sense of identity as 'good' employees. Still others were committed to the customer service discourse, yet frustrated by work pressures and intensification that restrained or prevented them from delivering service quality. Here staff are involved in different forms of struggle against 'forms of domination' and 'against subjection, against forms of subjectivity and submission' (Foucault 1982: 212). Thus, employees are not only resisting management attempts to secure control over work practices but are also struggling 'for control over their sense of self (identity)'. Employees resist the imposition of a regime that forces them to engage in shoddy practices which would threaten their sense of self. In various ways we can see individuals responding to the contradictory demands management place upon them, and their different responses only make sense in a context of differing subjectivities.

To conclude, TQM is distinctive from earlier more bureaucratic management approaches, as it targets much more completely and directly the realms of staff subjectivity. Through distributing the problem-solving function, for example, management can draw upon the sense of what it is to be human (e.g. identity, meaning, self-worth) as an effective tool of employee self-discipline in pursuit of the organization's goals. Paraphrasing a popular advertisement for Heineken lager, TQM can enter areas that other devices fail to reach; it can infiltrate what employees may previously have considered 'their' own private domain, an area to be protected from encroachment by work or management's control. Keeping quiet about such things as fiddling is often central to being a member of staff; ordinarily discussing them openly with management could be interpreted as tantamount to betraying other staff. Yet, through the empowerment process it seems that staff become more 'open' (see Knights and McCabe 2000b). Here we can see how the struggle 'against the submission of subjectivity is becoming more and more important, even though the struggle against forms of domination and exploitation have not disappeared. Quite the contrary' (Foucault 1982: 213).

Some may see these individual strategies or tactics of resistance as futile against the collective and institutionalized power of management to define organizational reality and control labour. While aware that they may not have the instant impact of industrial action (see Chapter 6), nonetheless the aggregate effects of uncoordinated or fragmented employee resistance can eventually have an important cultural influence.[10] Thus we have learned through Foucault's distinctive approach to power that global 'movements' (e.g. feminism, prison reform, anti-colonialism) arise and advance as broad ranging cultural transformations resulting from disparate, localized and often individual refusals to accept the subjectivity perpetrated by dominant groupings or institutions.

Part 2 focuses more specifically on our empirical research of management innovations. In the next chapter, we explore management interventions that have sought to transform organizations and reconstitute subjectivity through culture change and BPR programmes.

PART TWO

Manufacturing autonomy: re-engineering and culture change

Recent innovations including re-engineering and culture/excellence are replete with tensions and contradictions that may or may not undermine the very changes that are planned. One of the most significant of these is the appeal for staff to behave as responsible and autonomous individuals while simultaneously being tasked to submit to the control embedded in corporate strategies and goals. This contradiction mirrors what is, for us, a perennial tension between humanistic discourses that celebrate the individual and the demands of capitalism that subordinate everything to the dictates of profit. In this chapter we explore the resulting antagonisms in a call and processing centre of a major building society as a way of understanding the rise and fall of a set of management innovations.

Ever since the Enlightenment, the pursuit of rationality and reason has embraced a belief in the autonomous subject as its condition of possibility. This is reflected in modern management discourses such as culture/excellence and re-engineering. They proclaim the autonomy of the individual employee and demand that employees take individual responsibility for their actions in the name of anti-bureaucratic appeals to empowerment, delayering and flexibility. Hence, according to Hammer and Champy (1993: 65), as a result of re-engineering 'people who once did as they were instructed now make choices and decisions on their own'. Davenport (1993: 96) also argues that re-engineering promotes 'worker empowerment and autonomy' but argues that to achieve this, 'organizational culture must be adjusted accordingly'. Clearly the notion that culture can be 'adjusted' or controlled suggests that there are limits to the empowerment/autonomy that is on offer. This is evident in Deal and Kennedy's (1982: 32) prescriptions regarding culture change programmes: 'Since organization values can powerfully influence what people actually do, we think that values ought to be a matter of great concern to managers. In fact, shaping and enhancing values can become the most important job a manager can do'. Nonetheless, Peters and Waterman (1995: 72–3) continue to hold out the promise of autonomy, for 'Virtually all of the excellent companies are driven by just a few key values, and then give lots of space to employees to take initiative in support of those values – finding their own paths, and so making the task and its outcomes their own'.

Clearly there is a contradiction here between being 'driven' by values and the 'space' in which employees are supposedly able to find 'their own paths'. Du Gay and Salaman (1992: 625) explain how enterprising companies resolve the 'apparent contradiction – between increasing central control while extending individual autonomy and responsibility'. They argue, in their critique of Peters and Waterman (1995), that such companies make meaning for people 'by encouraging them to believe that they have control over their own lives; that no matter what position they may hold within an organization their contribution is vital, not only to the success of the company but to the enterprise of their own lives' (du Gay and Salaman 1992: 625). Thus through a culture of enterprise, employees must imbibe an 'enterprising relation to self' and so live values such as empowerment, autonomy and responsibility, seeing no separation between their own and corporate goals (see Deetz 1992; du Gay 1996).

Critics of re-engineering (e.g. Grey and Mitev 1995; Willmott 1995a, 1995b) and culture (Ray 1985; Willmott 1993) have been scathing of such attempts to manipulate the lives of employees. Grey and Mitev (1995: 13–14) assert that empowerment is really a form of control that is: 'Bestowed on individuals, rather than acquired . . . Employees are told to be empowered, so that, on the one hand, they acquire a (misguided) sense of "motivation" and, on the other hand, so that they are able to use "their" discretion to obviate the need to employ an overseer'. But, according to Willmott (1995a: 93), such empowerment is unlikely to proceed without resistance because 'in the absence of a shift in power relations [it] . . . will be assessed as a patronising act of false charity'. Despite these passionate denunciations of both re-engineering and culture, there is a paucity of research into how these interventions fair in practice. We believe that the contradictions are far more problematic and intractable for management than these critics envisage and, in this chapter, we seek to explore some of them.

One of the more stimulating ethnographic studies of corporate culture and management control is Kunda's (1992) research in a high-tech company. He shows how the attempt by management to transform the subjectivity of employees through what he calls 'normative control' has counterproductive consequences. Instead of highly committed, loyal, sincere and satisfied workers, normative manipulation produces subjects who treat the self as a dramatic or dramaturgical performance (Goffman 1959). They have internalized ambiguity and in questioning 'the authenticity of all beliefs and emotions' live their lives more through irony and the derision of, rather than respect for, authority (Kunda 1992: 216). In the following case study of culture change in a call centre, we found the same attempt to secure highly committed and satisfied staff through cultural change and the transformation of subjectivity.

We examine how management deployed the discourse of re-engineering and culture change to signify a shift away from bureaucratic, hierarchical control and towards autonomy, responsibility and self-discipline. For us, re-engineering signifies a change toward a process-based, rather than a functional, approach to the organization of work. But it is one that is facilitated by the increased use of IT. In addition, it includes teamworking, empowerment, flatter hierarchies, multiskilling and a customer orientation. According to Grint (1994), none of these alone are new; the novelty rests in the packaging of them together. Through considering how some staff embrace autonomy and self-discipline, we reflect upon how such discourses contribute to the reproduction of power, subjectivity and inequality in society. Rather than simply rejecting them as 'false charity' (Willmott 1995a), we argue that some staff may be enamoured by, or become embroiled in, such regimes. This is because, much like the American Dream, they support a sense of self that allows for feelings of dignity, self-respect and a sense of being in control over one's life that is rarely apparent in more traditional bureaucratic regimes. Nonetheless, we pay attention to the tensions and contradictions in such strategies that, as we shall see, emerged during the period of our research.

The chapter is organized as follows: before turning to our empirical research, we selectively discuss some of the recent literature on call centres. We then turn to the case study of a call and processing centre in a major UK building society[1] that has sought to introduce what management described as re-engineering. They have done so in a people friendly or more team-based way in that there was a concern, at least in the first instance, to take into account the existing corporate culture so as to effect a culture change. Finally, in a discussion and summary, we examine the impact of these ideas in action for our respondents and draw out some implications for studying organizations.

Call centre work

The financial services sector is the second biggest employer of call centre staff in Europe with 51,200 agents, 53 per cent of whom are in the UK (Skeldon and Johnson 1998). In financial services, call centres have been both a medium and outcome of branch closures and the increasing use of electronic and tele-communication forms of distribution. There is a considerable literature, both academic and journalistic (e.g. Baldry *et al.* 1998; Fernie and Metcalf 1998; Belt 1999), that has recently sought to describe call centres in extreme terms. Call centres are seen either as a restoration of the satanic dark age of 'sweatshops' or work camps, or as some future Orwellian nightmare where electronic surveillance and monitoring act as totalitarian controls over the lives of employees. According to such representations, call centres are 'white-collar factories' in which employees are arranged in serried ranks to handle a seemingly endless flow of customer telephone enquiries. The new generation of monitoring technology, or automatic call distribution (ACD), operates so as to ensure that, as one call is completed another demands an answer. Little or no idle time prevails. Furthermore, 'keystrokes' on a terminal are analysed to determine whether employees are making efficient use of their time between telephone conversations. Managers can listen in to calls so as to monitor not just the quantity but also the quality of telephone work; they can read email and monitor computer screens. The potential, and in some cases the actual, coercive use of surveillance techniques for call centre personnel is dramatic, intense and secretive.

While this kind of technological surveillance is potentially coercive, it is by no means totalizing in its effects (Knights and McCabe 1998b; Taylor and Bain 1999; Bain and Taylor 2000). Indeed, employers are often constrained by their dependence on the embodied labour and social skills of call centre staff to ensure that customers get the service they demand. This often means that the employee relationship has to be managed sensitively so as to secure a balance between the quantity and quality of work performance. Consequently, there are examples of companies adopting more humane approaches toward managing call centres (Korcynski *et al.* 1996; Frenkel *et al.* 1998; Hutchinson *et al.* 2000).

The problem, however, is that 'people friendly' accounts tend to make the same mistakes as the 'heavy duty control' accounts of call centres (Fernie and Metcalf 1998). They both assume that power is the polar opposite of freedom, and control is the denial of autonomy. Thus control, either through panoptic or bureaucratic means, is deemed to be a constraint upon what would otherwise be the autonomy and freedom of individuals. Consequently, we have either to move beyond bureaucratic approaches (Frenkel *et al.* 1998; Hutchinson *et al.* 2000) or indeed resist them (Taylor and Bain 1999; Bain and Taylor 2000) in order to rescue or secure human autonomy.

Such accounts of call centres neglect how power and freedom are contingent since in the absence of freedom or autonomy there is nothing to exercise power over and relations would be in a state of determination (Foucault 1982). Likewise, human freedom is a condition of power in that everyone is capable of exercising power even though its exercise may be constrained by inequality and the power/freedom of others. Thus it has to be recognized that the support of employees as 'autonomous' entities needs to be 'enrolled' or captured by management. It cannot simply be demanded, whether through coercive surveillance techniques or a set of values and norms during culture change programmes. Assuming that management *possesses* the power to switch regimes at will, many of the studies ignore the often precarious position management finds itself in when seeking to innovate or reform workplace practices. It is precisely this precarious position and the tensions management faces when managing autonomy that this chapter seeks to explore. For while management and employees are able to maintain a degree of autonomous thinking that enables critical self-reflection, they are not the autonomous entities that modern management discourses profess them to be. Power may be exercised to produce a particular sense of autonomy but those who exercise power are not free from the institutions and context in whose name they exercise it. Hence, as we shall see, they are often constrained in their purpose and the power they exercise is rarely unequivocal or without contradiction in its effects.

Case study: Loanco

During 1998, over a period of 12 months, interviews were conducted with 13 middle and senior level managers at Loanco's head office to gain an overview of the corporate strategy and change programme. A direct services unit was also visited (which will be called Salesco) and during the summer of 1998 21 team members (17 female, four male) amounting to a third of the Salesco workforce were interviewed. Management selected individuals to be interviewed largely on the basis of staff availability. The interviews took the form of group discussions with two to three staff for an hour at a time. Open-ended questions were asked such as 'What is it like to work here?' and 'How do management and staff get on?' in order to facilitate and encourage conversation. In addition, four team leaders and all four managers were individually interviewed for an hour. Group-based interviews were proposed because the comfort and stimulation of colleagues in an interview situation facilitates a more 'open' interaction. Indeed staff in this environment frequently talked among themselves, bouncing comments off each other that led in unexpected directions. All the interviews were tape-recorded. The interviews with senior level management were largely emergent as they sought to explore major changes in the company. In addition to interviews, use was made of audio- and video-recorded strategy presentations and training materials. The approach was broadly ethnographical and the representation provided is inevitably 'partial' because 'one cannot tell all' and 'no one reads from a neutral or final position' (Clifford 1986: 7, 18). We do not claim to speak on behalf of others and the interpretation we offer is inescapably our own.

Loanco has a network of 250 branches and employs 4000 staff. Strategic replacements in the senior management ranks in the late 1990s provided the impetus for a wide-ranging programme of change. At the vanguard of this change programme is Salesco − a call and processing unit. Salesco provides a direct savings service which offers customers premium rates of interest. It represents a new venture for Loanco in distributing its services through 'direct' means rather than through its branch network. It can be understood as an example of re-engineering for as Hammer and Champy (1993: 95) argue 'information technology, used imaginatively, has diminished the need for separate, fully-formed field units with their own overheads'. Salesco was chosen as a site for change because it manages everything from the customer's first call and application for a savings account, to opening the account, transacting, maintaining and charging details on the account all the way through to closure. Management initiated change in a highly participative and people-oriented way. Salesco's operations and re-engineering manager explained how her remit and the objectives of the change programme required that she take account of the human resource issues: 'I was set those objectives, 30 per cent improvement in cost, customer satisfaction and people satisfaction, that is, the people, the staff within the unit. So we're not focusing just on cost. It is about making people feel better about the way we do business'.

Loanco is pursuing an aggressive strategy of market expansion and so aims to avoid large-scale redundancies. In the short term, however, Salesco's management has employed temporary staff to make up for a staffing deficit so as to avoid redundancies. Salesco has a staffing requirement for 59 employees although it only has 46 full-time staff.

Salesco's management initiated change within Salesco through mapping 'as is' processes and designing new 'to be' processes. Five categories of change resulted from this process ranging from Category 1 changes that could be enacted immediately to Category 4 and 5 changes (e.g. replacing the work batching system with document image processing), which require major investments in IT. The simpler changes included reorganizing the unit to allow for more flexible working practices. For example, staff are now able to choose which processes they want to process such as opening an account or an account withdrawal, whereas previously these were separate sections with a rigid demarcation between them. Moreover, processes have been simplified so, for instance, while staff may now take a single batch of withdrawals for processing, previously there were 24 different batch types of withdrawals of varying complexity. Furthermore, clerks now have the authority to sign cheques up to £30,000 whereas previously only managers were authorized to sign cheques.

Call centre staff are able to authorize account withdrawals over the phone whereas previously they had to write a withdrawal slip which would then be sent to a postal unit before being batched for processing. Staff are also able to produce standard letters while on the phone, print out the letters, package them with relevant information and post them to customers. Previously requests for letters would have gone to a secretarial unit and then to a postal unit. Further changes include eliminating activities that do not add value and overcoming unnecessary functional 'hand-offs'.[2] As a consequence of these changes over a period of 12 months, Salesco has generated a 32 per cent saving in operating costs. The savings are as follows:

	Before	**After**
Processing staffing costs	819K	535K
Management costs	115K	80K
Total staff costs	934K	624K
Non-staff costs	474K	336K
Total costs	1408K	960K

Hammer and Champy (1993: 32) define BPR as 'the fundamental rethinking and radical design of business processes to achieve dramatic improvements in critical, contemporary measures of performance, such as cost, quality, service, and speed'. The above changes are by no means radical but everyone interviewed considered them to be substantial. More importantly, management defined the changes as 're-engineering' and they certainly fit with what Davenport (1993: 2) refers to as the design of new processes, which 'encompass the envisioning of new work strategies, the actual process design activity, and the implementation of the change in all its complex, technological, human and organizational dimensions'. Central to the programme has been a management concern to change the culture of the unit and fundamental to this is the notion that staff as autonomous beings must take responsibility for work processes and customer relations, as the Salesco manager explained: 'We had a culture here that said "You've got to check everything . . . you mustn't try to change things" . . . That's all Loanco of old and now we are asking them *to think for themselves* and challenge and take on responsibility that they never had before' (emphasis added).

Constituting the autonomous self

The appointment of a replacement chief executive (CE) in 1996 initiated a new approach within the company. The CE immediately began an extensive period of communication and consultation. Roadshows were conducted at different venues as a forum for communicating a corporate vision of planned growth, an essential component of which is to present the organization as 'one team'. This entails 'working as a team with clear individual roles and responsibilities' (Team brief, September 1997). The head of re-engineering reflected on the CE's message during these roadshows: 'if you don't change you won't survive and that was what he described as his platform for change, his burning platform. A real need *to drive us*' (emphasis added).

Change was presented as if there was no alternative and already we can identify a contradiction between the new approach (i.e. to encourage people to think for themselves – autonomy) and its opposite (being told how to think). This, for us, is a tension within innovations that have at their roots the ideology of the American Dream; for while everyone is supposedly a pioneer who is free to carve out their own world, in practice, there are considerable limitations upon what people can achieve, think, or do. The CE's concern to 'drive' others hardly fits with the discourse of responsibility/autonomy. During a tape-recorded brief to management in 1997, the CE elaborated the approach and stated his commitment to Salesco (emphasis added):

> There is an ongoing need to manage, to coordinate change . . . We have a vision . . . of finding, *with the people involved*, the best way of managing group staff activities and field activities   *Remember our commitment to head office, Salesco and acquisition X* . . . What's in it for me? First, that the commitment to *people first* as a philosophy in terms of investment in the people in this 'society' [i.e. company] is absolutely there.

The contradiction at the heart of the autonomous self is becoming clearer. It is apparent in the concern to engage the support of autonomous subjects ('finding, with the people involved the best way') while simultaneously outlining the forces that are beyond the individual's control ('an ongoing need to manage, to coordinate change') that limit autonomy. In conjunction with these roadshows, a video was prepared and made available to all staff. In it the CE introduced himself through elaborating aspects of his personal and employment background and his team-oriented philosophy on work. In the video, the CE asked staff to address him by his first name and he expressed a wish that staff might allow him to address them by their first names. The following quote is an extract from his closing address: 'My view is that *businesses are run by people out in the field*. I intend to get out and meet as many of you as I can in the next six months. When we do that I hope you'll share with me what you think about the society and where it's going and I'll share my thoughts with you' (emphasis added).

The CE is concerned to break down barriers between the staff and management so as to promote the notion that everyone is an equal working for the same team. Such an open approach is unusual in UK financial services and staff appeared to warm to this, referring to the CE by his first name. The suggestion is that it is the staff who 'run' the business and this inverts traditional assumptions that it is management that exercises power over others. However, it is only management that is in a position to issue such an authoritative statement and exercising power is the condition that makes it possible for them to enrol staff subjectivity. But employees may sometimes be complicit, as was the case for many Salesco staff who noted that the arrival of the new CE had been the turning point in the company's history. During one group interview the following conversation ensued:

> *Mandy:* You find in a lot of companies, you know, there is someone at the top there. They are a little unattainable and you can never quite get near enough to the office to meet them . . . 'He' was there. He introduced himself to all the staff . . . He has been down I don't know how many times to the unit. He will sit and talk to the staff.
>
> *Hilary:* He walked round in his shirtsleeves.
>
> *Lynn:* It was very authoritarian wasn't it? He has just changed all that hasn't he? He's part of the team. He is another worker.

For these staff, the fact that the CE is prepared to treat them with dignity has already gone a long way to breaking down some of the barriers between management and staff. So much so that Lynn considered the CE to be a part of the team and on a par with herself: simply 'another worker'. That the CE wants to talk to staff individually and on first-name terms symbolizes the company as a constituency of equals, each of whom is an autonomous agent that has a part to play in the company. Of course, this change only scratches the surface of inequality but by comparison with many companies it is quite radical. Being treated with respect and as if one were an equal, even where there are great disparities of power and wealth, is a condition of what it is to be human in post-Enlightenment western societies. Consequently, it is quite revealing to see that management can win such favour by simply treating their staff humanely.

In the company there began to be extensive employee consultation for the purpose of encouraging staff to suggest ways to improve existing work processes and for identifying more general improvements in the workplace. Staff were asked to identify those aspects of Salesco that gave them 'pleasure' and those that did not. Though seemingly insignificant, the eventual improvements provided important symbols that indicated to the staff that their voices were being heard and that management were prepared to act so as to meet their concerns. Changes in Salesco included the provision of new photocopying machines, water and coffee vending machines, improved stationery and private health care cover for part-time staff.

The other symbolic changes management initiated included abandoning preferential parking, toilet and restaurant facilities for managers, which Pam, the processing manager at Salesco, considered to be 'very refreshing things to happen'. Senior management are concerned that staff should have 'fun' while at work and indeed the spring 1998 edition of the in-house magazine *Team* almost instructed them to do so:

> All around the country, people get together to enjoy themselves at events supported and encouraged by the society – and the offer is open to you, too! All you have to do is get involved in the Sports and Social Club, an organisation with a single mission – getting people together to have a good time! . . . The Club's new chairman wants to encourage more branch staff to get involved . . . get ready to get sociable!

Though couched in a humanized language, here again is the contradiction, this time between enrolling the support of staff as autonomous agents and the injunction to have fun ('get ready to get sociable'). The new senior management visited Salesco regularly during the initial phase of change; they sat in the middle of work areas among the staff and demonstrated a willingness to listen and to get involved. Mandy, a team member from the customer service team, remarked of one senior executive, 'John will come in and chat to you just as if he is one of the boys'. This led some staff to comment that senior management are 'on your side' and are 'more friendly'. Part of the success of this more open management style is that it contrasts sharply with the past where senior managers had been invisible but authoritarian bureaucrats. Jane and Sue are both team members and the following conversation arose during a group interview. It is indicative of the change in management's approach (emphasis added):

Jane: Showing their face and introducing themselves, brings a nice feeling down. To see faces on the tele and pictures and that but to actually see 'em . . .

Sue: face to face and they seem more interested in what you do and if you've got any problems. They seem more open.

Jane: Which is nice because you are all one team.

Darren: What's this one team?

Sue: They are trying to encourage us to work as a team rather than us and the branch or us and the head office. *They are trying to make us as one.* Loanco working as one team to break down the barriers.

Interestingly, the sense in which management are seeking to unite employees under the teamworking banner ('they are trying to make us as one') appeared to be welcomed by the staff. One could, however, interpret this as an attack upon their autonomy in the sense that the notion of 'one team' seeks to impose a unitary way of thinking. Nonetheless, according to the Salesco processing manager, both the CE and the newly appointed director of customer services 'never made me feel small'. Thus, while exercising power over others, it appears that senior management did so in a way that obscured the 'reality' of its exercise. A more substantial development was that, following consultation with the staff, management recognized that pay was a major area of dissatisfaction. Subsequently, a pay review was initiated and in April 1998 all employees above the initial training grades were guaranteed a 3 per cent pay rise.

Concurrent with the re-engineering, a new manager was appointed over Salesco who shared the CE's more open management style. In contrast to her predecessor, she acted out the new approach. Staff remarked that whereas before it was 'an open door policy but don't come in' now the Salesco manager often sat among the staff. Rather than interpreting this as a coercive form of surveillance, staff warmed to the fact that she would often join in conversations about 'the weekend' or whatever. Lynn, a team member from the customer service team, remarked of the new manager: 'I was off on Tuesday, the day I was ill and she said to me today "Are you feeling better now?" That would never have happened before they wouldn't have even known I was sick'. These comments support the view that staff are being treated as individuals who deserve respect and this appeared to positively support their sense of self. Nonetheless, one could argue that now management are more aware of each member of staff's performance than before, including their attendance record ('before, they wouldn't have even known I was sick').

Manufacturing autonomy in Salesco

Management at Salesco adopted a more relaxed approach towards the supervision of work and this supported and reaffirmed the sense of staff autonomy. In the words of some employees, this means not having someone 'breathing down your neck' or 'looking over your shoulder'. In short, this shift from 'direct control' towards 'responsible autonomy' (Friedman 1977) was welcomed by staff because it indicated that they are trusted by management. Previously the staff had been subjected to excessive levels of 'checking' and this had reinforced 'low trust' relations between staff and management. Sue, a team member, commented on the changed regime as follows: 'They trust us to get on with it . . . [before] it was justify why it wasn't done at the end of the day whereas now you don't have to justify . . . it gives you more confidence as an individual as well'.

Sue's sense of an autonomous self seems to have been reinforced ('more confidence as an individual') by the reduced emphasis on checking and the following extract tends to support this interpretation (emphasis added):

Darren: How is work different then?

Vivienne: We've got more authority. We can make a lot more decisions ourself and, erm it's basically being given extra responsibility.

Helen: It's more efficient.

Darren: So are the demands greater than before?

Vivenne: You don't feel it like demands do you?

Martin: No. *They used to monitor us as well.* How long we were on the phone. If we were off the phone, for so long, we had to justify why. Now there's not. If you are off the phone doing a job you just say I'm going off to do this. You don't have to justify yourself.

Helen: I think the actual demands are greater but it doesn't feel it because you're busy but *you're in control.*

Vivienne: You don't feel that pressurized do you?

Helen: Whereas before you didn't know what was happening to anything. You didn't know when their (the customers) cheque was going to be processed. Now, although you are doing it yourself, so in effect you are doing more work, it's more relaxed but more pressured.

Darren: What was creating the stress before?

Vivienne: Before it was all demotivational. Erm, if you made a mistake it was logged. Anything you did wrong it was logged but anything you did right was just ignored, whereas now I think people are aware that you need the motivation so they have scrapped all that, you know, error logs and all that sort of thing.

This conversation reveals how the reduced emphasis on monitoring work and in particular 'error' rates has generated a sense of autonomy such that the staff feel they are 'in control' over what they do. In addition, the increased responsibilities or empowerment to sign cheques, for instance, quite literally means that they are in control over areas of work that previously they were not. These staff appear to have internalized work discipline such that they do not feel work pressure as 'demands' from an external authority. It seems that while staff are required to do more, this is not interpreted as 'pressure' or 'stress'; rather, it is understood as providing them with 'more authority'. Thus work demands are bolstering the staff's sense of autonomy and this appears to be welcomed because it confers a greater sense of being 'in control' over their life. It seems that management has successfully enrolled staff subjectivity such that their workplace identities are now bound up with the production and reproduction of power and inequality.

Intriguingly, the earlier emphasis on checking generated considerable pressure and this led to more mistakes, as Mary, a member of staff, explained:

I think more mistakes were made when you were under the pressure before because you were that worried about thinking 'Am I doing this right?' that it made more mistakes happen whereas now you look at things as you are putting them through. You know, you've not got someone watching over your shoulder all of the time. I mean when you're sitting at a VDU and you've got someone watching you doing it. You know you are not going to do it right. It's when they go away that's when everything starts to run smoothly.

Mary's comments reveal the threat that excessive checking can pose to one's sense of autonomy/responsibility. Indeed, extreme individual measurement and monitoring produced what one could describe as a sense of neurotic incompetence. Mary felt so isolated, so worried by the attention to her individual actions that she felt unable to perform. Once management relaxed their emphasis on direct control ('when they go away that's when everything starts to run smoothly') then her sense of composure returned and she was able to perform. She once again felt autonomous and capable of acting in a responsible way. This demonstrates that the subtle exercise of power through a relaxation of direct controls and surveillance, where individuality/accountability is obscured, can engender feelings of autonomy and promote a willingness to take on responsibilities. Staff appear to be able to embrace their individual responsibilities when they are not directly confronted with them.

Nonetheless, in either situation control or the exercise of power has not gone away and indeed one could argue that in the latter scenario it has been extended (see Willmott 1993). This tension suggests that a move towards greater individual surveillance through teamworking or technology (see Barker 1993; Sewell 1998) may ultimately generate resistance/inefficiencies because it gives rise to intense feelings of angst. The new regime elevates autonomy/responsibility and confers prestige upon such forms of employment while simultaneously disguising the fact that freedom is constrained. As we have seen, manufacturing a sense of autonomy is supremely useful to a capitalist regime where employee subjectivity is enrolled to ameliorate the indeterminacy of labour (Cressey and MacInnes 1980). But autonomy is often at odds with capitalism in so far as the imperatives of capital often require management to exercise power overtly – for instance, through 'checking' and close supervision and/or surveillance.

A number of staff remarks indicated a general change in the management style at Salesco. Staff commented how management 'seem to care', 'that their approach is nicer to you now' and that 'you feel more valued' and 'more appreciated'. Linked to this, in terms of the social organization of work, is the increase in 'discretion' and greater 'openness'. Abandoning the autocratic management style made some staff feel that the company is concerned with 'people not just work'. Staff commented on how they were now treated as 'adults', 'human beings' or 'equals'. They were 'not seen as robots' and were no longer 'having their knuckles wrapped' all the time. Thus the regime allows employees to feel that they are part of something while simultaneously conferring upon them a sense of autonomy or that they are no longer controlled. The comments of staff in the call centre confirm that change is beginning to be welcomed as is evident in the following discussion concerning the relaxation of controls over calls:

Vivienne: It used to be the time you logged on, the amount of calls you took, the amount of calls you had going out, the amount of time on not ready, the average time of a call . . .

Helen: It never stopped people going on not ready though did it? It never made people think they were tied to this headset, people still used to go on it even though they knew they were going to be, you know?

Martin: Which I think is another reason they scrapped it . . .

Helen: Because we feel that we've got more responsibility. They trust us more to write and sign a cheque. We sort of have accepted that responsibility and thought 'Well, I won't get off my chair if I need to use the toilet if there is a queue of ten'. You know, I'm an adult, I'll hang on a minute.

Martin: Before if it was a queue of ten and you're taking call after call after call you think 'Well I need a break I'm going to the loo' and now it's a case of 'We've got a queue. There's only three, right I'll get those out of the way and then go to the loo'.

Darren: Why have you taken that view on board?

Vivienne: Because I think the management have actually recognized that we are reasonably intelligent human beings who can make decisions for ourselves.

Despite the continued use of electronic overhead boards that inform staff of the number of calls pending, these staff do not seem to feel coerced by them. Indeed, Helen's comments indicate that staff were never forced to take calls if they needed to have a break. Nonetheless, now that management have stopped individually measuring performance, staff appear to have become more self-disciplining and so avoid going to the toilet either as an escape when they need a break or even when they physically need to go. It seems that staff are now using their autonomy in support of, rather than against, management. Thus before, people went into 'not ready' even though they may have been admonished for doing so; they were not 'tied to' the 'headset' and would also visit the toilet when they wanted to, irrespective of customer demand. Clearly they already had autonomy or an ability to exercise power, but now they seem to experience what was once a need to resist, in order to hold onto their sense of autonomy, as a reason to conform because the regime supports their sense of autonomy. Thus exercising choice to meet customer expectations allows them to feel 'in control' whereas before management sought to take away 'choice' in an endeavour to control staff. Staff resisted in order to restore choice or a sense of autonomy but now it seems that they have less need to do so.

Released from the twin burdens of isolation and control, staff felt able to embrace their condition by denying it. No longer isolated 'as robots' but instead made to feel like 'human beings' who are 'valued' and 'appreciated' as 'equals,' they feel part of a community. No longer controlled by 'having their knuckles wrapped' or disciplined like children they are 'individuals' who feel free from control. In so far as staff autonomy frees staff from the anxieties of surveillance and close supervision, the new regime may secure their consent. At the same time, it exploits staff's willingness to take on what previously were thought to be the responsibilities of management. It would seem that for some staff they no longer have to resist because they believe themselves to be 'in control' and are able to exercise choice/discretion through autonomy (see Burawoy 1979).

Restricting autonomy

Although welcomed, the changes were often double edged in that, on the one hand, they initiated a greater sense of autonomy while on the other they generated new restrictions, as the following conversation between two members of staff reveals:

> *Penny:* Because of the changes it's not as frustrating because you're not writing out this to pass on to Frank to pass on to Bill to pass on to Dave to go out. So in that way you think that's being done . . . like the fulfilments. We used to have to write out a slip that got passed on and you could get in to trouble, because your writing isn't clear, but now we can do it over the phone, which is really good. But they've now said that that doesn't go out today, that goes out a day later . . . the investor's [customer] saying 'I'm looking forward to reading this' and you're thinking 'Oh shit, I might be able to run over and get this put through especially for you but really I haven't got the time because there's a queue'. So I cannot go and make one person feel special I've just got to let it go . . . so that is stressful, so although one stress has been taken away another one has been introduced.
>
> *Heather:* We're paid to take calls you see and although we're not targeted and such, you know, there's a board saying if people are waiting for their calls to be answered. Basically the onus is on us to respond to calls very, very quickly so people don't just call and walk off. So the three of us have to sit in our seats and take calls. We cannot be roaming around the office trying to action things, get things done and it's frustrating if anybody wants anything out of the norm. You know, basically you haven't got the time, it puts you under pressure because you've got to take more calls.

As Heather's comments indicate, even though calls are no longer measured, the work itself continues to impose a discipline that questions autonomy and reveals it to be something of a myth. Staff do not have the autonomy to be able to treat every customer as a 'special' individual because of the pressure to take calls. Thus staff have a limited control over some decisions – for instance, regarding when fulfilments will be sent to customers. They face multiple pressures that both constrain and enhance their sense of autonomy. On the one hand, they no longer have to write memos out by hand and so avoid getting into 'trouble' for poor handwriting. This confers a sense of freedom. On the other hand, staff cannot afford to spend too much time away from the phones to ensure that each issue receives the priority that it deserves and this limits their sense of autonomy.

There were numerous contradictions between the control that the demands for profit requires, and the obscuring of such control through the elevation of autonomy that can secure staff commitment. This can be compared to Burawoy's (1979) research where consent was manufactured through participation in games that both secured, and simultaneously obscured, control. Through self-generated games around production, employees voluntarily engaged in a performance competition with each other that had productivity benefits for the company. In short, employees became so absorbed in the game as to forget or discount its effectiveness for corporate productivity. Similarly, in our case study and elsewhere (Barker 1993), staff were so pleased to be free of the previous regime of coercive control that they would forget or discount the degree of self-discipline that the appearance of autonomy stimulated. But not entirely and perhaps this is where a collective engagement in games, as in Burawoy's study, is more effective for management than feeding the individualized sense of self through the granting of autonomy and empowerment. In our case, there was a difficult balancing act for managers, between the need to maintain external control and the necessity of developing the conditions of autonomy that are conducive to self-discipline. This is indicated in the following dialogue (emphasis added):

> *Anita:* Before it was a lot of *duplication.* A lot of handwriting was involved but now it's all computing. But *now we find that we're not even moving from our seats are we? It's too much contact with the screen.*
>
> *Monica:* Before it was sort of long, drawn-out processes. I mean you would probably do things two or three times over, doing exactly the same thing, whereas now they have found a way of getting straight to the goal.
>
> *Anita:* There was a lot of checking wasn't there? *Checking, checking, checking and there wasn't any need for it,* so when the re-engineering was done it made the systems more slicker.
>
> *Darren:* So how come you don't have to move from your seats?
>
> *Monica:* Because a lot of the things that we used to do, for example going to the post room to pick up batches, well the post room has basically moved in where we are and if we had any queries we used to sort them out ourselves whereas now we are just directly processing. Before we used to run around.

The more efficient means of working that involves less duplication and less checking confers greater meaning to the work that these clerks perform. However, the more efficient organization of work also requires less physical movement, thereby removing one aspect of the employees' sense of autonomy. Although a 'slicker' system is conducive to the staff's identity, it seems to be slipping towards a more overt form of control. Once again, the staff's sense of autonomy is under threat and the control over their lives is becoming more tangible. It would seem that a more efficient means of managing would be to allow staff to 'move', even if this is not required in terms of the work processes or technology, because then they may deny the controls to which they are subjected. Allowing staff to move around physically seems to be consistent with manufacturing a myth of autonomy and facilitates avoidance of the fear of control and the isolation experienced while sitting at a VDU terminal.

Staff generally welcomed the opportunity to talk to all levels of management. Indeed, when there was any complaint it was that staff wanted more involvement. Specifically, they wanted more involvement in the design of new work processes and practices. Those staff that directly interface with the consumer wanted to be able to input more directly at the policy level on customer service as well as the level of delivery and enhancement. Staff, it appeared, wished to embrace the sense of control over their lives that such involvement confers – not least because the absence of involvement in decisions that affect their lives limits their sense of autonomy and control:

> *Angie:* We have to defend decisions we weren't part of making and don't know why they were made or who made them but we have to defend them over the telephone. I don't know who decided to put the fulfilment out second class post. I don't know why they made that decision. But sooner or later people are going to phone up and say 'I asked for my details five days ago, where are they?'
>
> *Penny:* It's trying to defend the indefensible a lot of the time. So we were empowered and we were asked what we wanted but we weren't, I mean we never would have come up with those ideas.

Despite the sense of autonomy or empowerment experienced by many, staff are clearly located within a hierarchical organization and are subject to control by others (Batt 1999). It appears that when this control is rendered visible then it rubs up against the staff's sense of autonomy such that resistance to control might be an unintended consequence of discourses of autonomy and empowerment.

Autonomy revisited?

Approximately a year after completing the case study an update was requested regarding Salesco's re-engineering programme. A report was received on 6 December 1999 from the customer services manager. The following is an extract from the letter sent to us: 'As promised some time last year a copy of the final report is enclosed for your records. You are no doubt aware that the unit is being relocated to the [building] society's head office . . . and as a result we are all being made redundant!'

A decision had been made during 1999 to close the unit that in terms of culture change had been considered to be the flagship of the company. In view of this paradox, we revisited Loanco during the spring of 2000. It was explained that the decision to relocate was essentially due to 'cost' considerations in that it is expensive to maintain a call and processing centre that is situated at a distance from the company's head office. According to the head of IT, it was 'Just too expensive basically, that's the bottom line. We've got to take some big decisions. None of these things are easy. The sort of mid-range business like us, there is a lot to do and a lot to spend money on. You can only do so many of these things'.

This act contradicts the strategic commitment made to Salesco's staff during the 1997 roadshow. In total, 250 people were made redundant and this included the entire Salesco workforce. The head of HRM talked about his 'sadness' in having to close the unit and he recounted the following anecdote upon announcing its closure:

> I pulled up outside Salesco just before the announcement that was to be made by the CE and myself. I saw a member of staff who I had got to know during the time of the re-engineering. She was waving and smiling. At the time of the re-engineering I had told her that if the photocopying machines had not been replaced by the following week that she was to come up and pinch me. Well, the following week she came up and pinched me. I got on to our suppliers and arranged personally for not one but two photocopiers to arrive by the same day. So here she was waving and smiling and I quietly passed by as I entered the building. I thought 'Would she be acting in the same way if she knew what I was about to announce?'.

It is interesting that when this manager was instigating the new regime he was accessible to staff. He sat among them, laughed with them, invited them to 'come up and pinch' him. All of this conveyed to the staff their autonomy, their equality with management, their rights as individuals to be treated with respect and their place within the community of Salesco. Now that the dictates of capitalism have exposed the myth of their autonomy, this manager felt uncomfortable even passing by a member of staff. By announcing the closure of Salesco, he was about to strip her of an immediate sense of control over her working life. While previously there had been a concentration on encouraging staff to be wholly committed to the Salesco community, here there was to be a sudden and almost inexplicable denial of that opportunity and a shocking illumination of staff vulnerability. Both this senior manager and the head of Salesco (neither of whom were to lose their job) expressed 'sadness' about the closure of the unit. They drew solace, however, from perceiving the staff in Salesco to be handling the redundancies with far more equanimity than did their peers in the other direct units. Indeed, they referred with pride to the final report prepared by the managers of Salesco that stated: 'Whilst we are now closing the Unit that proved some key principles in applying the disciplines of change through people, we are confident that every member of the team who experienced that change faces their new challenges stronger and better equipped to do so'.

Certainly, the managers and many staff had 'bought into' the autonomy but in the face of redundancy how long would it be before a sense of powerlessness reawakened for those both in and out of a job? How long before the sense of autonomy was displaced by feelings of isolation? The sadness expressed by these managers partly reflected an empathy for the staff involved but they were also disappointed that their cultural flagship would no longer serve as an example to others in the organization. The living testament to their efforts, successes and approach would no longer be evident. But both managers denied vehemently that there was any contradiction between the organization being 'one' team and the imposition of change and redundancy that undermines employee auton-omy. Thus change for the good of the business (i.e. cost cutting) was simply the way things are and it is necessary for managers to make these tough decisions. It is no good 'sitting on the fence', as one of them remarked. Illustrating the limits to autonomy, they stated that one either changes voluntarily or one is forced to change. Autonomy then, appears to be a convenient but subservient friend to capitalism.

Discussion and summary

Originally, it was our intention to argue that it is premature to say whether change has been successful at Salesco. Our intention was to reiterate the feed-back that was provided to management in 1998: 'unless the company delivers on its staff's expectations for continued autonomy, responsibility, openness, involvement, security and development, their willingness to support the new culture may abate'. Such sentiments seem somewhat in vain now that Salesco has closed. Before the last phase of our research in Loanco, we had been con-cerned to theorize the approach to re-engineering in Salesco as a superior style of management in terms of generating the kind of fully embodied and customer focused sales staff required of modern call centres. We refrained from endorsing the new regime as somehow a welcome diversion from the profit, control and cost-driven focus of conventional management and an escape from relations of power and inequality. Instead, following the inspiration of Foucault (1982, 1984), we understood it as particularly subjugating of employee subjectivity. Hence, in the name of autonomy and empowerment, it seemed that many employees had begun to be transformed into subjects who secured some of their sense of identity, meaning and reality through assuming personal responsi-bility for the success of the business. The case study is replete with examples of staff welcoming greater responsibility and enjoying the sense of autonomy that the new regime bestowed upon them.

Yet such autonomy is only available in so far as staff continue to embrace the new regime and this is also the case with regard to the American Dream. It does not extend to being able to challenge the existing relations of power and inequality. Staff derived a sense of autonomy through aligning their personal aspirations with those of the company. As long as management refrained from shifting back to an overt form of control and staff continued to enjoy benefits such as an increased income and less checking, the sense of employee autonomy was reaffirmed. For such staff, the absence of someone looking over your shoul-der allowed them to sustain an image of themselves as autonomous. We have some doubts that in the long term management could have maintained the favourable autonomous glow of the new regime. Nonetheless had that been possible staff may have been willing to allow management to continue to define their autonomy. For having embraced the discourse, many lived and at least partially were sustained by the identity it provided. We are not suggesting, however, that all of the staff were simply reconstituted, nor that the regime was unproblematic (see Knights and McCabe, 2003), and neither are we advocating a return to or celebration of bureaucracy (cf. du Gay 2000).

As we saw, an attempt to enrol subjectivity is not seamless and unifying in its effects and the processes of individualization that it engenders contain their own contradictions, tensions and inconsistencies. Our case study is a dramatic example of such contradictions in the sense that, having secured a transform-ation of subjectivity, whereby many staff were willingly committing themselves to their work well beyond any contractual obligation, their jobs were taken away from them. Yet even had this disruption of the programme not occurred, it is likely that the effects of individualization which lead subjects to embrace a belief in the autonomous self would have had some unintended consequences that were undesirable to management. For, as was suggested in Chapter 1, the process of individualization leads subjects to be so concerned about their own sense of themselves that cooperation and collaboration can become strained if not undermined. Certainly, there were already instances when staff had begun to question the autonomy and responsibility that they embraced, particularly as it threatened to tie them to a VDU terminal or exempted them from certain decisions.

Because of the closure, the new regime at Salesco did not last long enough for us to see the potential developments that we have discussed but perhaps there are other lessons that we can draw from the case. Salesco staff initially enjoyed the promise of secure employment and it was this combined with the new approach that supported the move towards re-engineering (see Chapter 7), as it has TQM elsewhere (see McCabe et al. 1998a). In other parts of Loanco, more substantial restructuring during 1999 already heralded future redundan-cies and this we believe would probably render employees less supportive of such changes. Under circumstances of redundancy/insecurity/closure, it does not seem to us that 'presenting employees with a prototype of how the reengi-neered organisation will work and conveying a sense of the project's urgency to employees may prove useful in overcoming resistance' (Grover et al. 1998: 56). Nor is it likely that such prototypes can serve to motivate employees. Essentially this is because communication cannot resolve the more fundamental tensions in the workplace. While it has been traditional for social psychologists to treat communication as a panacea, our own research here and elsewhere suggests that more or better communication cannot compensate for, or eradicate, the contra-dictions and conflicts that surround capitalist relations of production (see also Turner 1969). Although employees may prefer to be included in the loop of communication, if its content only conveys job insecurity then this far exceeds any positive benefits.

Nonetheless, the case of Salesco supports Drew's (1996: 34) finding that 'teamwork at all levels of an organisation is important to encourage innovation and radical improvement' and that 'senior managers play special roles in leading major change efforts'. It cannot be assumed that BPR in every instance 'displaces the attention that should be afforded to issues involving the people who will operate the re-engineered processes' (Blair *et al.* 1998: 118). Salesco could not claim to represent a case of radical re-engineering since it was a small unit and this facilitated effective communication and a team spirit. In the wider company, larger groupings of staff may prove to be more intractable in terms of securing their commitment to change. Prior to our knowledge of the closure, we argued in an earlier draft of this chapter that 'certainly, staff will be more critical and resistant if management fail to act consistently' and yet this is already the case. This study would indicate that appeals to autonomy cannot survive in a context of competitive capitalism, particularly at a time when corporate predators and merger mania threaten every organization that does not promise ever-increasing returns to shareholders.

To conclude, the new regime at Salesco was in many senses a breath of fresh air because it seemed to have few of the negative connotations that have been detected in other call centres (Fernie and Metcalf 1998; Bain and Taylor 2000). People welcomed the changes it brought including task flexibility, increased discretion, an enhanced sense of autonomy and greater responsibility. Call centres, then, may be construed positively if managed in a way that does not threaten or undermine the work experiences of those subjected to them (Hutchinson *et al.* 2000). Although management had initially secured their objective of a 30 per cent improvement in people satisfaction, more recent developments call this into question. The significant insight provided by this chapter is that those commentators who prescribe post-bureaucratic forms of call centre management need to reflect upon the assumption of greater autonomy within such regimes (Frenkel *et al.* 1998). Moreover, those critics who advocate resistance in favour of more humane working conditions should also be aware that such resistance (no matter how laudable) may reproduce the relations of power and inequality they wish to challenge (Taylor and Bain 1999; Bain and Taylor 2000). This is because such regimes have the potential to create and reinforce the myth of an autonomous self that secures, as it obscures, management control. Ultimately, however, such autonomy is replete with contradictions and tensions as we here sought to demonstrate in this analysis. The ultimate contradiction, of course, was the closure of the call centre because it conflicted with the overall profitability of the corporation. Marx may be dead but his legacy can hardly be lain to rest!

Given the promise of growth and the comparative success of the change programme, the closure of the call centre took everyone outside of executive decision-making circles by surprise (including ourselves). In the next chapter, we focus upon a number of unforeseen events following a diverse range of strategic interventions. In these situations, it was not only staff and local management that failed to anticipate the outcomes but also more senior corporate executives.

Tales of the unexpected: strategic management and innovation

Introduction

A number of critical commentators have highlighted the gap which often occurs between the 'rhetoric' and 'reality' of innovation. The focus tends to be upon the shortfall of management practice in relation to the claims of the quality gurus or management strategic designs and intentions. Here we identify such gaps or shortfalls but also extensions where practice often exceeds the aspirations of management. We argue that the problems facing managers when introducing innovations stem not only from the difficulties of implementation but also from flaws in their design. Equally, the failure (but also, in some cases, the success) of innovations is not always a function of inadequate implementation, so much as the unanticipated and unintended consequences of that implementation.

This gap between theory, prescription or aspiration and practical everyday organizational achievements is not new.[1] The academic literature on management and work is replete with studies that describe, for example, dysfunction in bureaucracy, targeting being undermined by output restrictions, the informal work group threatening formal leadership, line management disregarding personnel policy etc. But the discrepancies between theory and practice in relation to recent innovations are of an entirely different order because there is a promise that the discrepancies or inconsistencies in organizational life can be removed. Indeed, immersed as they are in the ideology underpinning the American Dream they rarely acknowledge any barriers to their fulfilment; for everyone has simply to work together to achieve unparalleled economic and individual success.

So far, critical research on quality management (e.g. Webb and Cleary 1994; McArdle *et al.* 1995; Tuckman 1995) has tended to concentrate on the failure of quality programmes to live up to the expectations that the advocates have built up around them and/or on the intensification of work for employees that are often their result (Delbridge *et al.* 1992; Sewell and Wilkinson 1992; Parker and Slaughter 1993). We seek here to add additional empirical support for these conclusions but wish to challenge some suggestions (Howcroft 1992; Boaden and Dale 1993; Hunter and Beaumont 1993; Zairi *et al.* 1993) that the failure of quality is primarily one of implementation. In our view, the limited success is as much related to problems surrounding the original design of, and beliefs regarding, such innovations as to imperfections in the process of implementation. Grey (2000a) has suggested that the whole ethos of change and change management that underlies innovation is misconceived. He argues that this ethos is built upon the idea that our age is one of unprecedented change. On examination, however, it is not clear that change and uncertainty is greater than at other times in our history – say during the two world wars or when communications were transformed by the invention of the printing press, radio and television. The selection of what constitutes the label 'unprecedented change' and why it is selected cannot be separated from specific political interests and power relations. As the ethnocentric West celebrates the global, digital and virtual revolution, it carefully neglects to acknowledge that 40 per cent of the world's population has never made a phone call. Similarly, whilst the American Dream celebrates Western "winners" it is silent with regard to the "losers" especially this 40 per cent. Our reflections on innovation in UK companies clearly need to acknowledge the ethnocentric and often hyperbolic character of managerial and guru claims about change. Having said that, the impact of innovations can often, and without explicit intention, extend beyond initial managerial expectations. This is largely because of the unanticipated and unintended consequence of strategic action, which can be positive as well as negative for organizations. Both the limits and the extensions of innovation in practice need to be documented by researchers in this field.

This chapter then has two major concerns. First is the matter of how to account for failure in the development of innovations. Until recently, a managerialist literature has dominated the field of quality. It has tended to attribute any failure of quality in practice to inadequate implementation rather than to flaws in the original quality designs (Gronroos 1982, 1984; Berry *et al.* 1985, 1988; Tilston 1989; Zeithaml *et al.* 1990). A growing critical literature (Webb and Cleary 1994; Wilkinson and Willmott 1995) challenges this assumption. While all failures of quality cannot necessarily be attributed to flaws at the design stage, equally all problems cannot be directed at the door of 'poor' implementation. Very often, the same limited understanding of organizational relations and organization politics accounts for flaws in the design as well as in the implementation of a particular initiative. The very idea that design and implementation or, as Mintzberg (1990: 184–7) puts it, thinking and action can, or should, always be separated off from one another runs counter to the view of strategy as emergent. It is also to impose a rigidity and inflexibility that denies the potential of employees to learn 'on the job' how to secure the best interests of the organization.

The second concern relates to the failure in both the literature and among practitioners to examine the unintended consequences of innovative strategies. More particularly, there seems to be little recognition that although the unintended is often negative in its impact, sometimes the actions of employees far exceed the anticipated expectations or outcome of those who instigate a new initiative. Part of the reason for this neglect, it may be argued, is a paucity of empirical research that is independent of, or free of, vested interests in the prescriptions of quality initiatives. Another explanation is that when interventions appear not to work, there is a tendency to shift to some new fashionable innovation rather than investigate the reasons for failure of the one abandoned or marginalized.[2] Consultants clearly encourage this but, with their eye on what will have a readership appeal, academics are also not averse to the 'fads' and 'fashions' of management innovations (see Abrahamson 1996, 1997; Huczynski 1993a; Jackson 2001, Newell *et al.* 2001).[3]

This chapter is structured as follows. First, our approach towards strategy in relation to innovation is discussed. Here we pursue our interest in problems of design as well as implementation by examining a debate between Ansoff and Mintzberg regarding the importance or otherwise of design in strategic management. The next section examines the context that has given rise to the introduction of a range of innovations intended to improve service quality in UK financial services. Then, in the main section, we explore findings that draw selectively on three case studies from this sector to illustrate some of the unintended consequences, both negative and positive, of introducing and developing a variety of innovations. Finally, in a discussion and summary, we argue that it is not simply design or unintended consequences that plague management innovations but also the political context of their design, development and distribution.

Strategic planning and innovation

The line of argument in this chapter draws partially on Mintzberg's (1994) view that management should adopt a more flexible approach towards strategic planning. He believes that managers should seek to 'find' strategies lower down the organization rather than simply trying to impose formal plans from above. This approach seeks to remedy the failings of formal strategic planning, which include its inflexibility, its preoccupation with management control and the problems that these generate for creative and innovative work. This approach is a development of Mintzberg's well-rehearsed belief (Mintzberg and Waters 1985; Mintzberg 1987, 1990) that strategies are largely *emergent* within organizations and not simply predictable outcomes of formal hierarchical plans.

There is some consensus that inflexibility and a preoccupation with management control constrains creativity and innovation in organizations, yet they continue to be central features of strategic planning. While Mintzberg subscribes to a more flexible 'bottom-up' approach to strategy, he still tends to project onto management precisely the same rational and 'objective' motives that, when criticizing the formal view of strategic planning, are considered inappropriate. In short, although recognizing that organizations do not work like machines, Mintzberg still seems to share with the formal theorists an omnipotent, if not omniscient, view of managerial power. This presumes that managers can easily remove organizational deficiencies by incorporating informally derived solutions into the strategic plans of a company.

We suggest that a more flexible approach towards strategic planning may remedy some of its problems. However, it is difficult to imagine that the promised benefits of empowerment, for example, can be delivered while operating within the same hierarchical power relations that existed prior to the change. Thus we question whether 'emergent' strategies 'can be managed', as Mintzberg (1994) suggests. Nonetheless, we endorse the spirit if not the exact content of Mintzberg's 'emergent strategy' thesis. This is because, although often more as an unintended, rather than an intended, consequence of a new strategic initiative, employees may find space in which to be creative and innovative.

Mintzberg clearly recognizes that strategic planning is more messy and contested than the traditional formal approaches towards strategy making imply (Ansoff 1965, 1991; Andrews 1971; Hofer and Schendel 1978; Porter 1980, 1985). Indeed, a quite rancorous debate took place in the *Strategic Management Journal* in the early 1990s in which Mintzberg (1990, 1991) set out his own distinctive approach to strategy in contrast to what he described as the 'Design School'. The thrust of Mintzberg's critique is that the formal and rational model of strategy is only appropriate to organizations in stable environments. Since these are quite rare, it is necessary to criticize the premises of the design model for denying important aspects of strategy formation such as 'incrementalism and emergent strategy, the influence of existing structure on strategy, and the full participation of actors other than the Chief Executive' (Mintzberg 1990: 181). The design model of strategy is built on a view of the organization as a machine bureaucracy where strategic designs and decisions are made at the most senior levels and are expected to be implemented in a rational manner without divergence or disruption. Even if these assumptions held, the model would still be problematic because it assumes not only a knowable but also an unchanging and predictable environment (Mintzberg 1990: 184). This knowledge is partial and uncertain even for those (e.g. sales and marketing personnel, public relations people) working at the boundary of the organization and its environment; it is usually no more than speculation for senior management operating at a distance. This all leads up to Mintzberg's own view that incremental and emergent conceptions of strategy, where design and implementation go hand in hand on a trial and error basis, are best suited to organizations operating in turbulent environments.

While there is no doubt that Mintzberg sets up a 'straw person' in attacking the Design School, the counter critique by Ansoff (1991: 457) also involves a polemic whereby he criticizes Mintzberg for returning to an existential model of learning. This, according to Ansoff, is a 'rudimentary model . . . that has been replaced in the age of enlightenment' by a rational model. The advantages of the rational model are that it is less time consuming than trial and error, can save further time through anticipating the need to act, and limits errors and costs by eliminating inappropriate strategies. Through the use of empirical studies in six distinct settings, Ansoff (1991) then demonstrates that Mintzberg's prescriptive model is *not* appropriate in turbulent environments, as he proposes. Rather, Ansoff suggests, it fits the situation where the speed of environmental change is slower than the speed of the organizational response so that strategic developments can be incremental (1991: 459). Clearly the emergent strategy approach of Mintzberg and the Design School of Ansoff are polarized around the issue of stable or turbulent environments. Each considers their own perspective to be appropriate for the strategic management of *turbulent* environments and the opposite to be the case for their opponent.

In our view, the heat of this debate masked the extent to which when, standing back from the fray, the design and emergent approaches share more in common than that which separates them. They clearly differ in that Mintzberg views strategy as emerging through 'bottom-up' trial and error procedures in contrast to the 'top-down' rational planning approach of Ansoff. Nevertheless, Mintzberg does not depart very far from a rational and linear approach to implementing the strategy once it has been identified, formalized and resourced. Moreover, neither of these theorists questions the hierarchical structures of inequality that inform the production and reproduction of organizational strategies.

Recognizing that innovations such as BPR and TQM are part of the strategic focus of a company, we part company with Mintzberg in his assumption that the political context of their formation, implementation and development can be readily neutralized or ignored. Mintzberg fails to study in any depth the complexity of managerial power relations that are the condition and consequence of organizational practices and the politics of change. Despite his recognition of informal processes within organizations, he seems to treat the implementation of solutions to organizational problems derived from such processes unproblematically. Moreover, Mintzberg presumes that the context wherein strategies are implemented is that of a pluralist organization where all 'voices' are heard and balanced through compromise so as to 'chase out' or neutralize political contests and conflicts. Mintzberg does not analyse the political dynamics of organization as both a medium and an outcome of the 'environment'. For Mintzberg, then, the 'environment' – whether it is stable or turbulent – is an independent variable that (should) determine(s) the form of strategic management. Our view, in contrast, is that interpretations of the environment whether, for example, they are seen as 'stable' or 'turbulent' mediate the strategic management process. Consequently, variations in environment between the extremes of 'stable' and 'turbulent' are a part of the politics of organization and cannot, therefore, be treated as independent determinants of the nature of strategy. Having said this, the value of this debate on strategic management is that it focuses attention on the dominance of a rational paradigm that the innovation literature shares with these authors. Rationality is presumed not only at the point of initial intervention (Ansoff) but also in the processes of implementation (Mintzberg). Moreover, when initiatives clearly fail, there is no admission that the rational model is problematic. Rationality is not in question for it is assumed that poor implementation can be corrected by adopting a greater degree of rationality. What is not considered is the degree to which there is a diversity of rationalities and interests within an organization and that many of them are incompatible with the objectives of senior management.

This debate between Ansoff and Mintzberg provides us with an ideal platform from which to examine innovations as a strategic issue. As we have already indicated, the advocates of initiatives such as TQM cannot so readily attribute the relatively 'poor' success rate of quality as exclusively the responsibility of management and inadequate implementation (see Wilkinson and Willmott 1995: 12–13). For part of the problem resides in the very programmes themselves and their design by those who have an engineering-based, mechanistic understanding of organizations combined with a vested interest in maintaining the status quo. To argue otherwise is to take the design of initiatives for granted whereas we would wish to focus critically on the design as well as the problems of implementation. Fundamental weaknesses are present in theories of TQM and BPR which ignore the complexity of culture (Smircich 1983) and politics (Knights and Murray 1994; Knights and McCabe 1998d; McCabe *et al.* 1998a) in organizations and assume that a given strategy will simply override and eradicate the problems that preceded it.

We believe that the formation of strategies is more complex than much of the literature suggests. Conversely, the presumed failure of a number of strategic interventions (e.g. TQM, JIT, BPR) cannot be readily attributed to a single factor such as an inadequacy of implementation. Following Max Weber (1947) it has become a sociological commonplace to recognize how the unintended consequences of aggregated social interactions render prediction somewhat perilous. Specific outcomes frequently belie original intentions (Boudon 1981). To take a recent widely exposed example from the UK banking sector, it is extremely doubtful that activities amounting to the infamous rogue trading of Nick Leeson would have been pursued if the outcome could have been anticipated. This is not to argue that each step on the way was unintentional but merely that the unintended consequence of one action led to ever escalating attempts to retrieve the situation which, through unintended consequences of mounting proportions, resulted in the collapse of Barings Bank. Likewise, it could not have been anticipated that the government-stimulated changes in regulation within UK financial services in the 1980s would have resulted in the size and number of mergers that have occurred in the banking and building society sector.[4] While not quite on the scale of these examples, unintended consequences also arise from the introduction of innovations. For instance, shortfalls occur when initiatives promise to 'empower' staff and improve 'service quality' but, at the same time, increase work pressures. For the latter often renders service quality unattainable (Howcroft 1992). Similarly, a context of job insecurity generated through strategic restructuring or downsizing may undermine the unity and creativity that management aspire to promote and draw upon through a strategy aimed at improving service quality (McCabe and Wilkinson 1998).

Yet, as has been intimated, innovations may also extend beyond their original strategic designs. So for example, Kerfoot and Knights (1992) found that team-working in an insurance company became the norm partly because it worked effectively as a result of employing a large number of 'mature' women returnees during a period of labour shortage. Once it was discovered that these women possessed skills ideal for managing teams, the effectiveness of teamworking was reinforced, but this was an accidental or contingent consequence of a recruitment decision in the comparatively lower ranks of the organization. What we are arguing here is that strategies are neither the exclusive prerogative of the most senior management nor effective merely by virtue of their introduction into the organization. What is effective is often the consequence of accident or chance, but certainly the importance of employee involvement and commitment in the design and development of strategies and practices should not be underestimated. Indeed, as we saw in chapter three, committed employees may well resist managers who fall short of, or disrupt the potential for, delivering service quality. However, since such employee involvement and commitment cannot itself be anticipated to follow directly as a consequence of the corporate strategy, it is worth considering some of the ways in which it might arise.

The context

The growing trend towards innovating so as to improve service quality in UK financial services stems from the competitive pressures which swept through the sector during the 1980s and 1990s. Deregulation (e.g. the Building Societies Act 1986) and re-regulation (e.g. the Financial Services Act 1986) blurred the boundaries between the hitherto distinct spheres of banking, insurance, credit and mortgage provision. This opened up the financial services marketplace by allowing banks, building societies and insurance companies to invade one another's territory, encouraging new entrants, and stimulating mergers and acquisitions as a means of withstanding the increased competition. It is here that service quality has gained in strategic importance as companies have sought to differentiate themselves on the basis of customer service. Previously, customers were forced to accept poor quality and, with limited competition, companies were guaranteed healthy profits. Customers are now increasingly prepared to switch suppliers[5] and experiment with new channels of distribution such as e-commerce, supermarket banking and telebanking. Also, new market entrants such as Virgin, Marks and Spencer and the retail supermarkets (e.g. Tesco) have reinforced the competitive climate that emerged after deregulation in the 1980s. In effect, the financial services has become a battleground for market share, especially at the higher ends of the market, where suppliers seek to attract the highly profitable high net-worth customer.

The banking sector, for example, has responded by instigating massive waves of redundancy following branch closures. NatWest closed 1200 branches in the

1980s, Lloyds TSB closed 977 and Barclays shut 723 (*The Sunday Times*, 7 May 2000). Partly, this was to cut costs and partly it reflected a belief that customers can be better served through large back-office processing and telephone call centres. The criticism of Barclays' closure of 170 branches in one day (*The Sunday Times*, 30 April 2000) suggests that this route offers no simple means of improving customer service, as many customers who live in rural areas no longer have local access to the bank. Barclays justified their restructuring on the need to invest in new technology and the shift towards internet and telephone banking. A spokesman said, 'We will respond to *changing customer demands* by focusing our resources on *what people want.*[6] Over time there will be fewer branches' (*The Sunday Times*, 7 May 2000, emphasis added). Barclays had already justified a plan to cut 6000 jobs or 10 per cent of its workforce in 1999 as part of a 'strategy to refocus the business on the needs of its *customers*' (*The Sunday Times*, 23 May 1999, emphasis added). These moves are not unrelated to the threat of takeover and Barclays' plan also involved cutting 12 regional centres to 6 and centralizing processes within back-office centres. Such initiatives are, according to Hammer and Champy (1993), examples of re-engineering and they are legitimized on the basis of improving customer service. Improved customer service may be the outcome for those seeking alternative channels of banking but not for those who want to use more traditional channels. Branch closure is inextricably linked with profitability. Thus for branches to remain open, they must sell additional products such as mortgages and insurance and therefore branches in mature areas are not seen as desirable locations (*The Sunday Times*, 7 May 2000). Questions of quality and customer service are, therefore, bound up with concerns over profitability and one must avoid accepting corporate rationalizations regarding strategic moves at face value.

The recessionary pressures of the early 1990s added to the trends of intensified competition and corporate restructuring. The pre-eminence of improving service quality in financial services also increased following the trends of greater customer awareness and expectations regarding quality (Lewis 1989). These transformations were accompanied by a growth in customer complaints according to both the *Independent Consumer Guide* (*Which?* 1993, 1994) and industry ombudsmen. For example, complaints to the banking ombudsman rose 7 per cent in 1999 to 12,700 and investigations increased by 14 per cent to 846 (Bankingliaison, December 1999: see www.bankingliaison.co.uk). This is perhaps the clearest indication that strategic moves to improve service quality did not have the desired consequences. As we shall see, tensions arise between service quality, customer care, culture change and concurrent strategies of cost cutting, downsizing or redundancy and restructuring. Consequently, the context which gives rise to new innovations is politically charged and rarely devoid of contradictions.

The case studies

The research was conducted between 1994 and 1998. This section focuses on vignettes from two banks and one insurance company. These are given the pseudonyms, in order of presentation, as follows: Qualbank, Medbank and E&M Insurance. In order to explore the introduction and operation of a variety of innovations such as TQM, customer care and BPR 'an array of interpretive techniques were deployed' so as 'to describe, decode, translate, and otherwise come to terms with the meaning, not the frequency' (Van Maanen 1979: 520) of such innovations. This approach requires 'an understanding and interpretation of how members of the culture see and describe their world' (Smircich 1983: 346). The case studies involved formal and informal interviewing techniques, documentary investigation and observation. Observational research was possible through attending a variety of team meetings. During these meeting, copious notes were made of the conversations that ensued, which provided dynamic insights into the nature of work and employee relations. The aim was 'to gather first-hand information about social processes in a "naturally occurring way"' (Silverman 1993: 11). Documentary investigation made use of strategy statements, training materials and the minutes of various meetings. Our concern is not to offer a total or complete picture of innovations for each case 'has to be understood in context' (Silverman 1986: 21) and multiple methods do not and cannot render understanding unproblematic or cases somehow definitive.

Qualbank

Between 1986 and 1989, Qualbank's cost/income ratio rose from 66 to 75 per cent. A strategy was put in place of which TQM was an integral part and the objective was to 'drive costs down and increase quality, sustainable income', as the CE put it. Between 1990 and 1995, 8500 jobs were removed from the branch network through restructuring and 19 per cent of branches were closed. The company launched TQM in 1990/1 by training all of its 23,000 staff over two years in 'knowing what is required and meeting that requirement first time, every time' (CE). We visited Qualbank over a six-month period during 1994 and according to a corporate quality document the aim of the intervention was to reconstitute employees as unquestioning TQM subjects: 'Quality improvement is a challenge facing all of us. It is not an extra task to do but a whole new way of working . . . when we as individuals make a commitment to improve quality, we promise to do everything in our power to meet customer requirements and continually look for ways to improve quality'. This extract is redolent of the enterprising individualism and success ethic that imbues the American Dream. Indeed, the ideas of the US quality guru P.B. Crosby (1979) inspired the programme itself. As the extract indicates, everyone was to unite to meet the single goal of meeting customer requirements.

To facilitate and encourage problem solving, a 'top-down' initiative with an elaborate hierarchical infrastructure was introduced throughout Qualbank's branch network. Staff were allocated an hour each week to brainstorm and identify problems that were perceived to impair the 'smooth' running of the branches. The intention was for these ideas to be directed upwards throughout the hierarchy via meetings between staff quality representatives and management. The initiative aimed to encourage local-level problem solving while ensuring that issues which had a company-wide relevance were implemented throughout the organization.

Problems arose, however, as insufficient resources were allocated 'within' the quality structure. Thus, according to an area manager, problems once raised 'disappear into a black hole and we don't quite know what happens to them'. Upon investigation, it was found that the problems, once identified, were simply 'stored' due to a lack of staff resources for dealing with them. Consequently, both staff and branch management began to be disillusioned as the void between problem raising and subsequent feedback and actions became ever wider. Moreover, given the operational demands on both staff and management, disillusioned branch managers soon reduced the frequency and duration of quality meetings, and the initiative was on the wane.

The intention behind the hierarchical structure of the initiative was to support staff empowerment and secure a culture change that entailed a 'shared' interest in quality. It served, however, to reinforce distinctions between management and staff, as branch staff were excluded from high-level quality meetings and decision making. Likewise, senior figures from both within and without the quality structure were not involved in the daily operation of TQM and it was these managers that had the political clout to provide the necessary investment in TQM. Thus, TQM mirrored the hierarchical structure of the organization and did not remove, so much as reinforce, divisions and tensions between staff and management. There was also a hierarchical divide in terms of the knowledge base regarding quality. Management had far more training in the quality ideas and concepts compared to the staff. Once operationalized, it became apparent that the full-time quality staff had a good understanding of the quality concepts as did those staff who were actively involved in quality teams. However, staff that were not directly involved tended to have a limited understanding of both the quality concepts and of the processes involved in problem solving.

Other negative and unintended consequences resulted from the use of inter-branch league tables. These were used to record the number of 'snags', or problems, raised by employees in each branch of the bank. The intention behind pitting one branch against another was to motivate staff to identify problems (or 'snags') but the league tables served to reduce the quality of the issues raised. Staff endeavoured to generate as many snags as possible, irrespective of how useful/important they were, simply in order to climb or maintain their position in the league table. This they did in order to avoid letting down either themselves and/or their branches but it often wasted considerable time during meetings. Large numbers of relatively minor issues were raised as snags thus displacing the attention of staff on more serious matters. Moreover, a number of staff expressed concern that league tables militated against the team spirit that supposedly underpinned the quality initiative, as indeed Deming (1986) has argued in relation to work quotas. Thus, rather than sharing problems staff tended to hoard them so as to get the credit either for themselves or their branches.

Clearly these consequences were neither anticipated nor intended but arose largely because managers failed to monitor or reflect adequately on their actions and/or inaction. The TQM initiative was designed to break down divisions between staff and management by encouraging a 'team'-based approach towards problem solving throughout the organization. Yet, the structure served to reinforce such divisions and distanced management from the operation of quality, leaving them unaware of the damage that the lack of feedback and inadequate resources caused to the quality programme. While having made an initial multi-million pound investment, inadequate resourcing of the everyday quality activities created frustrations and tensions that undermined both staff enthusiasm and commitment and, eventually, the programme as a whole.

Despite these negative tensions and disruptions to the programme, we found instances within the bank where local level dynamics served to generate (albeit temporarily) solutions to the problems. These could be understood as the type of 'emergent' strategies that Mintzberg encourages managers to exploit. For instance, within one area of the bank, local level staff and management displayed a keen interest in problem solving and produced an in-house magazine to publicize TQM and the achievements of local staff. The motivation for doing this was the lack of feedback once problem solving suggestions had moved up the hierarchy, but also a general concern to maintain the momentum of the quality initiative. However, the magazine could not be sustained or expanded because it was never resourced as a company-wide newsletter. Another example was when local quality representatives sought to extend quality meetings to include local inter-branch meetings. In doing so, the intention was to improve the awareness and understanding of quality in relation to local conditions. Thus, at the local level, it was recognized that many branches share similar problems and how, by combining forces, these could be addressed more effectively. So, for instance, within a single area there may be pockets of affluence or poverty that have particular shared requirements. The suggestion was never implemented due to pressures upon staffing within the branches. Moreover, there was a belief among branch management that staff were merely wasting time by attending such meetings.

These positive unintended consequences were not even acknowledged let alone promoted by more senior management. Partly, perhaps, this was because they were unaware of them but also continuous programmes of restructuring left many managers feeling 'uncertain' about their careers and 'unwilling' to risk criticizing existing procedures. The case of Qualbank is illustrative of the need for management to carefully monitor the outcomes of strategies; however, it also suggests that doing so offers no simple solution to the difficulties facing managers.

Medbank

At the time we visited Medbank during the mid-1990s it had already gone through a major programme of restructuring whereby branch processes were centralized into back-office locations and the workforce had been reduced by a third. Such moves are consistent with what Hammer and Champy (1993) describe as re-engineering, although management did not, at that time, use this term. TQM had also been launched as a response to the demands of the marketplace and as a means of integrating a number of innovations as the following extract reveals:

> Our competitors are . . . augmenting their markets; restructuring; paying attention to customer requirements and improving their image and products . . . We intend to use TQM as a vehicle for improvement throughout our organisation. Regional management, head office functions, all branches and outlets, the Customer Services Bureau. Everyone will be invited to involve themselves in making the group a more competitive one and one in which employees can thrive and prosper.
>
> (Internal communications booklet 1988 quoted in McCabe and Wilkinson 1998)

Here we see how TQM, as with the American Dream, sells success and does not anticipate any barriers to breaking down political and functional groupings within the organization. Everyone is simply expected to benefit and the resulting environment is to be one in which 'employees can thrive and prosper'. Yet, given that nearly a third of the workforce was made redundant shortly after TQM was launched, this does not bode well for the intervention or the ethos. Medbank initially introduced TQM within its 'branches' to 'empower' staff and improve service to its customers. However, the training of branch staff in concepts such as 'right first time' had the unintended consequence of giving them a 'stick' with which to 'beat' head office. Head office staff were neither equipped to deal with the problems raised by the branch, nor had they been trained in quality concepts. Therefore, when head office staff made errors or were unable to provide support to the branches, the branch staff retorted that 'that's not right first time' or they asked 'how about the customer first?' The head office staff were not only ignorant of, and nonplussed by, these concepts, they also resented the way branch staff goaded them and wielded the quality discourse as a weapon to criticize the service they delivered. This created inter-organizational tensions that served to undermine relations between the branch and head office staff. The lesson we can draw from this example is that partial rather than comprehensive quality programmes are problematic inasmuch as they may stimulate interorganizational frictions.

Ultimately, TQM failed and the training manager explained that although the company introduced a comprehensive training programme, once individuals went back to the branches they simply worked in much the same way as before. Hence, TQM was never really operationalized: 'We won the training award. I wish we'd won the war, we got our troops on, they knew what it meant, putting it into application, we weren't so good at that'. In contrast to Qualbank, Medbank did not put an infrastructure in place to ensure that quality was enacted. It was thought that quality would simply emerge but this was far from the case, as a member of the TQM training team indicated:

> I'm not sure that we actually got the message to them that this was ongoing . . . I think you've really got to work hard at saying to the person who actually speaks to the customer, 'you know, this is your issue, not my issue'. I'm not that sure that, at that time, that we actually managed to do that as well as we could. I think some of it was seen as 'well it's management tools to get more out of us' – the staff can be cynical about these things.

Here, although management could have learned from the failings of TQM it was simply abandoned in favour of the next innovation. Hence there was no comprehensive post-implementation review. The above quote suggests that there was some considerable distrust between management and staff and this appeared to have impacted upon the success of TQM. Thus, it seemed that some staff did not buy into the ethos and instead saw it as a tool of oppression whereby management sought to get 'more' out of them.

Although the initial phase of restructuring in 1989 could be understood as re-engineering it was not described as such. Subsequently, in 1994, management introduced what was labelled 'BPR' in one of its newly created back offices. The programme entailed delayering, restructuring the organization of work to produce multiskilled, process-based teams and the introduction of team meetings. Senior management within the back office were particularly concerned to bridge the 'them and us' gap between management and staff, which had historically prevailed. Doing so was considered essential to the smooth running of the BPR programme and so management stressed that the organization should be managed as a 'team'. Team meetings between line management and staff aimed to break down hierarchical distinctions; however, these meetings were organized in such a way that they reproduced existing hierarchical structures and power relations. Hence, team members met with team leaders, team leaders met with customer service managers (CSMs) and the CSMs met with the back-office manager. Consequently, middle and senior management remained comparatively distant from the staff. In view of this and despite management's assertions to the contrary, staff did not consider that management-staff relations had become closer or that a more team-based culture had evolved. The intention was for these team meetings to convey problems and issues upwards as well as downwards. However, our observations revealed that both team leaders and CSMs tended to suppress or deny problems. If the staff complained of excessive levels of stress this was not communicated upwards. Partly this reflected existing hierarchical power relations but also career interests and concerns. Faced with such dynamics, it seemed that senior management would not hear of, let alone address, such problems.

Unintended consequences also arose out of the productivity measures that were used to record the number and duration of telephone calls taken and not the quality of the service interaction in the back office. These measures, combined with mounting volumes of work, placed pressures on staff that forced them on occasions to deal abruptly with customers over the phone. Indeed, some staff even disconnected customers whom it was thought would take up too much time. This was completely inconsistent with the ethos and intention of the BPR programme, which sought to render the organization more customer focused and committed to service quality. Clearly, productivity measures designed to enhance customer service can have the desired effect, but if the nature of the service interface and existing pressures of work are not taken into account, then such measures and pressures may detract from service quality. The failure of the organization to break the them and us divide between management and staff, and the reproduction of hierarchical tensions, served to prevent these problems being properly exposed. This reinforced the distance and tensions between the objectives and outcomes of the BPR programme. Nonetheless, we have considerable doubts as to whether greater awareness of the problems faced among the middle to senior management ranks would have remedied the problems. Unlike Mintzberg, and other processual commentators, it seems to us that communication cannot resolve more intractable problems such as the pressure to cut costs, increase output or to maximize profits. Indeed, management seem oblivious or unwilling to recognize the contradictions such pressures create when they simultaneously call for improved service quality.

E&M Insurance

We visited E&M Insurance during 1998. The company had gone through a substantial restructuring programme in the early 1990s that involved reorganizing from four business focused divisions. Each division (agency, independent financial adviser, direct sales and corporate) had a 'separate personality' and each had its own general manager. The divisions also had separate IT, sales, marketing, customer services, human resource, finance and actuarial support functions. This organizational structure had 'emerged' during the 1980s following considerable growth in the market for life insurance. Consequently, each division or market niche was deemed to require specialist support functions. Interestingly, these are precisely the organizational conditions advocated and described by Hammer and Champy (1993) as 're-engineering', in that the company was organized around business processes. The company subsequently moved towards a more traditional functional structure in response to the near collapse of its market in the 1990s. There was a perceived need to cut costs and consultants recommended that the support functions should be centralized within a client services area. Thus, from 1992, distinct customer services, sales, marketing, human resources, actuarial and finance departments were introduced. Reflecting the scaling down of operations in client services, 25 per cent of the cost base was taken out which led to 3000 redundancies.

The organization then began a major review of its IT structures as it was recognized that the 'multiple' systems it had in place were inflexible and incompatible with one another. Fifty business and system developers were deployed from a variety of functions to develop a new 'single' IT system to support the business in the future. Simultaneously, elements within the company were endeavouring to introduce TQM and had proposed to the board of directors that the company adopt a more process-based structure. The initial proposals to do so had been rejected on the basis that TQM would simply entail returning to the older business divisions or 'channel' structure. As the IT systems review advanced, it became increasingly apparent to the members of the IT development team that the structure of the organization would need to be changed if a new, single IT system was to be introduced. The head of IT explained:

> This is when we said, as we roll out this new way of working, in terms of our systems, 'We really have got to challenge the current functional organization'. We've got to because if we've got processes that go from A to Z they have to pass through six functions, this is not the way to do it, we should have the process going from A to Z and anybody who needs to work in that process should work in teams together.

A growing realization emerged that there was a need to reverse the recent shift towards a 'functional' organizational structure. To do so, however, was politically problematic. The quality director remarked that 'none of this happened sequentially, there were lots of things happening at the same time'. The concern to attack the 'functional organization' had not been the intention of the original IT systems review. Nonetheless, the need to do so, as the head of IT argued, became increasingly apparent:

> it's a big challenge when you say 'We're going to have this new system, there's nothing you can see yet' . . . We've got to develop it all, the functionality to support all the products we want to put on it . . . 'Well OK, what should this functionality be?' and it makes you say 'What should it look like, what is it that we should be doing in the future, what are the things to give us sufficient flexibility?', it forces you to look at the processes.

Following the IT review the impetus for change grew not least because the type of changes advocated by the head of IT corresponded with the earlier proposal by the quality director: 'a couple of things came together and we thought well here's an opportunity to re-engineer the processes; we also wanted to reorganize our company on a process basis, so let's capitalize on both of them to push the organization forwards'.

Before a major reorganization programme could be enacted two issues emerged. First, a provisional completion date for the new, single IT system had become 'set in stone' following its initial approval by senior management. Second, it was recognized that if a more ambitious programme of re-engineering was to go ahead then 'deliverables', whether real or otherwise, would have to be demonstrated. Thus, in order to illustrate a quick 'result' and to maintain the momentum for change, the IT team decided to re-engineer its pensions products. The quality director explained that the decision to re-engineer pensions was eventually a political one. It did not involve a fundamental reorganization, as both the IT and quality staff were proposing, but it would produce a deliverable because it was easy to take 'an existing process and bung it through and say we'll look after that afterwards'. It became apparent, however, that even if one does not re-engineer the whole organization it is still possible to derive benefits from a more moderate form of re-engineering.

A more process-based approach allowed a flexible pension product to be designed. The pension product had previously been rigid in that one would pay contributions over a lifetime and receive a pension at age 60 or 65. Greater system flexibility meant that multiple pensions products could be designed to accommodate greater consumer variability, such as individuals who change their place of employment, who may have periods of unemployment or who may want part of their pension paid before they formally retire. The flexibility of the system, however, had another unintended consequence: it forced the marketing department to specify in advance what product they wanted whereas previously the choice was limited. There had been flexibility about what rate to charge but not about the product (i.e. whether to front-end load, spread the cost etc.). The outcome was that the systems team had almost to begin developing the product because the marketing department was unwilling to specify the product they wanted in advance. Thus, in designing a system, the designers were forced to define the product. Similarly, financial issues became involved as the finance department needed to know what product was involved in order to cost it. We can see then that the pension product's flexibility created unintended consequences and also uncertainty for departments hitherto unused to flexible conditions of work.

This case illustrates a number of unintended consequences. Far from being 'planned' or 'emergent' (Mintzberg 1994), we see management stumbling and politicking. Here management cannot simply be understood to be learning but rather they are reacting while manoeuvring against and within hierarchical and functional power relations. A number of consequences that were not necessarily intended occurred as a result of the creation of a divisional or business focused organization during the 1990s, following advice from consultants. First, it was recognized that there was a need to return to a process-based structure partly arising from an IT review. Second, barriers to becoming process based emerged due to the 'functional' organization structure and the 'deadlines' set for the IT system. Third, a set of deadlines for product deliverables led to the re-engineering of pensions and finally, the flexibility of IT resulted in a more exacting demand for product specifications from marketing.

The importance of this case study is that it demonstrates how power may be 'productive' despite the occurrence of consequences that were entirely unanticipated. Thus, innovations provide management with a sense of meaning in an otherwise uncertain world; they present challenges and offer direction to management seeking to generate certainty in a context that is often beyond their control. Moreover, unintended consequences can give rise to new innovative developments such as the implementation of an IT review that generates insights into process re-engineering. Here we see that unintended consequences are not entirely negative and that indeed they can be productive of creative changes that might not otherwise have been considered. Yet we could not envisage a situation where the IT review would be wholly embraced as an 'emergent' strategy because the politically charged nature of organizational life meant that it threatened some interests while supporting others. Ultimately, however, in 1998, E&M Insurance was subject to a successful take-over bid and this meant that re-engineering had to be shelved, as more pressing needs arose such as unifying existing products under a single 'brand'.

Discussion and summary

In this chapter we have provided some brief illustrations of the unintended consequences of a variety of innovations. We have followed the spirit of Mintzberg's (1994) thesis where he argues that in practice strategy takes a more 'emergent' form arising out of localized solutions to specific problems rather than reflecting a formalized plan designed by executive senior management. From our research, it would appear that innovative strategies in the area of quality or re-engineering often begin their life as a formal scheme that originates with senior management. However, in the process of their implementation, such strategies are subjected to a variety of modifications and/or lose favour because of the failure to deliver the promised outcomes. In other circumstances, innovations may be 'driven' by managers lower in the hierarchy who have to compete for senior management commitment and resources with those fighting for alternative strategies. But no matter where they originate, or whose support is mobilized, innovations will rarely deliver precisely what was intended.

This is because the consequences of aggregated actions can never be entirely anticipated or controlled; unintended consequences are an inevitable feature of organizational life. Moreover, their negative impact can be exacerbated where managers are insensitive to, or unaware of, their existence. As we have suggested, some of the problems of innovations such as TQM are evident in their design. For it is quite contradictory to deploy detailed prescription and hierarchical control methods when seeking employee empowerment and a more participative organizational culture. A partial and inconsistent implementation, as well as managerial insensitivity to staff commitment and their desire for feedback, only serves to undermine morale and enthusiasm for quality. In particular, it puts the 'poor' quality of management practice under the spotlight. Moreover, when one considers that implementation has tended to occur in a context of redundancy, cost cutting and job insecurity, the barriers to success seem more apparent than ever.

One needs to recognize that quality or re-engineering initiatives are not politically neutral management techniques. Innovations are introduced into politically charged organizations where vested interest groups, relations of conflict and accommodation between labour and management, and intense pressures around cost reduction versus service quality prevail. These tensions and pressures invariably serve to constitute and reconstitute organizational forms, inequality, power relations, and innovations, rendering management's planned intentions open to disruption. This is not simply to support Mintzberg's 'emergent' strategy thesis because, as should be apparent from our analysis, unintended consequences cannot always be managed or eradicated by more attentive management. Of course, a lack of awareness about the possibility of unintended consequences can result in their negative implications being exacerbated. But, by definition, the consequences of strategic innovations can never be entirely predicted. Nor can it be known in advance whether what is unintended will support, undermine or extend the objectives of management. Ultimately this produces a situation of uncertainty that may or may not be productive for the organization. This is not to argue the case for chaos (cf. Peters 1987). Indeed, in the above cases, despite the assertion that we all can be "winners", management have successfully restructured, closed hundreds of branches and shed thousands of jobs. They have successfully reduced their cost base but perhaps the ultimate unintended consequence is that, while innovation and rationalization has been carried out in the name of service quality, the public seems ever more disenchanted with the service provided. Moreover, the 'most important asset' of staff has often been depleted and frequently neglected, and these "losers" are rarely mentioned.

To conclude, we have identified numerous instances where the unintended consequences of innovations serve to interrupt, disrupt or extend management strategies. For advocates of innovation, the phenomenon suggests a need for vigilance regarding the outcomes of any strategy. For the critics of quality, it suggests that management control may not be nearly as effective as they seem to believe. Thus there are always disjunctures within management strategies that create space and opportunities for a variety of responses including outright resistance. Of course, such dynamics could lead to further innovations that enhance management control but there is rarely a guarantee on outcomes. Our research reveals that a situation of uncertainty prevails and, whether 'planned' or 'emergent', strategies are subject to a variety of unanticipated consequences. Some of these may rupture, or generate resistance to, managerial objectives and others may take a strategy well beyond the dreams of its designers.

In the next chapter, we focus much more specifically upon an instance where there was resistance to managerial interventions around teamworking in a manufacturing context. The case once again illuminates the unintended consequences of the exercise of power.

Teamworking and resistance

Teamworking is not a new phenomenon at work as it was critical to the human relations and socio-technical movements, and it is central to a number of recent interventions including TQM, JIT, excellence and BPR. However, as an innovation in itself, teamworking seems to have been given a new lease of life over recent years (Barker 1993, 1999; Pollert 1996; Procter and Mueller 2000). Despite this growth in the popularity and proliferation of teamworking in practice and in academic discourses, with few exceptions the literature has developed at a fairly leisurely pace in terms of theoretical analysis. Teamworking tends to be seen as a homogenous and universal phenomenon. In so far as some diversity is recognized, it is quickly captured within a classification scheme or typology that is rarely subjected to an analysis beyond that of contextual or contingency variables.

We will also produce a classification but it is one that reflects similar assumptions to those that have informed much of the empirical research in this book. It does not see teamworking as a homogeneous or universal phenomenon although through an examination of a cross-section of the literature, it identifies concepts such as power, knowledge and subjectivity that are invariably embedded, often implicitly, in recent analyses. By re-examining teamworking through considering relations of power, knowledge and subjectivity, we seek to move beyond contingency theory.

The chapter begins by seeking to develop a history that contextualizes the current preoccupations with teamworking as a significant modern management innovation. In a sense, we focus on a 'history of the present' (Foucault 1980) and attempt to identify, within diverse texts, their focus on one or more of the concepts of power, knowledge and subjectivity. We do this by linking the various understandings of teamworking to particular problems that seem in need of solution while, at the same time, showing how these are related to conceptions of power, knowledge and subjectivity. The chapter then focuses on our empirical case study of workplace resistance to some aspects of a teamworking programme and its associated innovations. The empirical analysis is divided into four sections ('Innovate to subjugate'; 'The Business Performance Reward Scheme (BPRS)'; 'The wildcat'; and 'The trimshop experience') that respectively follow through first the strategies of management innovation and then a one-day strike. Through their teamworking innovation, management articulated a dream whereby they sought to internalize the corporate norms of profit and productivity among shop-floor employees. In the summary, we draw out the implications of the case study for a discussion of power, knowledge and subjectivity and examine their relationship to resistance at work.

Teamworking in retrospect

It may be argued that teamworking has a history stretching back at least as far as the Hawthorne experiments and the human relations movement that followed. At this time teamworking was associated primarily with a literature on leadership and the belief that a reassertion of management control required informal workplace leaders to be replaced by managers or first-line supervisors. This was to ensure that shop-floor work group norms could be channeled toward the formal requirements of the organization (Likert 1961, 1967). Later, human relations scholars became preoccupied with studying the role of teams in generating and sustaining job satisfaction (Hertzberg *et al.* 1959). While these studies were well researched, eventually there were questions raised as to whether a satisfied worker was actually more productive or simply content, in which case they might suffer a dearth of motivation. A more scientifically sophisticated direction followed in the form of 'expectancy theory' (Vroom 1964), which perceived motivation to relate to expectations that a particular behaviour would lead to a highly valued outcome. These psychological studies tended to concentrate on the individual and they were soon challenged by a social psychological approach which argued that work groups and teams were organized as an 'an interdependent socio-technical system' (Burrell and Morgan 1979: 146).

Since the 1970s, the teamworking literature has been almost inseparable from a political promotion of participation at work either for conservative/ managerial or democratic/liberal objectives, but a contingency approach has tended to dominate the theoretical thinking. Contingency theory insists on checking 'grand narrative' universal claims against detailed empirical knowledge. It also avoids the crude deterministic kinds of analysis that were prevalent in earlier research. However, in place of any attempt to theorize the growth and development of teamworking, research often ends up endlessly repeating the conclusion that everything is contingent or dependent on its context.[1] That is to say, arguments are advanced such as teamworking will be successful if there are group – rather than individual – based rewards or if the team has greater autonomy/responsibility/involvement. Alternatively, there is an attempt to quantify every contextual variable and every dimension of teamworking to produce the ultimate scientific account of its causes and effects. Both Imperial

College (Woodward 1958, 1965, 1970) and the Aston studies (Hickson et al. 1969; Pugh and Hickson 1976) took this approach in seeking to measure organizational structure in terms of size, hierarchical levels, spans of control, number of teams etc. Taking account of their environmental contingencies in relation to the constraints and opportunities of markets, supply chains and regulations, there was an attempt to correlate a range of these variables with performance and profitability.

While these studies complied with the demand for social science to emulate the physical sciences to produce quantitative analyses in pursuit of causal explanation, the meaning of the correlations was not clear and their significance for management practice even less so. A major problem for studies that attempt to find the determinants of performance and profit in one or a small number of variables internal to the organization is that it is almost impossible to isolate their effects from more global changes in the economy locally, nationally and internationally. It is also impossible to be exhaustive with respect to all possible influences and their complex interactions one with another. Finally and most importantly, it is not clear that the variables selected for inclusion are in any way significant for the practices and interventions of the members of organizations, and yet these behavioural activities are probably some of the most important factors in assessing organizational performance. We would argue that these difficulties follow at least partly from the fact that the studies cited above involved the quantification largely of descriptive concepts in an empiricist fashion and lacked any depth of theorizing.[2]

An alternative approach adopted here is to theorize the basic concepts that we find continually cropping up when researching teamworking. We wish to argue that relations of power, knowledge and subjectivity can help us to understand teamworking. While these relations can be identified in large numbers of studies, it is rare that they assume anything but an implicit status. Moreover, even when explicit, the concepts often remain under-theorized, treated independently of one another or as binary oppositions (Knights and McCabe 2000a). Table 6.1 shows our selection of studies and their focus in relation to power, knowledge and subjectivity. Included in the table are the two most dominant perspectives – the human relations and sociotechnical systems approaches – that occurred prior to the 1990s. As was argued in Chapter 1, the human relations movement created the conditions that made it possible for the development of innovative interventions such as teamworking. In resisting the technological determinism (e.g. Woodward 1958) that had captured academic research in the 1950s, the sociotechnical approach (Emery and Trist 1960) drew on the idea that teamworking was an important socially mediating factor in terms of the relationship between technology and workplace performance or productivity. These two early perspectives were broad-ranging in terms of the focus of study but they have been included because they were so influential in the development of subsequent teamworking ideas. Our selection of subsequent studies has been restricted to the vehicle manufacturing industry, partly to limit the number of studies examined but largely to prepare the ground for this chapter's case study of an automobile factory.

Table 6.1 Examples from human relations, the sociotechnical approach and the vehicle manufacturing teamworking literature: power/knowledge/subjectivity

Research perspective	Example	Power	Knowledge	Subjectivity
Human relations	Mayo (1933)	Management concern to infiltrate groups so as to utilize peer pressure	Group norms	Group identity
Sociotechnical	Trist *et al.* (1963)	Focus upon maximizing production through both social and technical means	Work as a social and technical system	Workers who prefer autonomous teamworking
Lean production	Womack *et al.* (1990)	Demands for flexible automation, multiskilled workers and devolved responsibility	Knowledge of production processes and utilizing employee know-how	A unitary single subjectivity oriented around commitment towards the goals of profit/productivity
Critics of lean production	Berggren (1993)	Developing more rewarding forms of work to secure continued increases in productivity	Understanding of more rewarding forms of work	Resistance in Japan due to work intensification
	Stewart and Garrahan (1995)	Focus on control over the labour process	Focus on methods of working	Cultural hegemony versus resistance
Managerialist	Wickens (1992)	Humansitic leadership aimed at maximum productivity through accountability	Methods of securing accountability	Individuals working in the same direction towards goals determined by management
Labour process	Thompson and Wallace (1996)	Governmental	Technical	Normative

In abstracting from these studies the bare bones of what we find relevant for developing ideas about power, knowledge and subjectivity, the result is quite clearly a particular and limited reconstruction of each work and one that the various authors will possibly not recognize. But all accounts involve such a reconstruction and we believe that they should be judged not on the 'accuracy' of the representation so much as on what is its outcome in terms of theoretical insights.

We now proceed to elaborate the work of these research perspectives or authors to show how their particular concerns depend implicitly on one or more of our three concepts when making sense of teamworking. For example, the human relations, sociotechnical and managerialist literatures all share a basic belief in providing business or organizations with knowledge that facilitates the management control of labour. Within human relations, this knowledge derived largely from the bank wiring room experiments. Here it was found that work groups function through a series of informal norms that exercise considerable power and control over group members who apparently conform due to peer pressure. Subsequent human relations advocates saw that if managers could infiltrate these groups and, better still, take on a leadership role, they would be able to transform the group into a team thus reconstituting their subjectivity. In short, through teamworking and effective leadership (power), management could use their knowledge of group behaviour and social identity to reverse workplace restrictions of output so as to stimulate new, high levels of productivity.

The sociotechnical theorists were reacting to a strong belief that technology was the most important impetus to work group performance (Sayles 1958; Woodward 1965). Indeed, the approach had its embryonic formation prior to the technological determinism that it sought to challenge, for the classic study of Longwall production methods in mining (Trist and Bamforth 1951) had been published much earlier. This study, which can be seen as the source of the 'modern concept of teamworking' (Huczynski and Buchanan 2001: 287) had shown how teams, organized around particular tasks and technologies, were effective largely because of the social arrangements. As an early application of systems theory to organization and work, it identified how the technical components (e.g. picks, coal-cutting machinery etc.) had to be compatible with a parallel social organization (e.g. emotional and psychological needs, communications, meaning etc.). The traditional 'hand-got' approach to mining was replaced by the 'longwall' method in which each miner had a single task and place to work along a long wall at the coalface. In one of their studies, Trist et al. 1963 found that automation had created certain dangers with the longwall method and the miners responded by developing a teamworking approach that involved multiskilling and interchangeability of tasks along a short coalface. When, because of costs, the mine tried to return to longwall methods, the miners resisted and negotiated a formal recognition of their methods of autonomous self-regulating teamworking. Clearly, here was a case of miners drawing on their knowledge of work and exercising power to resist changes to practices with which they had developed a very strong identification. Not only was the work safer, it was also more socially collaborative and could be seen to enhance team solidarity as mutual identities were confirmed through incorporating the new automated technology into a teamworking social arrangement. While power, knowledge and subjectivity were clearly evident in this example of organizational change and innovation being stimulated from below, the authors of the study neglected them in favour of systems concepts of equilibrium and integration. As sociotechnical theory developed, this systems theoretical approach of drawing analogies with a biological organism (Emery and Trist 1960; Trist *et al.* 1963; Miller and Rice 1967) was broadened from teams to encompass the whole organization. Its functionalist and value consensus orientation meant that concepts of power, knowledge and subjectivity were unlikely to be considered as potential ways of understanding the empirical material from the original research.

Autonomous teams were, of course, prominent in the Swedish auto industry in the 1970s and had been adopted as a way of overcoming the tedium and negative effect on productivity of the assembly line under mass production. The Swedish system was predominantly about improving the psychological and social conditions of work through autonomy, job rotation and employee participation in decision making. By contrast, however, the Japanese model has gained far more popularity, especially due to the threat posed to western markets, and the extent of this partly reflected the debate over the 'Japanization of British Industry' (Oliver and Wilkinson 1988). The Japanese approach to teamworking became known as 'lean production' and was proselytized by American authors such as Womack *et al.* (1990) not *only* as the 'one best way', but as the *only* way for the future of industry worldwide. In particular, it was a call to the auto industries of North America and Europe to recognize that their techniques of mass production 'were simply not competitive with a new set of ideas pioneered by the Japanese companies . . . Lean production calls for learning far more professional skills and applying these creatively in a team setting rather than in a rigid hierarchy' (Womack *et al.* 1990: 3, 14).

The research by Womack *et al.* reflected a long-standing fear in America of the Japanese juggernaut for, as Peters and Waterman (1995: 132) put it, 'The automotive industry is under attack. Virtually everything American automotive management does seems to be a day late and a dollar short'. Teamworking emerged as a key component to combat this, reflecting certain beliefs about how Japan gained economic superiority. For as Ezra Vogel (1979: 143) stated in *Japan as Number One: Lessons for America*, in Japan 'The essential building block of the organisation is the section. A section might have 8 to 10 people, including the section chief'. For it to work, 'leading section personnel need to know and identify with company purposes to a higher degree than persons in an American firm' (p. 145). Company officials 'reinforce company identification with the company' (p. 146) and promotion is linked to one's ability to 'cooperate with others in finding a conclusion satisfactory to everyone' (p. 150). Ultimately, according to Vogel, the success of the Japanese corporation is 'not because of any mystical group loyalty embedded in the character of the Japanese race but because it provides a sense of belonging and a sense of pride to workers, who believe their future is best served by the success of their company' (p. 157). Following similar warnings and exhortations, there was a veritable explosion of teamworking approaches in companies such as Ford and General Motors.

While longitudinal and extensive, the research that led Womack *et al.* (1990) to their 'end of history' conclusion was based only on a study of the auto industry. Also, it conveniently omitted research that pointed towards work intensification and the dehumanizing effects of Japanese management practices (see Kamata 1983; Dohse *et al.* 1985; Parker and Slaughter 1988). For as they state, lean production will 'become the standard global production system of the twenty-first century. That world will be a very different, and a much better, place' (Womack *et al.* 1990: 278). By 'better' they mean that it provides 'the opportunity for the prosperity and more rewarding work that these new techniques offer' (p. 4). Yet again, another innovation, this time teamworking, promises that everyone can be a winner. Despite its rather lengthy history, team-working became the flavour of the month and this was consolidated as the West continued to import Japanese management ideas. Yet many of these ideas were already at least shared by Americans, as our discussion of the human relations movement has indicated. Moreover, quality circles (group problem solving forums) arose in Japan as a result of their original importation from the US. Through deploying the ideas of Deming (1986), 'the structured and controlled development of practical production skills . . . [were advanced] in a way that was dictated and controlled by management' (Tuckman 1995: 62). Womack *et al.*'s production of knowledge about teamworking aimed to assist managers in exercising power over employees, although they did not articulate it in this way. The implications of their prescriptions and those of Vogel (1979) are that employee subjectivity is to be realigned in accordance with management objectives both in terms of how individuals perform their tasks and in how they think about and make sense of their work. Rarely in the managerial teamworking literature is this acknowledged or understood; instead it would seem that teamworking exists in a power-free vacuum.

Critics question the universal claims of lean production arguing that, for example, Japanese production methods produce both negative as well as positive results (Berggren 1993) and/or that the effect of 'lean and mean' techniques of production is to undermine employee morale and commitment, leading to work intensification (Stewart and Garrahan 1995). Where Japanese transplants have been successful, Berggren (1993: 169–70) argues, it is because they were non-unionized, greenfield sites and virtual clones of their Japanese counter-parts, having transplanted not only the technology but also the manufacturing culture and suppliers. Clearly this can be understood as ensuring that the manufacturer could readily exercise power and control over both its labour and suppliers partly through the knowledge that they were comparatively dependent but also by conditioning their subjectivity through culture such that resistance would be outside their horizons. However, Berggren also provides evidence in the late 1980s in both Japan and the US of a simmering discontent and negative attitudes towards the industry (Berggren 1993: 183).[3] Similarly, Stewart and Garrahan (1995: 533) criticize the rhetoric of the Japanese methods of working including teamworking and JIT as 'smart' and affording employees greater opportunities for 'creativity and satisfaction'. Instead, confirming their earlier research at Nissan UK (Garrahan and Stewart 1992), their survey found that auto industry jobs adopting new management techniques were as demanding and work intensive as before and provided few opportunities for upskilling and problem solving. Employees comparatively free from the cultural hegemony (subjectivity) that lean production seeks to impose were more likely to see the new management techniques as 'mean' rather than simply lean. Employee resistance occurred despite unions generally cooperating fully with management in developing the lean production methods (Garrahan and Stewart 1992: 534).

Wickens (1992), a practitioner with Nissan, has sought to defend lean production against its critics, arguing that efficient volume production is necessary for the auto industry, as long as it can be 'managed by people who care about people' (p. 89). He suggested that a crucial element of this more humanistic approach to lean production is to provide a degree of security and discretion for employees. However, the main focus was on how employees can be made accountable (subjectivity) to a particular leader or sets of leaders (power) who are responsible for the work being conducted (1992: 86).

A less sympathetic approach is offered by Thompson and Wallace (1996) in their research at the Volvo Truck Corporation in Sweden. In their study they attend to the way in which power and knowledge operate through:

- transforming the *technical* division of labour in favour of flexibility, delegated responsibilities for resourcing, scheduling and discipline, and a collective framework for competence development; and
- *governance*, in placing strict limits on delegated powers.

Thompson and Wallace found no evidence of *normative* or subjective regulation by which they mean 'the changes in attitudes and behaviour necessary to make teamworking operate effectively' (1996: 107). Yet it seems highly unlikely that 'transforming the technical division of labour', for instance, will not affect employees' subjective experiences of work.

As a practitioner, Wickens confirms this when he argues that 'Teamworking is not about organization structures nor changing the technology from sequential to cellular manufacturing systems' for 'A team begins with a group of individuals whose individual contributions are recognized and valued and who are motivated to work in the same direction to achieve clear, understood and stretching goals for which they are accountable' (1992: 86). Wickens might not have viewed the concern to render employees 'accountable' as an exercise of power; nor would he necessarily understand that a preoccupation with ensuring employees 'work in the same direction to achieve clear, understood and stretching goals' is an attempt to reconstitute subjectivity. Nonetheless, it may be claimed that Wickens' deliberations of his practical experiences illustrate how management were concerned to exercise power so as to transform individuals into subjects that identify with organizational goals. Because subjectivity is not an analytical focus of either Wickens or Thompson and Wallace, it is not seen as a condition and consequence of securing the accountability, discipline, flexibility, governance and goal-directedness of employees. It is the limitations of such research that we seek to address in this chapter's case study.

The American Dream

There are, of course, a large range of studies of teamworking that have been neglected here as our intention has simply been to elaborate the value of our approach and how it relates to, and could enhance, earlier studies of teamworking. A paper of particular interest to us, however, is that by Reich (1987) because it allows us to explain the relevance of teamworking to our central critique of the unreflective adoption of the contemporary American Dream. Reich has written a managerial polemic that challenges the individualism of the American Dream with its focus on upward mobility through heroic effort and entrepreneurial flair. He seeks to displace this with a more collective ideology in which the team becomes the heroic entrepreneur. In a similar vein to Womack et al. (1990) but without the detailed research, Reich sees collective entrepreneurship as the ultimate panacea where everyone becomes a partner in the enterprise. Reich (1987: 83) prescribes 'continually retraining employees for more complex tasks, automating in ways that cut routine tasks and enhancing worker flexibility and creativity'. This is not unlike the 'new management' criticized by Stewart and Garrahan (1995) where teamworking resulted in an intensification of work rather than employee autonomy and engagement. Reich's prescriptions echo those of Vogel (1979: 235) in that he suggested that American individualism 'In the guise of pursuing freedoms' has 'supported egoism and self-interest' and that this has 'damaged group or common interests'. Vogel, though not uncritically, applauded the Japanese, who 'from an early age are taught the values of group life'. For Vogel, 'America would do well to follow the Japanese model and rely on moral suasion, on creating a consensus of concerned people who can exert their positive influence' (p. 236). Yet this would not mean giving up the American Dream for it is suggested that it would entail revitalizing 'communitarian values so essential for group living' that 'is an integral part of the American tradition, going back to the early New England village' (p. 255).

We have to conclude that both Vogel and Reich's collective dream may be no more likely to be realized than the contemporary individualistic American Dream. It is understandable that both wish to displace the heroic individualism that reflects and reinforces the myth of the American Dream and we fully endorse their view that collective, creative interdependence is the condition and consequence of a successful organization. However, both are managerialists who believe that such interdependence is realizable within the status quo, which we doubt. As both authors and Womack et al. (1990) prescribe it, teamworking is yet another means whereby corporate America can attain economic dominance over its competitors – the main threat in relation to teamworking at that time being seen to come from Japan. In the decade following the popularity of these authors' celebration of Japanese management methods, the Japanese economic miracle collapsed, partly because of the conservative, collective traditions of personal loyalty, trust and nepotism (Scher 1997).

As an exercise of power, teamworking is deployed to transform subjects and their attitudes, as well as their behaviour. It requires employees to draw upon their knowledge of production or service provision, to remedy or smooth problems, to take up slack and improve products and processes through the power of working together as a team. This collective enterprise, as with human relations before it, in no way questions the underlying tenets of the contemporary American Dream – indeed it reinforces them. Individuals are to consume and subsume themselves within teamworking as a means to procure both their own individual and corporate success. The status quo, with its gross inequalities of wealth and power, is to remain unchallenged and we are to throw ourselves into teamworking pursuits from which the victors will be those individuals who hold the largest crumbs, while the cake itself remains untouched. As we shall see in our case study, teamworking can stimulate some employees to demonstrate their commitment but, for others, there is resentment or resistance against the exercise of power. Here the limitations of teamworking as a mechanism for reconstituting employee subjectivity arose when labour was expected to collaborate in a systematic loss of income through the removal of bonus payments due to profits falling below a given threshold. Teamworking had been imposed and coincided with an autocratic management approach and employees were only willing to accept the linking of their bonuses to profits when the latter were rising. The interesting point, however, is that employees only really questioned teamworking when their individual earnings were threatened, demonstrating the effectiveness of individualistic ideologies if not necessarily a wholesome belief in the American Dream.

Case study: Intermotors

A variety of methods were deployed during the conduct of this case study including formal and informal interviewing techniques and documentary investigation. Strategy statements, corporate memos and briefs, training materials and union-management documents were particularly useful. The research involved an extensive period of interviewing over a six-month period from July to December 1996. It included interviews with 30 middle managers from a variety of functions including quality, personnel, engineering and production, and 30 shop-floor employees including ten team leaders and 20 shop-floor employees. Each individual was interviewed for an hour. Employees were generally asked to outline what they saw as the major changes the company had gone through, and they were asked their opinions as to the variety of innovations the company had introduced during the 1990s. It is important to note that the employees interviewed were selected by management and so one might expect that the results would favour the corporate line.[4] That in practice this was far from the case perhaps reveals much about the general support for teamworking within the factory. Of course, it is difficult to generalize but this interpretation is consistent with a employee opinion survey conducted by management in 1995. It found that 'people do not feel that morale is very high', 'there is uncertainty about the future', 'dissatisfaction with pay', and that 'levels of trust' in management are 'low'. The clearest support for our interpretation, however, was a one-day walkout during the summer of 1996 following a management decision to withhold a corporate bonus payment. This was the first industrial action within the company for 15 years and reflected frustrations that had built up since the early 1990s.

Intermotors is a large UK-based automotive manufacturing company which underwent a period of substantial change in the 1990s. Intermotors is atypical because the international nature of its market meant that the domestic recession of the early 1980s had a relatively minor impact upon its performance. The 1980s were the best years of sustained growth and profitability in the company's history. The worldwide recession of the 1990s, however, had a significant impact and sales collapsed by two thirds, plunging the company into the red. Intermotors is a multi-union site and the unions exercised considerable power within the company during the 1980s. Partly this was because management had been unwilling to confront the unions as, at the time, the demand for sales far outstripped production capacity. To avoid closure in the early 1990s, however, the company initiated a period of rapid and extensive change which presided over the introduction of more flexible working practices, trade union marginalization, outsourcing, delayering and substantial job losses that reduced the workforce from 4000 to 2000. These changes were imposed on employees and trade unions. In view of this, many employees expressed considerable resentment towards management as of late 1996. It seemed to them that they had been ill-treated by what appeared to them to be ruthless management practices.

Employees resented not just the redundancies but also the autocratic approach that management had adopted towards them. This was apparent in management's refusal to negotiate with trade union representatives and the imposition of pay awards during the 1990s. In this context we can begin to see that common-sense notions of the positive implications of teamworking may be somewhat inconsistent with the 'lived experiences' of employees. Once the recession began to 'bottom out' in the mid-1990s, a more conciliatory approach towards the unions began to be adopted. Nonetheless, management were considered by many employees to have 'ridden roughshod' over them. This context shaped their experiences of teamworking and it is impossible, therefore, to disentangle employees' past experiences from the practice of teamworking.

Increased work flexibility had a profound impact on the workplace as it threatened existing trade skills and identities. Even as late as 1990, strict skill demarcations still applied in terms of skilled, semi-skilled and unskilled groups, and within this there were distinct trades such as turners, fitters and coach builders, each with their own separate skills and trade identity. In theory all of these divisions were replaced with the introduction of a 'new labour agreement' (NLA) in the early 1990s, which demanded complete flexibility. In practice, however, many of the skilled divisions still apply. Nonetheless, employees are now bound to work anywhere within the factory at management's behest. In February 1991, a document was presented to all employees to accompany the NLA. Here the then personnel director outlined the new approach indicating how teamworking was a central feature:

- A simplified, single cycle assembly process.
- A commitment to continuous improvement with changes as necessary to assist productivity and product quality supported by an operator-supervisor-management structure with more accountability and responsibility at every level.
- Shop-floor teams led by a team leader. Within each team the members will be totally flexible and responsible for all the activities which take place in that department including process (assembly, machining, painting etc.), maintenance, quality/inspection, cleaning up, work recording and reporting.

In the early 1990s production was reorganized into zones which encompassed approximately ten teams of 10–15 workers. Previously, work areas had grown like topsy and although grouped around the paint, trim, wood, machining and assembly areas, production involved a complex movement of parts. The restructured work organization more closely corresponded with the flow line of production. A decision to outsource major areas of manufacturing was to lead to the closure of the machine shop and this had a profound impact upon employees. Layers of shop-floor supervision were also taken out including leading hands, charge hands and foremen. These were condensed and replaced with working team leaders. In some areas of the factory, team leaders were elected while in others they were appointed.

The quality of work processes was a major preoccupation throughout the 1990s and most employees had been through a two-stage quality training programme. Natural work teams (NWTs) were introduced whereby individuals engaged in problem solving. Such teams were widespread in the early 1990s when workers and management came together in the face of financial disaster to ensure a return to profitability. Management also delegated engineering expertise to the shop-floor so as to assist with problem solving. Linked to these developments were 'plan, do and review' (PDR) meetings where team leaders, in conjunction with their team members, set weekly production targets and reviewed their weekly performance in terms of cost, delivery and quality. Despite being widespread within areas of the factory, NWTs were unevenly spread. Moreover, many supervisors simply set targets without consulting team members, while some teams were not involved in NWTs at all. In view of this, as has been found elsewhere (Thompson and Wallace 1996), teamworking was uneven, even within a single factory. Teamworking requires employees to think about the world in new ways and this has been promoted through training employees in quality ideas and concepts. Hence, in relation to 'zero defects' a training document stipulated: 'All the results of the Company are made by people . . . We must understand that the zero defect concept means all of us must commit to meet our agreed customer requirements all the time'. Here we can see the company seeking to reconstitute the way in which its employees think about and understand the world of work. Interestingly, there is an authoritative, almost hypnotic propaganda in the assertion that 'we must understand', 'all of us must commit', 'to meet our agreed customer requirements'. It seeks to remove any questioning with regard to 'ends'; instead, attention is focused only on the means to achieve the pre-given goals of productivity and profitability. Teamwork was heavily promoted during the quality training sessions at Intermotors and the dream of teamworking is apparent in the following extract: 'Teamworking is a guiding principle for the Company that allows individuals to increase the scope of their skills and experience and provides a foundation for continuous improvement'.

Teamworking was therefore presented as being innately good for both individuals and the company. Thus, corporate training materials presented the benefits as greater 'ownership', 'involvement', 'quicker decision making', 'being competitive', 'improved communication', 'motivation', 'skills' and 'information sharing'. Such gains make the dream of teamworking difficult to argue against, for who would prefer 'poor communication' or a failure to be 'competitive' and, as such, the discourse of teamworking is persuasive. Not least this is so when one considers some of the attributes which are said to make 'an effective team':

Humility	Learning
No blame	Creativity
Desire to win	Team spirit
Leadership	

Again we can see teamworking presented as a way of unifying the organization by benefiting everyone; the 'desire to win' that it endeavours to promote speaks volumes and echoes the American Dream. In addition, a mission statement, corporate goals, a corporate vision and values and a company uniform were introduced at Intermotors. An in-house employee learning centre was also established where employees could attend courses ranging from languages and computing to golf. In addition, management began to address all employees irrespective of rank or position as 'associates'. Overall, there was a concern with changing the culture of the organization whereby everyone was to embrace the dream, as the quality director explained: 'Above all we've been working with people. We've been working on the minds of people because we needed a new attitude, old attitudes don't work in this new creative environment'.

At Intermotors, teamworking was central to new ways of working that involved greater task flexibility, enhanced skills through training operators to set up machines, flatter structures of control, problem solving via the delegation of engineering expertise and involvement in planning. But teamworking also generated for staff a way of understanding and making sense of the world. This is because these methods of working invariably impinge on employee subjectivity. Teamworking was promoted at Intermotors during quality training courses; it was a corporate value and goal; it was embedded in the unitary thinking behind the corporate mission statement, the corporate uniform and the nomenclature of *associate*. In view of this, the employee experiences explored below are all related to teamworking as a concerted attack on existing traditions and ways of working. Nonetheless, this is not to suggest that all aspects of teamworking gain the same reception; slotting individual experiences into categories is problematic and individuals rarely fit neatly into any one grouping. The complexity of teamworking and experience itself renders understanding problematic and ultimately all we can do is to offer our interpretation of the events within Intermotors.

The response of employees to the teamworking innovations varied dramatically and this is something that the literature tends to underestimate, partly because more attention is given to the changes than to responses to them. While there may be numerous different responses, we were able to identify three prominent ones that we have characterized elsewhere in the words of a popular song from the past: 'Bewitched, bothered and bewildered'.[5] The 'bewitched' were a comparatively small minority of employees who usually had benefited in terms of career progress since the introduction of teamworking. They welcomed the changes and, despite occasional lapses and inconsistencies in their accounts, generally emphasized positive features such as 'empowerment', 'communication' and 'less dotting of the cap'. The employees who were 'bothered' tended to see through the gloss of the teamworking discourse and felt that its lack of genuineness was a major obstacle to realizing its objectives. Typical was Ian who argued that employees did not trust management. 'Bewildered' employees tended to identify an absence of change and Frank, for example, had 'always cared' about his work. Moreover, he had always worked in a way that was consistent with the aspirations of teamworking. We turn now to a more in-depth analysis of the developments leading up to and including a one-day industrial dispute at Intermotors.

Innovate to subjugate

During the 1990s, Intermotors sought to marginalize its unions. This was against a background in which the workforce had experienced large-scale redundancies and pay awards had been imposed without consultation or negotiation. The marginalization of the trade unions was integral to instilling a new discipline where 'each individual has his own place; and each place its individual' (Foucault 1977: 143). It required that management 'avoid distributions in groups' and demanded that they 'break up collective dispositions' − or, at least, groups that might question the status quo as defined by management. Simultaneously, management sought to build a team spirit and to promote enhanced employee identification with, and commitment towards, the company. By restructuring the organization of work from a multiplicity of groupings that had evolved in a relatively unplanned fashion to a distinct pattern organized around workflow and teamworking, management sought to observe/survey the operation of work more effectively. Associated with this restructuring was a delayering which replaced a system of 'direct control' with a form of 'responsible autonomy' (Friedman 1977). This involved replacing leading hands, charge hands and foremen with team leaders supporting a regime of self-discipline through the norms and values of teamworking. It is important to note that despite flattening the hierarchy, 'hierarchized surveillance' did not disappear. This is because 'it is the apparatus as a whole that produces "power" and distributes individuals' (Foucault 1977: 177). Thus despite the most visible distinctions and layers of hierarchy being removed, surveillance is reinforced: 'It is a power that seems all the less "corporal" in that it is more subtly "physical"'. One could argue that delayering consolidated control by rendering work a more visible target of strategic intervention, especially through simplified work flows and patterns of production, and new video surveillance techniques. At the same time, however, the new emphasis on self-discipline made the outward manifestations of control appear less tangible.

In conjunction with delayering, management had been preoccupied with wrestling control over working practices away from the shop-floor. Central to this was the introduction of video surveillance techniques to obtain knowledge about (and so aid the analysis of) job/task performance. Employees initially resisted attempts to video them by a series of sectional walkouts and subsequently management sought to soothe disgruntled employees by allowing them to video each other. Such a humanistic tactic of facilitating autonomy can be very effective as employees are drawn into the events of self-surveillance. For despite the appearance of employee participation, the aim was the same: 'to know where and how to locate individuals . . . to be able at each moment to supervise the conduct of each individual, to assess it, to judge it, to calculate its qualities or merits. It was a procedure, therefore, aimed at knowing, mastering and using employees' (Foucault 1977: 143).

New corporate norms and values were promoted more generally through a corporate strategy and set of key goals that were outlined in annual presentations to employees, supported by glossy booklets. For instance, the 'people' strategy was as follows: 'to provide an environment in which we can unlock the potential of all our people'. Linked to this was the following 'key goal': 'Our goal is to create an environment in which more of our employees can take responsibility for their own development and be proud of the more open atmosphere which they have helped create'.

Here we can see that despite an emphasis on teams, there was a preoccupation with developing an individualistic outlook among employees in terms of development, responsibility and pride. Again drawing on Foucault (1977), there were a variety of ways in which employees were individually encouraged to accept and identify with the corporation. As outlined above, these can be understood as part of an endeavour to transform individual employees into subjects who secure a sense of meaning and identity from participating in new workplace practices. This was made explicit in the 1994 key goals statement at Intermotors:

> If you consider each key goal carefully you will see that you can make a contribution to some, if not all, of the key goals. We can all impact customer satisfaction by doing our job right first time. We can all have an influence on cycle time and delivery, and if we manage our area or job as if it were our own business, then we can reduce our costs.

It was not sufficient for employees simply to engage in teamworking – they had to demonstrate to management their commitment to the new ways of working by treating the job as if it were their own business. Hence employees were tasked to become entrepreneurs even whilst they are excluded from the rewards of such endeavours. Here Foucault's concept of the *examination* is appropriate: through a diverse range of channels, management provided the opportunity for those individuals who embraced the new approach to come forward and express their support. There are a number of examples of this: an innovation was launched whereby volunteers were asked to attend working groups in order to develop the *vision* and *values*; an 'open' forum was introduced whereby each Monday, in their own time, employees had the opportunity to discuss issues of concern with the managing director and his colleagues. Moreover, concurrent with the introduction of a new automated production line, employees were asked to attend working groups that would discuss new methods of working. Involvement in determining new working practices and establishing a corporate vision and values reflected an endeavour to 'bind' employees 'by the chain of their own ideas' (Foucault 1977: 103) to the new corporate approach. Here we see not only how power stimulates new kinds of knowledge (ideas) but also a knowledge that is drawn upon in the exercise of the power of self-discipline. As Foucault argues, this chain of ideas is 'all the stronger in that we do not know of what it is made and we believe it to be our own work'. Thus the danger is that we become chained to new innovations such as teamworking, never stopping to reflect upon how such innovations change or reproduce the world we inhabit.

Simply by attending meetings, employees were able to reveal their commitment/conformance and held themselves up for examination. During the meetings, management discouraged employee dissent by dismissing challenging comments as being 'negative'; non-conforming employees were cajoled by management assertions such as 'don't you want to come to the party?' or 'don't you want to get on board?'. Such forums can be understood as involving the examination of employee commitment, aimed at normalizing individuals through *dividing* the 'good' from the 'bad' (Foucault 1982) so as to silence those who might question management. Judgements were made during these meetings as to who might be selected to work on the new line and who would be 'tomorrow's' team leader. Many employees expressed fears that dissent today would mean selection for redundancy in the future. The cost of such dissent reveals the high price to pay if one fails to conform and it is indicative of how difficult it can be to resist. Teams were encouraged to use notice boards to display a celebration of their support for the new teamworking approach, exemplifying the effects of the processes of examination, normalization and surveillance. It would be these teams that 'passed' the 'examination'; these teams would be 'rewarded' by being selected for work on the new line. By contrast those that failed to 'come to the party' would await closure of the old line and faced possible redundancy.

Individuals who appeared to revel in the teamworking ethos were rewarded in a variety of ways. One reward was for employees to be invited to show customers around the factory. This task was described as 'swanning' about the place by many of the other factory workers. A number of employees expressed disdain for this practice of turning the factory into what Foucault (1977: 126) would describe as 'a sort of permanent observatory'. Perhaps the ultimate accolade was for an employee to be promoted to a team leader or to a managerial position and, in one case, to the 'quality team' that devised new innovations. In so far as many of these managerial techniques separated individuals off from one another, they can be seen to have had individualizing effects. In such cases, the key goal of encouraging 'responsibility' for one's 'own development' would have been achieved. In effect, 'Discipline rewards simply by the play of awards, thus making it possible to attain higher ranks and places, it punishes by reversing this process' (Foucault 1977: 181). In this section we have elaborated how, despite calls for unity, teamworking can serve to reinforce individual preoccupations.

The business performance reward scheme (BPRS)

In the early 1990s management at Intermotors 'suspended' a bonus payment for employees due to the need to cut costs in the face of recessionary pressures. Then in 1991 management promised to restore the bonus so as to procure cooperation with the introduction of new working practices: 'The suspended bonus will be re-introduced and consolidated at the rate of £10 per week from 1 August 1992. This is subject to the successful introduction of . . . [new models] and the full co-operation with all the changes in manufacturing' (Company statement, 28 October 1991). Subsequently, despite continued cooperation, the bonus payment of £10 per week was withheld due to the sustained effects of the UK recession: 'The level of sales activity and the subsequent production levels, and their effect on business performance make it impossible to increase costs further. Consequently, the increase of £10 per week, which was due to be paid from the 1 August, will not take place' (Company statement, July 1992).

Withdrawing the bonus was a continuing source of discontent among the workforce as many had come to view the bonus as something that was theirs by right.[6] The decision not to pay the bonus, the personnel manager argued, was due to 'financial constraints', intimating that it was therefore outside of management control. In 1993 the company imposed a two-year pay deal which reintroduced a bonus element as the following extract reveals:

Despite the absence of a pay review in 1993 and the loss of the bonus, our wages and salaries are still very competitive, both locally and nationally . . . Nevertheless, the Company recognizes the need to reward people for their major efforts over the past 12 months and the need to maintain this commitment during 1994/1995. Achieving break even in 1993 will not generate the resources to fund a pay review but despite this, and on the basis that break-even is achieved, the following will apply. A basic pay review of 2% will apply to all grades. Additionally, a bonus will be

introduced which will be paid subject to the Company achieving its
targeted profit at mid year and year end.

(Company statement, November 1993)

The bonus scheme was introduced as part of an attempt by management to
procure employee commitment to corporate profitability. It was seen as a
means to reward employees for the efforts that they had made during the 1990s
and as a means to improve the much flagging employee morale. However, it
neglected the fact that employees had come to expect the bonus as 'of right'. In
this sense, the bonus could never procure employee commitment because it was
seen as simply a case of restoring that which had been taken away. Indeed,
employees were likely to remain disgruntled, not only due to the original
withdrawal of the bonus but also because of the loss of earnings that had
occurred since it had been withdrawn, combined with the successive
imposition of pay awards. The bonus needs, however, to be understood as being
integral to an attempt by management to mobilize the employees around the
corporate goal of profitability.

The earlier bonus was linked to production in terms of employee output. By
contrast, the new scheme was linked with corporate profitability and represented an attempt to align employee 'hearts and minds' with the wider corporate project of increasing company profits. In this sense, it was a departure from
the past – a past that employees were expected to forget. This was a clear sign of
attempts to transform labour subjectivity so as to transcend narrow interests in
wages and internalize the business ethic in order to become self-disciplined
with regard to *profitable* production. It can also be understood in the context of
the concerted move towards teamworking during the 1990s. The personnel
manager was explicit about this when he outlined management intentions for
introducing the bonus: 'The company decided that there ought to be a business
focus to tie people into and help people to understand that we are a bottom line
organization and that whatever people do within their jobs it impacts upon the
profitability of the business'. This comment reveals a lack of understanding on
the part of senior management regarding what could be achieved through a
bonus scheme, especially given the recent history. In the first year of the BPRS,
the company set itself a target of £10m profit for which each employee would
receive a £500 bonus. The profit target was exceeded with the company making an £18m profit and the bonus was paid biannually. In 1995 the company set
itself a £20m profit target and offered employees an increased bonus of £550.
The target was met and the bonus paid. Then in 1996 a £30m target was set and
employees were again offered a bonus of £550. The system itself was deemed to
be iniquitous by many employees as the amount of profit made, and the increase
in effort demanded, was not reflected in the bonus paid. Roger Wilky, a team
member of 12 years from the machine shop, lamented the inconsistency
between the bonus scheme and the corporate teamworking philosophy: 'Now
this is investment in people, trust, communication. It's not working'.

It is these kinds of inconsistencies that leave space for, or encourage, resistance. Making demands for increased profits that do not correspond with an

equitable increase in the bonus seemed likely to stimulate a sense of injustice. The inconsistency and sense of inequality was compounded by the fact that employees' efforts had only a tenuous influence on corporate profits. Two bonus payments were to be made in 1996, one in June the other at Christmas. Each payment amounted to £275 for each employee. Employees were individually informed as to when the payments would be made:

> The scheme will continue during 1996 with a payment of £550 for the year, again payment in two instalments subject to the Company achieving its half-year and full-year profit targets. Achievement of these profit targets is essential to *our future* and consequently no part payments will be made if profit targets are not met.
>
> (Company statement, November 1995, emphasis added)

The attainment of 'profit' is firmly wedded to the collective future ('our future') of the corporate entity. Thus there is no distinction between individual and corporate performance. Individuals must visualize corporate performance and subsume themselves within it. Company success is to equate with individual success, as in the American Dream.

During the first quarter of 1996, management informally indicated to employees that they 'did not think' the bonus would be paid. It had become clear that the company would not meet its profit targets and that therefore the bonus would not be paid. Senior management was uncomfortable with employees perceiving the bonus as theirs 'by right' rather than being linked to corporate performance. Subsequently, the personnel manager formally told employees that the bonus would not be paid: 'I influenced the decision because there were people down there that did not believe that we were not going to pay the bonus. I think that if we are not going to, then we need to say it clearly. So we did it'. In June, all management were briefed in a letter from the CE that the summer bonus would not be paid because the company had failed to meet its profit targets. Management then cascaded the information to the workforce. Zone managers read out a statement to teams of workers explaining that the bonus would not be paid. This was only two days before the bonus was due to be paid and the personnel manager admitted that the announcement should have been made six weeks before but management 'didn't have the bottle' to do so.

Advance notice that the bonus would not be paid was particularly important since it was treated by many of the employees as their summer 'holiday money'. The loss of bonus highlighted to employees how unjust it was to deny payment for any output short of 100 per cent of the target – for instance, if the company made £14m as opposed to £15m profit for that half year then the bonus would not be paid. It is critical to understand, however, that the decision not to pay the bonus was bound up with management's concern to introduce a new teamworking discipline. Thus, managers were concerned to demonstrate how 'serious' they were about transforming employee subjectivity or, as management would say, the 'mindset' of employees. In the next section we discuss what happened after management made the announcement.

The wildcat

The buzzer went for the morning tea break and employees began to talk among themselves. Many were disgruntled by what they saw as a gross unfairness. A number of issues arose. Many employees considered that 'the goalposts had been moved' because the company had set production targets of X number of vehicles which had been met. Yet, management stated that the mix of vehicles, which had been sold, was such that the profit targets had not been achieved. The CE had already received a bonus of over £100,000 because his bonus was linked to units produced. It is interesting that Gouldner (1954) in *Wildcat Strike* reported similar inequities in that Gypsum's board of directors had voted themselves an enormous bonus shortly before the dispute that he described occurred. This was particularly frustrating for employees at Intermotors because the CE was considered to be in a better position to influence sales levels than employees. John Brown, the works convenor, recalled employee reaction at the time:

> It was unofficial. We hadn't called a ballot or anything . . . That was the first time we had any sort of reaction. As you walked round, people actually said 'Redundancies'. Everything was coming out. 'Let's all take our workwear off and burn it in a big pile'. This was the final straw, not getting the bonus. That was it. All the things that had happened to them. Then all of a sudden we [the union] were given a bit of respect . . . that was it, better start talking to these guys.

Many middle managers were as shocked by the decision not to pay the bonus as the employees. The directors made a decision but did not effectively communicate the reason for it even to their own managers, indicating that management are rarely the homogeneous and unified force that is sometimes assumed by those who subscribe to 'heavy duty' conceptions of management control. As has been argued elsewhere (Knights and Murray 1994; Watson 1994; McCabe 2000), management are far from being an undifferentiated and cohesive block and, of course, it is their inconsistency and incoherence that gives rise to, and provides the space for, resistance (see Collinson 1992; McCabe 1996; May 1999). Stuart P., a shift manager, reflected on the walkout:

> We had a walkout but it wasn't union pushed. The people decided to do it off their own back because they were just sort of frustrated. It was like a blotting paper effect. Things happened all over the factory at the same time and within a few hours everyone was of the same mind. 'Cos when I came in at 2.00 p.m. to cover the shift no one was here. I didn't know what had gone on . . . the way it was briefed, it wasn't explained correctly . . . But then the union, or the people representatives came into their own, because they had to talk to top management. I would say it's a one off, it won't happen again.

This quotation reveals how 'power is exercised from innumerable points, in the interplay of nonegalitarian and mobile relations' (Foucault 1979:94). Power acted 'like blotting paper' and without organization from either above or below, individuals walked out and became an unorganized collective. A common explanation offered by management for the walkout was to dismiss the action as following on from the way in which the information had been communicated to the employees. It is a common response of managers (and politicians) to assume that conflicts are a result of failed communications rather than real differences or disputes. Thus the problem is seen in terms of something which could have been resolved if managed better. But this is to be dismissive of how the conflict had been brewing for some considerable time. It also denies the legitimacy of the workers' concerns and ignores the contextual issues that gave rise to the action (see also Gouldner 1954). The employees and trade unionists confirmed the 'spontaneous' nature of the action. One way of understanding this spontaneity is to see it as one consequence of management at Intermotors marginalizing the trade unions. Effectively this rendered employees bereft of a collective voice through which conflict could be channelled. The works convenor intimated how he had had to respond to the actions of the workforce. His account is clearly indicative of a classic wildcat strike in that individuals had acted without recourse to formal union demands:

> it got out of me hands 'cos I hadn't experienced it before . . . We handled it best we could. I marched them down to the main gate 'cos where they walked out was deep in the factory. Nobody could see really. So I thought 'We'll have some impact on this'. I felt like the Pied Piper, I marched them all through the factory to the main gate here so that they could be seen. The main managers' offices are over the main gate. So I thought 'They can see this, so I'll get them down there'. Very visible. Next minute the reporters arrived – there was method to that. I stood in the flowerbeds by the canteen.

Here the convenor is indicating how, despite having initially been surprised by the shop-floor 'walkout', he quickly began to organize the action. Thus, workers were 'marched' to the factory gates. That he felt like the 'Pied Piper' indicates something of the mystery and power of individuals acting spontaneously as a cohesive, collective force. It also suggests something of the magical feeling the convenor experienced during the conduct of the industrial action. Like the Sorcerer's Apprentice, once the magic of collective action was unleashed it was simply 'out there' and beyond his control. His only recourse was to use his initiative to bring it to the attention of senior management and the wider public through the media. One way to make the strike 'very visible' was to stand 'in the flowerbeds' at the main factory gates below the 'managers' offices' and to ensure the reporters from the press arrived. The senior managers' offices are situated near the main gates and so marching to them provided a potent symbol of opposition. The flowerbeds, as Gouldner (1954: 17) noted, mark the entrance building and the executive offices 'off from the dinginess of other buildings'. In this sense, standing in the flowerbeds posed a challenge to the existing relations of power.

The trim shop experience

The trim shop is a close-knit community that produces leather fixtures for Intermotor vehicles. The experience of trim shop workers ('trimmers') is particularly relevant when considering the inequity of the bonus system. This is because each group of employees within the factory is paid a bonus according to the overall factory performance. Different sections, however, performed in different ways. Thus some areas met their targets while others failed to do so. The trim shop had met its targets in terms of production for the year. In view of this, the section was particularly aggrieved that management withheld the bonus payment. Jane Spencer, the team leader, commented (emphasis added):

> That is a prime example of trust. You get briefings all year to say that you've turned out X number of cars and you are on plan until two months before. Suddenly you're not on target for your bonus even though you've trimmed more cars than we asked you for originally. How can people out there understand that, when they have trimmed more cars than they thought they were going to have to do, and you're still not going to get your bonus. *Now we all know it's linked into profit but that is not what they are interested in. What they are interested in is what they have produced.*

Although as a team leader Jane is first line management, she clearly identifies with the concerns of the workers in her section. Here we can see that the line between 'management' and 'workers' is a tenuous one. Despite being aware of management's concern to concentrate minds on profits, she is also fully aware that workers are more concerned with meeting production targets.

The management explanation that the mix of vehicles sold had not yielded the profit targets was met with derision from the trim shop workforce. For example, Robert Markus, a team member within the trim shop, suggested that the shop-floor had little control over sales, and therefore should not have their bonus linked to them (emphasis added):

> Unfortunately we didn't reach their *target* since we didn't know what their target was. We weren't happy at all because in the trim shop we had met every *target* they put to us. Week for week we did it. So we said 'We have, we've done it. We've got our *worksheets . . . You've got the cars down there. Where's the money . . .* We decided to take a little bit of fresh air and we all wandered out . . . It was just like they had kicked the stuffing out of you. You know, you've done *all this work for six months* and you're not getting acknowledged for it. It just seemed to happen. There was no one waving a flag saying 'all right boys let's make a stand'. It was just this feeling of discontent.

Here Robert displays how his worldview contrasts sharply with that of the idealized team player that management seeks to create. Production targets, the worksheets that record and specify his work performance, the manufacture of cars and the payment of money for this work, suffuse Robert's world. By contrast, the managerial worldview of profits, teams, visions, values and strategies bears little relation to his daily lived experiences. After the morning break, when the buzzer to return to work went, many employees recommenced working: 'There were still lots of staples going', Robert reflected. But gradually people began to stop work. The paint shop and the trim shop walked out. These are two key groups within the factory because they feed the production line and therefore their actions have a 'domino effect'. Jane Spencer again:

> I was doing a spray test and so I was in a project area away. For a couple of weeks, leading up to that, they had said 'You are not on plan for your bonus'. Although they were grumbling, people were accepting the fact that maybe they weren't going to see it in the summer. Then what did they [management] do? Without any consultation with the zone manager or team leaders, the manager came out and said 'I'm going to be briefing the teams with this, you're not going to get your bonus'. It was, full manager sits there, briefing. Not the team leader sits down and has a chat: 'OK guys I don't think we're going to get it'. It was, the manager comes and briefs . . . I came out of the project area and the whole place was completely empty. 'What's gone on?' 'Well everyone's completely cheesed off' and they've walked out.

Jane considered that if management had handled the situation in a more devolved way then a walkout could have been avoided. Although the action was not dismissed as irrational, Jane clearly saw it as marginal, as reflected in her belief that devolved team briefings could have prevented it. Jane even commented to the zone manager before the briefing that it would undoubtedly affect production targets for the day. Nonetheless she did not anticipate the extent of the reaction that the briefing would provoke. Groups of workers began to coalesce both inside and outside the factory so as to talk. As they did so, the senior management negotiator sought to bully and single out workers. He attempted to walk through and brush past groups and pockets of workers: 'To try and intimidate them to go back to work. The silent touch. Just wandered through like stern. Cold as ice like' (Robert Markus).

The coercion that lies behind such management strategies is not difficult to detect; equally, the 'surface' calm of workplace relations is all too misleading. The convenor explained what happened next:

> The lads took it on themselves basically. It was like an area of the factory walked out and it sort of snowballed. It just became something. It just happened. It really did just happen . . . the trim shop went and stood outside. The body line said 'What are they stood outside for?' They came out and joined them. Before you knew where you were there were 1000 people standing in the yard. The manager came in my office and said 'What's happened to them? Go and get them back in'. I said 'I didn't put

them out there you go and get them back in. It's you who didn't pay the
bonus not me'. I had to go and address them and say things like 'Get back
to work you're in breach of your contract'. These sort of things that they
ask you to do. You have to repudiate the action.

Here we can see how fragile the power of management can be in the face of
resistance or the exercise of power by employees. Management were forced to
appeal to trade unionists to exert their power over the employees, for they did
not consider this to be within their grasp – a clear indication of how power is
dispersed and 'points of resistance are present everywhere in the power network' (Foucault 1979: 95). The action taken here does not reflect 'a single locus
of great Refusal' but rather a challenge to particular local circumstances. The
need to consider the local context does not mean that change of more revolutionary proportions can be ruled out but rather that 'more often one is
dealing with mobile and transitory points of resistance, producing cleavages in a
society that shift about, fracturing unities and effecting regroupings' (Foucault
1979: 96).

Jane Spencer indicated her mixed loyalties during the walkout. On the one
hand, she wanted to avoid the action, not least because she had aspirations to
secure a managerial position and was comparatively anti-union. On the other
hand, however, she sympathized with the plight of the union that had been
forced to react to the members' actions and she also empathized with her team
members:

> Through all that, I felt quite sorry for our union guy [shop steward]
> because he was in the middle of a situation that had gone completely out
> of his control anyway and he was like trying to talk people to go back to
> work. He was the only one working actually . . . it was said you are all in
> breach of your contract, go back to work . . . I think I was right to go out.
> My team had already gone out . . . I am not paid that amount of money to
> sit that side of the fence. Far as I'm concerned my loyalty lies with that
> team. I expect them to work with me every day and I expect them to
> bend over backwards sometimes. The way not to do that is to go and stand
> opposite them when they are genuinely concerned and as I say the major-
> ity of people on my team are moderate . . . So I was right to go and stand
> with them on that because they felt that it had got to the point where they
> could get somebody to come and have a chat with them.

Jane weighed up carefully her strategic options once the walkout took place,
finally believing that her best interests were served by supporting her team
colleagues, since not to do so would only result in terrible tensions once work
resumed. First, she reasoned that she was not paid to support management.
Second, she rationalized that she needed her team's support in order to be an
effective team leader and so was prepared to act against management to
maintain the team's support. Nonetheless, by apparently challenging management along with her team colleagues, she was acting in both her own and the

long-term interests of management, because her actions would maintain the cohesion of the team and secure her position. Clearly, in matters of power/ knowledge relations, nothing is straightforward. It is necessary to reflect on how different individuals might calculate the conditions that make certain commitments to practices possible and plausible. Individuals draw upon their knowledge of the material circumstances of the work situation but also on the sense of their own identity. Therefore, social practices and exercises of power and resistance have to be contextualized in relation to the symbolic as well as the material aspects of self and social relations. Resistance, then, can be seen 'furrowing across individuals themselves, cutting them up and remolding them, marking off irreducible regions in them, in their bodies and minds' (Foucault 1979: 96).

Discussion and summary

Throughout this chapter we have examined teamworking both in the literature and through an empirical case study by drawing on Foucault's conceptualizations of power, knowledge and subjectivity. While virtually none of the teamworking writers in motor manufacturing theorize their research by the direct use of these concepts, all of them can be reinterpreted from this perspective. We sought to show how their different analyses implicitly relied on notions of power, knowledge and identity while neglecting to theorize these concepts. Our argument was that through these concepts, teamworking theory could escape the limitations of a contingency approach. We proceeded to apply these insights to an empirical analysis of employee resistance in the context of teamworking. The objective of the profit scheme 'to pull the company together' so as 'to operate as one team' had precisely the opposite effect than that intended. It might be argued that the bonus scheme was an additional factor introduced into the teamworking equation, the non-payment of which would inevitably lead to the outcome we have described. Yet, one needs to understand that the bonus scheme was not distinct from, but was integral to, and indeed was the culmination of, the teamworking ethos. Non-payment of the bonus was perceived as a defining moment within the new approach whereby all employees would realize that the world had been created anew. Resistance in this Brave New World was not envisaged, and absolutely not of the type that would involve trade unions, which were believed to have been displaced by the 'New World order'. It was this belief in a workforce subjugated to the demands of teamworking that drove the directors' decision not to pay the bonus, and as such, for these managers, the outcome was entirely unexpected.

As we have suggested, not all management at Intermotors shared the directors' naïveté but the speed, spontaneity and passion of the reaction shocked all. We would argue that no one anticipated a return to collectivism in the decisive and rapid way in which the unions were returned to power – not even the works convenor or the shop stewards. Here resistance can be seen to traverse 'social stratifications and individual unities' (Foucault 1979: 96) in that the employees reacted outside of traditional union boundaries. Sections such as the trim shop took action independently of one another, team leaders reacted against management and shop-floor workers expressed their demands in opposition to sales and marketing staff. In view of this, we believe that the outcome was entirely unanticipated. It is apparent that points of resistance and exercises of power rarely act in a way that is predictable.

The case reveals how teamworking and the bonus scheme failed to transform individuals into subjects whose sense of reality, meaning and identity was completely tied to a conception of the company and themselves as one single unit. While teamworking generated higher levels of self-discipline than before, this was not sufficient to remove the sense of separation between employees and management that is summed up in the phrase 'them and us'. Hierarchical surveillance, normalization and continuous processes of examining performances were seen to have some impact but not exactly what senior management would have preferred. Nonetheless, senior management attributed the problem not to any flaws within the project itself but largely to a failure of communication. But this is to negate the power relations and the resistance that is in operation in organizations. It suggests that despite several decades of pluralistic thinking within management discourse, some managers are still unable to understand that employees may view the world in a way different from themselves.

One could argue that, because ultimately the employees went back to work, this verifies a 'deterministic scenario' and gives credence to those who perceive Foucault's analysis to be deterministic. The question we have to ask here is what determined what? As we suggest below, teamworking did generate new levels of self-discipline among some employees but their lives were not determined, for when 'push came to shove' they saw their relations with management as somewhat antagonistic. This was a shock to a number of managers for they had begun to believe that employee conformity to the norms of teamworking had transformed traditional antagonisms. Likewise it was a shock to the union leadership who, having been marginalized, seemed to rule out the possibility of such collective action. It only goes to show that compliance is not the equivalent of consent and that there is a thin line between compliance and resistance. Although employees did not like the way that the union had been marginalized, they could not have anticipated that the walkout would lead management back into the arms of the union and thus restore some semblance of 'normal' industrial relations.

Only by imposing a broad generalized abstraction from these diverse discursive configurations would it be possible to conclude that events were determined. This is precisely what the deterministic supporters or critics of Foucault do – the supporters reduce everything to panopticon-like surveillance. By contrast, the critics see power and resistance as polar opposites of one another, thereby arguing that there can be no space for, or agents of, resistance (Knights and Vurdubakis 1994) if, as Foucault (1977, 1979) suggests, power is everywhere and exercised by everyone. In answer to supporters of Foucault that subscribe to a deterministic analysis, we would argue that surveillance is not exhaustive of possible discourses and practices *even* in prisons or other total institutions, let alone in factories and offices. In answer to the critics of Foucault, the ubiquity of power only precludes resistance if power and resistance are seen as independent and mutually exclusive of one another rather than simply two sides of the same coin.

What we have sought to describe here is the complexity of an event that in industrial relations discourse assumes the label 'strike' or 'walkout'. We have not attempted to provide a causal explanation of the strike in terms of the failure of management to pay the bonus. For, as Foucault would argue, there is a panoply of complex and contingent conditions that give rise to any event, none of which can readily be seen as pre-eminent. Of course, the convenor had stated that 'not getting the bonus was the final straw' but he also pointed out that it was not the only concern, for people were talking about the earlier redundancies, the introduction of workwear or company uniforms and 'all the things that had happened to them'.

It has to be remembered that specific accounts of events are often selected for their plausibility not just to those immediately implicated in a particular exercise of power but also to significant audiences – management, journalists, the public, and lesser ones such as researchers. These audiences might be less sympathetic to the strike if accounted for by a more complex set of contingencies – undermining of the union, redundancies, transformation of the mindset of employees, profit-related bonuses – that could not be reduced to a single cause. Simple causal accounts may distort events but they mobilize support, as newspapers and politicians are well aware. By refusing to perform reductionist causal interpretations, Foucault's analysis resists a common sense that has been formed and furnished by positive science. Positive representations seek that which is pre-eminent or causal in any set of statements. Causal analysis is always going to be attractive to human beings in so far as the construction of an orderly world is dependent on identifying determinants, the tweaking of which can 'restore normality' whenever things go awry.

To conclude, although contested and far from realized, we can see some of the effects of discipline upon employees and it is here that free market, individualizing discourses such as the American Dream can be said to have an insidious grip upon our subjectivity. Despite being aggrieved, employees and trade unionists never questioned management's right to manage. Shop-floor employees simply wanted bonus payments to reflect their achievements and efforts in terms of production. Unionists wanted an opportunity to represent their members and to negotiate or have a voice in the process of change. Neither questioned managerial prerogative, indicating the deep internalization of property values and the principles by which contemporary capitalism functions. In this regard, a majority of employees are self-disciplined, having internalized the norms of property ownership and recognizing them to be realistically outside of the domain of legitimate resistance. More than this, we can see how power is 'sometimes extended by the position of those who are dominated' (Foucault 1977: 27). Thus, the convenor and shop stewards took on board the identity of trade unionists, and as such acted in a way that reinforced existing inequalities. These individuals simply wanted to be able to act like trade unionists; indeed they proposed an alternative bonus scheme, which would minimize conflict. Similarly, some workers continued to work (even though they felt aggrieved and sympathized with the action their colleagues had taken), essentially because they feared for their future job security.

It is the individualizing effect of power that leads us all to be susceptible to the promise that hard work and endeavour can enable us to rise to the top. Fear of lost employment and income forces our heads into the sands of capitalistic desires and security. At least one team leader walked out despite holding anti-union views because she felt that their case was necessary in order to retain the loyalty of the team. Robert Markus, despite taking industrial action, was preoccupied with targets and production. We can see that power 'invests' these individuals, 'is transmitted by them and through them; it exerts pressure upon them, just as they themselves, in their struggle against it, resist the grip it has on them' (Foucault 1977: 27). Nonetheless, in their preparedness to take action against the disciplinary effects of management strategies, we cannot remain oblivious of 'the distant roar of the battle' (Foucault 1977: 308). That is to say, the grip of the American Dream in its most unreflective and self-interested guise is not total; it can be shaken off.

In the next chapter, we turn to one of the most contemporary interventions in the 'new' economy – knowledge management or KM. As we shall see, KM suffers from many of the tensions and contradictions that earlier innovations posed for management and staff.

A 'one team' approach to knowledge management

Both in the literature and in practice, technology has tended to be conceived as a determinant or driver of the business in private sector organizations. Partly this is a reflection of a human preoccupation with finding simple causal explanations for complex realities. But it is also a function of new or changing technologies appearing to be more easily captured than more broad ranging organizational or social change. Criticisms of such approaches have been vociferous in recent years (MacKenzie and Wajman 1985; Knights and Murray 1994; Grint and Woolgar 1997) yet just when we think that technological determinism has finally been buried, it rises from the ashes. Hot on the heels of BPR (Hammer 1990; Hammer and Champy 1993; Hammer and Stanton 1995), the current craze emerging from developments in IT is 'knowledge management' (KM). Technological panaceas appear irresistible despite their tendency to promise more than they can ever deliver.

KM has recently enjoyed a favourable reception within the more esoteric realms of the trade, consultancy and academic press. While the term can be traced back to the late 1980s with the publication of *Knowledge Management* by the *Harvard Business Review* (1987/1998), it still has a fairly short history. It was not until the mid-1990s that 'a surge of publications, conferences, and consultant activity' (Quintas 2002: 2) began to mark it out as a distinct field of study and innovation practice. According to Chumer *et al.* (2000: xv), this was partly a result of work by Leonard-Barton (1995) and an influential report by the Economic Intelligence Unit (1996).

Considering the volume of material written on KM there is rather a paucity of empirical research on its use and development in practice (cf. Coombs and Hull 1998; Davenport *et al.* 1998; Carter and Scarborough 2000). For example, none of the chapters in Little *et al.*'s (2002) report detailed empirical research of the kind presented here. Yet it has to be recognized that research undertaken before the term KM was coined is now categorized as within the mainstream of the literature. Some of this work, in particular that of Nonaka and Takeuchi (1995) involved empirical study and, as the KM movement has progressed, these authors were happy to be seen almost as the founding fathers of the movement, despite having emphasized the *creation* of knowledge not its *management* in their classic book *The Knowledge Creating Company*. Davenport *et al.* (1998) claim empirical research of 31 projects in 24 companies but their work is primarily concerned to describe and classify types of KM. In so far as they engage in analysis, it is largely to link KM projects to measurable success for purposes of providing prescriptive recommendations. This is in sharp contrast to our own intensive case study work in a single company that is concerned to understand the conditions and consequences of KM interventions.

While we did not set out to study KM so much as innovations more broadly and business re-engineering specifically, the managers within our case study saw themselves as exploring the potential of KM for the changes they were seeking. Indeed, we observed them grasping for yet another dream of innovation whereby everyone would be able to share knowledge and readily gain access to each others' expertise. This chapter is therefore concerned to contribute to the literature on KM by returning to the case of Loanco, a major UK-based building society (i.e. mutual mortgage lender), that we initially presented in Chapter 4. In particular, we explore how KM reflects and reproduces the inequalities, subjectivities and power relations already embedded in the organization where it was introduced.

Our research demonstrates how an emphasis on a preoccupation with cost and benefit measures of output, or what has been termed 'performativity' (Lyotard 1984) can undermine the potential, or the claims of, KM to transform organization relations in the direction of sharing knowledge irrespective of hierarchical position or privilege. This is clearly a contradiction since KM can be seen to derive precisely out of a belief in performativity as a universal legitimation. In this sense, we suggest that KM may be sowing the seeds of its own demise.

Secondly and relatedly, we consider how, while eschewing any 'techie' associations, KM can reproduce ways of thinking and acting that are difficult to detach from what we know as 'technological determinism'. This is particularly intriguing because, in our case study, there was a concerted effort to manage change through 'people' and to avoid a traditional technicist approach towards technology. We discuss the dangers of technological determinism but argue that it is difficult for management to avoid this way of acting and thinking as the demand for profits almost always pushes management toward 'quick fixes' of the kind that technology appears to promise.

The chapter is organized into three sections. The first provides a limited review of the literature on KM as a preparation for the case study presentation which follows. There is a longitudinal aspect to the research since while the main study took place in 1998 as reported in Chapter 4, we revisited the site in 2000 to evaluate the aftermath of some of the significant changes such as the closure of the call and processing centre. The third section provides a discussion and summary to the chapter.

Knowledge management in perspective

KM has been seen as perhaps one of the most important management panaceas for the new millennium. As with many management panaceas, there is not much that is new other than the attention being given to knowledge and a belief that it can be formally managed. For over a hundred years economists have staked their claim on the importance of knowledge for economic growth and corporate profitability (Quintas 2002). Even before the last century, in 1890 the famous economist Alfred Marshall declared that 'Knowledge is our most important engine of production'. But the subject matter was left dormant until quite recently perhaps because, unlike most economic concepts knowledge does not lend itself readily to quantification. This is even more true when knowledge is seen to consist of a tacit or informal as well as an explicit or formal content (Polanyi 1962, 1966). Considerable time elapsed before the development of this insight had any impact on the study of management and organization, especially in the form of industrial anthropological observations of work.

Of course, knowledge that working practices are not always what they seem in terms of the formal role obligations of employees goes back to scientific management (Taylor 1911) and the Hawthorne experiments (Roethlisberger and Dickson 1939) discussed in Chapter 1. Frederick Taylor was clearly concerned with the knowledge that shop-floor workers utilized in restricting their output and, for this reason, advocated that management appropriated total responsibility for the planning and organization of work from employees, leaving them with just the execution of tasks. This restoration of managerial prerogative was to be complemented by close observations of the fastest workers, the knowledge of which could then be used to allocate tasks efficiently and price them in accordance with normalized time schedules. The Bank Wiring group experiments at Hawthorne also revealed to management, knowledge of how informal norms and behaviour on the shop-floor conditioned levels of productivity and output. Although these researchers did not emphasize the distinction between tacit and explicit knowledge, a central feature of their findings was the existence of informal work behaviour.

The focus on knowledge management could be seen as a function both of the dramatic growth in the sophistication and usage of micro-electronic technology and of its limitations. IT developments created electronic information networks that could serve as a medium through which knowledge in an organization could in principle be captured and transferred, or at least made generally available at the flick of a switch. In the early days, it was simply assumed that the power of IT would alleviate much of an organization's dependence on its employees. This was soon seen as a false dawn when it was realized that there is a world of difference between information and knowledge. While electronic media can readily store, retrieve and communicate information, the creation, transformation and often the communication of knowledge is not easily shifted from human beings to machines. This difficulty is exacerbated and multiplied when the distinction between tacit and explicit knowledge is recognized. While some aspects of explicit knowledge can, in principle, be codified and thereby digitized, the same is not the case for tacit knowledge since it ordinarily exists beneath the level of practitioner conscious awareness. The current attention given to managing knowledge was anticipated by Peter Drucker (1969: 6) as he saw knowledge increasingly as the most important resource in a modern economy. His work certainly influenced the practitioners and consultants but there are two significant contributions that probably had more impact on the proliferation of interest in KM. First was the work of the Xerox Corporation's Palo Alto Research Centre (PARC) where, by 1990, anthropologists worked closely with computer scientists, physicists and engineers to advance knowledge-intensive work (Brown 1998, 2002). Second was the more theoretical work of Nonaka and Takeuchi (1995), which combined the insights of Berger and Luckmann (1966) on the social construction of reality and of Polanyi (1966) on the distinction between tacit and explicit knowledge.

KM shares with many other so-called innovative moves a lack of precise definition, for it is indeed 'slippery' (McInerney and LeFevre 2000: 1). The problem of definition is not surprising given the comparatively long history in which the terms have been used independently of one another. Some authors begin their analysis by drawing a distinction between information and knowledge, arguing that information is giving 'form to our experience, the form of language which can be communicated' (Allee 1997: 42). It is 'organised data presented in context' (Brooking 1999: 4).[1] In this sense, however, the distinction between information and knowledge begins to break down and indeed Bukowitz and Williams (1999: 4) argue that information can be seen as explicit knowledge. From this point of view, the important distinction becomes not so much between information and knowledge as between explicit and tacit knowledge (see below). But this can also, in effect, reduce knowledge to information (Fuller 2002: 16) since the latter is capable of being managed much more than the former. This is perhaps why 'in many organizations, a legitimate interest in knowledge creation has been reduced to an over-emphasis on information technology or measurement tools' (Von Krogh et al. 2000: 4).

Most of the literature sees the difficulties to lie in the term 'knowledge', rather than 'information'. Knowledge has generally been understood by philosophers from Plato onwards to be 'justified true belief' (Nonaka and Takeuchi 1995: 21). This means a belief that is true in so far as it can be justified through evidence that supports it. Positivist philosophies that see no discontinuity between what is natural and what is social (Douglas 1970) have tended to dominate the literature on knowledge in western social science. Largely they have understood knowledge to consist of accurate representations of the objects to which they refer. The truth of such knowledge depends upon rational models constructed by the scientist coinciding with the representations of reality acquired through empirical research. This combination of a rationalist and empiricist epistemology (Nonaka and Takeuchi 1995: 21–2) relies entirely on a 'closure of meaning' (Derrida 1982) such that there is rarely any dispute in interpreting the terms and arguments on the basis of which the models and representations are constructed. The supply and demand models of economics are a good example of this form of knowledge and since such knowledge is adopted by government agencies, its 'truth' can be self-fulfilling. This is because once knowledge is drawn upon in the exercise of power, individuals change their behaviour to accommodate it. Whether or not the assumptions of the model about economic rationality were valid prior to the application of the knowledge matters little once power enters the equation to secure its self-fulfilling 'truth'.

An alternative social constructionist view of knowledge does not share this belief in the possibility of accurately representing reality.[2] Since all representations are constructed and share the contestable and precarious character of meaning that characterizes social relations, knowledge is simply a transitional intervention, break or disruption in the complex flux and flow of meaning. It is thus of value largely as the condition of bringing about its own demise through the knowledge with which it is displaced. In this understanding, knowledge is neither true nor false for it is no more than a narrative (Lawson, 2001) that makes claims to plausibility in so far as it can mobilize resources and enrol supporters (Callon 1986; Knights 2002).

While purporting to be constructionist in their approach, Von Krogh *et al.* (2000: 6, 265 n.7) continue to support the definition of knowledge as 'justified true belief'. For they are unashamedly *prescriptive* in their recommendations to management about knowledge creation and how its tacit quality has to be converted to an explicit form. However, their insistence that knowledge cannot be managed, only created, presents the literature with a paradox in that they have been elevated to guru status in an activity (KM) that they self-consciously deny. While we find their argument convincing, the certainty with which they present it sits uncomfortably with their older views that the truth of a belief can never be guaranteed, and that 'the pursuit of knowledge within western philosophy is heavily laden with skepticism' (Nonaka and Takeuchi 1995: 21). Bathing in their elevated status as a result of the growing interest in knowledge by managers and consultants at the end of the twentieth century, these authors seem to keep this scepticism well at bay. Their belief that the creation of 'new knowledge boils down to *the conversion of tacit knowledge to explicit knowledge*' (p. 11) is unshaken by any sceptical stance. Admittedly, they contrast their own analysis with cognitive psychology, which concentrates on the unidirectional transfer from explicit to tacit knowledge, whereas Nonaka and Takeuchi (1995: 62) see the transformation as interactive and spiral but largely flowing in the opposite direction.

This absence of a sceptical let alone critical stance is even more marked within the KM movement in general. For the philosophical and epistemological roots of a discourse on knowledge, at least recognized by Nonaka and Takeuchi (1995: Ch. 2), are more or less ignored by other KM advocates. Typical of the literature is the conventional way of understanding knowledge in terms of a hierarchy (see Figure 7.1). Within such analyses there is attention not to knowledge itself but to the various forms it can take. Knowledge is simply taken for granted and what is addressed is the relative value and accessibility for an organization and its management of the different forms. Of the greatest value to an organization yet clearly the most difficult to access is wisdom, as a 'synthesis of knowledge and experience'. In principle, then, a major objective of supporters of knowledge management would seem to be that of rendering accessible more of the knowledge that has a higher value to the organization. It is not clear whether this means converting it into explicit knowledge or simply providing the conditions wherein, while remaining tacit or restricted to particular individuals or groups, knowledge is channelled in the direction of achieving the organization's goals, as defined by senior management. Nonaka and Takeuchi (1995: 230–1) are firm in the belief that the process of creating knowledge is quintessentially that of converting tacit into explicit knowledge. This would seem to be the most common approach adopted by those promoting KM as a management tool or strategy.

In this sense, Nonaka and Takeuchi (1995) appear not to see their own knowledge as a construction so much as a commodity that can be acquired and controlled by management. When claiming 'the organization that wishes to cope dynamically with the changing environment needs to be one that creates information and knowledge not merely processes them more efficiently' (p. 50), there is no sense of irony about the certainty of their representation about uncertainty and change! Nor are Nonaka and Takeuchi able therefore to reflect on the politics of their own thesis and, more importantly, on how even were they to mobilize the support of practitioners to its cause, alternative constructions and political rivalries might disrupt intentions and predicted events. In this chapter's case study, it will be seen how it is not some fixed representation of reality, whether or not described as dynamic, that intervenes to disrupt specific plans and designs on knowledge and its management. Rather it would appear to

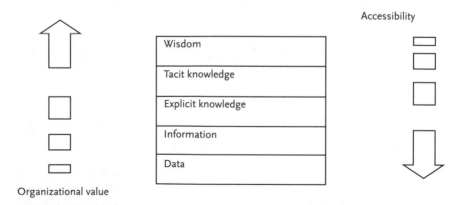

Figure 7.1 The knowledge hierarchy in terms of value and accessibility
Source: Wilson (2000: 12).

be alternative constructions of reality, reflecting diverse political interests which tend to create sudden changes in direction and undermine innovations that have previously been resourced both politically and economically.

KM supporters routinely draw a distinction between tacit and explicit knowledge from Nonaka and Takeuchi (1995) with little or no reference to its origins in Polanyi (1958, 1966).[3] There is good reason for this since Polanyi's endeavour was holistic in nature. This informs his understanding of tacit knowledge as an unconscious, randomly evolved 'whole' that would probably be destroyed by a self-conscious and analytical breakdown of its content into its component parts.[4] In other words, rather than a revelation of how it works as a basis for instrumental usage, too much rational analysis of tacit knowledge may be self-defeating. The overall meaning would be lost in the endeavour to grasp fragmentary parts. Given Polanyi's views about the emergent quality of tacit knowledge, it is unlikely that he would have approved of the preoccupation within KM to convert it into explicit knowledge. For this demands breaking knowledge down into its particulars for purposes of codification and translation into an explicit form. If this is so, it might be argued that KM has been misled by its reliance on Nonaka and Takeuchi's (1995) interpretation of Polanyi's distinction. While the KM literature takes licence with Polanyi, it also seems to ignore Nonaka and Takeuchi's rejection of the idea that knowledge can be *managed* as opposed to *created* (see also Von Krogh *et al.* 2000).[5] Von Krogh *et al.* (2000: 4) argue that, 'the term *management* implies control of processes that may be inherently uncontrollable or, at the least, stifled by heavy-handed direction'. Their view is that while knowledge cannot be managed, it is possible to *enable* its creation by establishing appropriate organizational conditions that facilitate the transformation of tacit into explicit knowledge.

In order to illustrate this critical analysis of KM, we return now to the case study of Loanco that was initially presented in Chapter 4.

Case study: Loanco revisited

The 'one team' vision and strategy

> *We have crossed the Rubicon.* We are seriously committed to developing people . . . this is the toughest job to do. You cannot reverse a trend of under-investment overnight but by 2001 there will be real progress . . . that's the essence of this credo . . . This is about 3800 people . . . *working together* to deliver on *a single vision* of the business. The key thing is that it's *one team* that is going towards 2001.

The above extract is from a tape-recorded speech made in 1997 by the CE of Loanco to his senior management team (emphasis added). Following a cascading approach, these managers (complete with transcribed copies of the speech) in turn delivered the CE's vision and strategy to their staff. The dream of 'working together' to achieve 'a single vision' that we discussed in Chapter 4 is all too apparent. The phrase 'we have crossed the Rubicon' seeks to convey the sense in which 'everyone' in the company has taken a decisive step forward. Yet, it must also be understood as a command to those who are in doubt about the proposed changes: culture as control (see Ray 1985; Willmott 1993). Both believers and non-believers alike must accept that things are different now. As we shall see, this one team approach was bound up with the CE's vision of transforming information services, reflecting a belief that 'knowledge management is best practised in situations that are collaborative and team-oriented' (McInerney and LeFevre 2000: 15). However, his rhetoric can also be interpreted as a dividing practice (Foucault 1982) where anyone deviating would be immediately labelled as disruptive. In the speech, the CE outlined his vision for the future and described his strategy under the acronym for growth, efficiency and managing effectiveness (GEM). The company was to achieve growth and improved efficiency through managing effectively. Clearly, this vision is imbued with an emphasis upon performativity and ultimately it requires that everyone think of the company as 'one team'. Thus staff and management were to achieve direction and purpose through embracing GEM and embarking on a journey whereby the potential of IT was to be exploited. Hence, the CE outlined what he referred to as 'the big stuff' which amounted to how the company was going to achieve this vision (emphasis added):

> Let's look at the big stuff. At this stage all they [staff] need to know is that there is some serious big stuff going on . . . they need to get a sense of the commitment we have when they look at the big stuff . . . There is a lot that has to be done on *efficiency* . . . business and IT architecture, if you don't have a spinal cord for the business or your operating systems, you've got a problem because you put the leg on where the foot should be. That's all that means, you've got to assemble the body in the right place . . . common customer data access means one set of data at the front end for customers, we only enter data once . . . The information network that drives our business. We are *one step better than the quill*, at the moment . . . the fact that we can't all communicate to each other electronically is an unsustainable position going forward.

The use of the body as an analogy is reminiscent of a discredited functionalist sociology that sought to promote order and consensus by treating society as if it were an organism, where the coordination and consistency of the parts are prerequisites of survival. Leaving this imagery aside, however, the substance of the CE's statement is the focus on technology. He outlined the view that improved IT was central to the company's future progress. In terms of technology, he described the company as being 'one step better than the quill' and this signifies that substantial investment and change is required. It should be clear from the evangelical way in which the CE speaks that he was (and is) a visionary. His speech was 'big' on inspiration but was far less clear on the details of how to realize the vision. Of course, one might expect such details to be worked out by less senior managers but one thing that was clear was the coercion that lingered behind the inspirational rhetoric. Hence, the CE continued his communication by saying (emphasis added):

> I expect you will have no trouble communicating to your colleagues that the goals are modestly stretching. I hope you will help them understand that growth equals opportunities and by the way no growth leads down a much less attractive path and *no efficiencies* leads down a much less attractive path. In fact it leads down a path that means we haven't got a future. So not only is it the best thing for them it's the only thing for us.

Thus, despite the rhetoric of the 'one team', hierarchical control and power relations remain unchallenged by the vision. Control, especially over costs through efficiency gains, is firmly wedded to the unitary vision. The thinly veiled threat of the failure to achieve growth applies to the managerial audience but the intention is for them to communicate this threat to the staff. This vision is inscribed in the KM innovation. It is here that one can already begin to glean some insight into the failures of KM and other innovations such as TQM or BPR.

KM, like the innovations before it, is nothing if it cannot legitimize and intensify the demands of capital accumulation involving increased growth, cost reduction and improved efficiency. Despite the rhetoric of the 'one team', profit, performance and productivity are the ends for which KM is the means. Yet it is not always possible to 'cost', particularly in the short term, either the benefits or the losses associated with a specific innovation (see Knights and McCabe 1997). Embedded as it is in the strategic vision, KM is not intended to pose a threat to the existing hierarchical power relations (though there is no guarantee of this). But, KM must be able to demonstrate that it contributes to growth and efficiency. A 'particular' social world is inscribed in the birth and genesis of 'one-team information services' (OTIS) (see Grint and Woolgar 1997), which is bound up with the demands of performativity. The next section will examine OTIS as it emerged and developed at Loanco.

OTIS and KM[6]

Traditionally Loanco was organized along functional lines that were referred to as 'silos' and these had generated a 'silo mentality'. Consequently, there were a number of distinct functions each having a separate 'sub-culture' that presented a considerable barrier to internal communication and knowledge sharing. In view of this, in October 1997, the CE organized a conference to which the key players from each functional group were invited. The head of IT explained the rationale for the conference:

> Rather than just say things like lack of communication, we used a sort of knowledge theme as a way of getting people bought into the idea that there was a lot of knowledge in the business . . . there were some shared resources but not a great deal of them. And wouldn't it be a good idea if we could free up some of that knowledge and share it with other people?

Instead of confronting the participants of the conference with their limitations, there was a concern to engage them in designing a solution. The participants were involved in drawing up a picture of the business that went outside of the traditional organizational boundaries and this pointed towards the need for improved communication. It served as a springboard for OTIS and the delegates were prompted to identify the need for a single method across the group for moving information and sharing knowledge. Two key elements of the new system were to be a group intranet and a single group-wide email. Although a number of systems were already in place, they were often incompatible with one another.

In March 1998 the OTIS project began to be rolled out. The project had two objectives: first to deliver benefits in terms of reduced costs and second to demonstrate that OTIS could be used to change not only the way that people worked but also their attitudes *to* work. The latter aim was made explicit in a corporate brief to all staff issued during May 1998 (emphasis added):

> The aim for OTIS is that eventually we will *all be part of an online community*. With everyone swapping ideas and best practice, publishing information about their departments and linking to our customers and business partners directly. Working in a way which develops new relationships and *drives change in the society's culture* – in other words: the way we work, our attitudes and how we interact.

We can see that the CE's corporate vision and strategy had a major impact in terms of defining OTIS. Here the aims of OTIS were expressed in the dreamlike terms of everyone being part of an 'online community'. It would seem that everyone was a potential beneficiary as they would swap 'ideas and best practice'. The head of IT explained that OTIS was not simply about 'technology implementation' as there was a concern to 'change the way people actually did their jobs'. Nonetheless, there was an element of technological determinism here as it was thought that the introduction of OTIS would 'drive changes in the society's culture'. Thus 'the social' and 'the technological' were still considered to be distinct from each other: the latter determining the former. The attention to culture was firmly wedded to the need to cut costs and this also reflected the corporate vision and strategy: 'we need to grow OTIS into a thriving community. If the pilot is successful and identifies business benefits across the society *including cost savings*, then the community will widen, and everyone can look forward to moving into OTIS' (emphasis added). We can see here that the creation of a unitary, 'one team' culture is not sufficient; there must be 'business benefits', 'including cost savings'. Thus the 'bottom line' was clearly inscribed in the OTIS project. At the same time, management were conscious that culture and technological change can rarely be achieved where those who are its target are excluded from the process. But, as is often the case with new technology developments, it was difficult to secure the interest and involvement of staff initially as few people actually understood anything about the intranet. Although people eventually came up with ideas about how to use the intranet it was not until they actually engaged with the technology and had learned how to use it, that its relevance became apparent. As the head of IT commented:

> We did spend a long time with a core group of people taking them around on visits and showing them what they were likely to get. To get to stimulate their imaginations, start to get them thinking about what that sort of technology could do for them. So they came up with ideas, initially, of how they might use it but we never really got to the nub of it until we'd given them the technology and the tools.

Here is some clear evidence that the meaning of a technology only becomes obvious with its use and that any attempt to treat it independently of the social relations through which it is developed and applied is likely to result in failure. Even with the best intentions the social ground cannot be prepared so as to be compatible with the technological, for what is technological is already social immediately it is made sense of (or not) in practical everyday affairs. While 'techies', consultants and the media tend to create representations of technology that are irrepressibly positive and 'progressive', in practice the benefits revolve around users finding the technology 'useful' and managers finding it cost effective.

In terms of the 'roll out', various types of users were identified and different forms of technology and training were issued accordingly. The first group were defined as 'management' users. These were individuals who managed others and took decisions. Managers were provided with a mail client and a web browser. The second group of users were defined as 'knowledge workers'. These were described as specialists, individuals who had an analytical content to their job, who needed information from a variety of sources and might therefore benefit from having access to the web. They were seen as information gatherers, disseminators, people who made recommendations, and were usually IT business analysts, legal staff and human resource personnel. These individuals had a powerful, full-blown client on their desktop. The third group of users were defined as 'core workers' who were primarily customer-facing people. These members of staff required a PC and needed access to information and mail via a browser, though their work did not involve a great deal of processing. Of the users, 25 per cent were management, 25 per cent were deemed to be knowledge workers and 50 per cent were core workers. We can see that users were clearly distinguished on hierarchical and functional grounds and this served to reinforce earlier stratifications and divisions. It was not the case that everyone would have equal access to knowledge as the vision and indeed KM suggests.

A small project team of 20 staff oversaw the pilot, each of whom now runs an intranet site but, at the time, they engaged with users to determine how the Intranet should be structured, its appearance and content, and how it would be organized. The approach was described as being 'business-led' rather than 'technology-led'. A pre-eminent concern was that OTIS should 'deliver benefits' and these had to be tangible benefits. This was a question that continually confronted users. Thus staff were asked to think about their everyday jobs, about the documents they produced, how they were produced and whether they could be put on the intranet. This contrasts with the method adopted by some KM interventions where an anthropological observation of existing practices is conducted in order to become aware of the tacit knowledge and innovative intuition that might be deployed (Brown 2002). At Loanco, improvements in productivity of between 10 and 50 per cent were expected. It was thought that staff who spend a great deal of time communicating with other people, and also individuals on help desks who spend a huge amount of their time answering queries, could be freed up by putting information onto the intranet, thereby reducing phone calls. The staff were also asked to document their work both before and after OTIS so as to estimate the amount of time saved following its introduction. The procedure for documenting these benefits proved to be highly complex and this discouraged a number of people. Subsequently, it was considered that before a full roll out could take place a more simplified procedure would have to be found. Nonetheless there was an attempt to list the benefits by identifying things that could be displaced by the intranet such as producing reports, printing letters, using paper and making phone calls.

The bulk of the savings were in people's time but, according to the head of IT, the problem was convincing management that the time saved could be used productively rather than simply 'wasted'. It became apparent that although the staff were willing to adopt the technology and to change the way they worked, there was not a similar degree of support from the management to enact the changes necessary to turn the time saved to other productive uses. The project was dogged by the intangible nature of the savings leading to questions about how to make use of this spare 'time'. Management could either cut the number of staff employed or they could encourage staff to deploy their time more productively. The former would be unsavoury for both sides as well as being inconsistent with the 'one team' vision and the notion that everyone benefits from KM. The latter was incongruous with the culture of Loanco. As a number of managers pointed out, 'there is no tradition of cost benefit analysis in Loanco and, in the past, projects have simply been introduced rather than carefully costed'. Although a demand for cost savings and 'benefits', as outlined in the corporate vision was embedded in the rationale for OTIS, this rationale proved difficult to operationalize. At the grass roots level it seemed that the managerial culture had not been touched by the corporate vision; consequently, management were loathe to take advantage of the possible benefits OTIS had to offer. After all, they were intangible benefits and management at all levels were seemingly unwilling to commit themselves. According to the head of IT: 'To do this successfully means that you have to change the way that managers' manage in this place . . . So suddenly this becomes more than just implementing an intranet and a mail system'. This suggests that even when it is endorsed by staff, the introduction of technology and the attempted management and sharing of knowledge does not necessarily shift attitudes and behaviour that are deeply entrenched in culture. However, this is the case for management every bit as much as for staff.

OTIS post-pilot scheme review

Following the pilot, which had been completed between September and December 1998, it was initially agreed that OTIS should be fully rolled out across the group. The key theme reported in a management summary of the pilot was that 'People want OTIS. They can see the future benefits and the way it could make communication easier'. In terms of the branch users, however, it was stated that: 'The culture of people being responsible for ensuring that they access information being provided and ensuring that they take care to keep themselves up to date by using the system has not been universally successful'.

This is an interesting finding given the apparent support for OTIS. It suggests that staff may have considered OTIS to be an undue imposition upon their time. The report underlined the importance of committed local leaders to ensure that there was sufficient support for OTIS (as with TQM in Chapter Five). These leaders 'must be advocates, enthusiasts, and *have time to make the most of the role* to maximize the benefits achieved' (emphasis added). Having the time to ensure that OTIS worked effectively seemed to be important even for enthusiasts and so we can see that there were decisions and choices to be made between the pressures on work output and for there to be sufficient time for effective communication through OTIS. To date, work pressures seemed to have taken priority over communication even among the local leaders for, as the management summary of the pilot continued, there were those: 'who feel that it is another responsibility, which had no customer priority and defer from any ownership of the service being provided'.

This reluctance among some local leaders to take OTIS on board supports our interpretation that for some individuals OTIS was seen as an additional burden. A conference that included several workshops was conducted after the pilot as a post-pilot implementation review and a report of the conference findings was compiled in December 1998. It identified what people had done differently since the introduction of OTIS. Of the 68 uses that were identified the most popular were use of the calendar facility (13), sending external emails (11), attaching documents (10) and also making use of the electronic phone directory (9). Only four respondents felt that there was a general improvement in communication while only two considered that they had shared knowledge as a consequence of OTIS. It does not seem therefore that technology in and of itself is sufficient to promote KM. A context of insecurity, job losses and increasing work pressures seem to have prevented the spirit of KM being adopted at Loanco.

During a benefits realization workshop, OTIS was found to have a number of 'business benefits problems' including 'identifying the benefits', 'difficult to cost benefits' and identifying 'who actually benefits?'. This led to questions such as 'How do we measure the benefits as they cascade through the business?'; 'How can the saved time be used more profitably?' and 'Do we need to measure everything financially?'. Despite the absence of a historical culture of cost-benefit analysis (reported above), we can see that OTIS reflected the performativity embedded in the corporate vision in terms of the preoccupation with efficiencies, cost cutting and measuring benefits. Yet a substantial problem was to quantify the benefits. One could argue that the preoccupation with cost cutting is antithetical to sharing information and improving communication. Indeed for employees to share tacit knowledge requires trust and a spirit of cooperation. However, it seems that identifying the financial benefits of OTIS would only lead to yet more cost cutting measures, for once they were identified it seemed likely that cuts would follow. Some supposedly 'non-financial', or at least intangible, benefits of OTIS were also identified, including:

- aiding public relations of support functions;
- ease of administration;
- incremental savings of many small things;
- openness is generating questions – a need to affirm 'the new way';
- debate and discussion encouraged;
- better quality service.

These intangible benefits reflect the limitations of the strategic vision and strategy in that it is not always possible to identify efficiencies. Yet these efficiencies needed to be shown in order to confirm that OTIS was contributing to corporate growth. Thus the vision and strategy were not only inscribed in the rationale for OTIS but they were also its measure of success or failure, adoption or otherwise. It is intriguing that the benefits of OTIS were self-evident (i.e. improved communication). Hence, at the post–pilot implementation review conference the human resource director reiterated the importance of OTIS and restated the link between OTIS and the corporate vision:

> Without fast, clear, appropriate communication it would be impossible to become 'the mutual which really can meet the needs of everyday customers throughout Britain' . . . He reminded us that *we are all pioneers* and that we will face personal challenges before our vision of OTIS will become a reality.

On the one hand, we see here a blind faith in technology following a perception that technology in and of itself is a means to improve communication and to secure competitive success. On the other hand, however, it seems that OTIS will only be implemented if it meets the imperative of delivering tangible savings. Thus it would seem that the 'pioneers' will only have a new frontier to follow if financial benefits can be shown. The problem, however, is that this may well lead to some 'pioneers' losing their jobs. A closet technological determinism leads some managers down the path of thinking that IT can solve all their problems. However, the intangible benefits outlined above reveal that OTIS is bound up with the social fabric of the company. As such, its benefits cannot be neatly defined as if they exist outside of the social context of their application and use. Because measurement demands that technology is treated as a variable that can be identified as discrete from its effects (dependent variables), the complex relations and benefits go unrecorded. In short, the problems for OTIS are tied to a commonsense (epistemological) faith in causal analysis and quantification.

The tension between the costs/benefits of OTIS and the conception of KM being a solution in and of itself was apparent during an 'Internet searching workshop'. In the workshop report, a feeling was expressed that 'the internet should not be used as it is not part of the job'. A cost-based explanation for this comment is apparent in the 'concern over the time it takes to hunt for information'. Thus the miracle cure and benefits of KM were brought into question by the potential costs involved. Indeed, OTIS also appeared to introduce new uncertainties for management as it presented new freedoms for staff over which management had little control. Consequently, concerns were voiced with regard to 'searching' on the internet, as expressed in the following guidelines for staff:

- there is no guarantee that the information you require is actually available or that when found it is correct;
- initially you should restrict the amount of time that you 'surf' when trying to get information:
- the intranet and internet are only another source of information.

These guidelines provide direct evidence of how, despite the apparent intensification of surveillance made possible by ICT (e.g. Sewell and Wilkinson 1992), management are often unable to control the use and outcomes of the technology itself. For not only is the technology difficult to cost, it also creates new space and scope for staff resistance and autonomy (Knights and McCabe 1998b). Perhaps this is why in the *OTIS Pilot Roll Out: Feedback Report*, it was stated that 'the promotion of the use of the service and the resolution of any issues should come from the top'. It seems then that management at all levels were anxious about committing themselves to OTIS because neither its costs nor its benefits could be accurately accounted for and controlled. Moreover, the prerequisite that authorization comes from the top underlines the continuing importance of hierarchical structures and power relations.

OTIS: the aftermath

After the pilot for OTIS was complete, the company began to face intense pressures to transfer from being a mutual organization to a PLC and at this time, as a full roll out, OTIS was effectively shelved. Its demise was explained in terms of the need to conserve 'costs' or that it was a 'business decision'. Although approval to go ahead with full roll out was not granted, the number of users was extended from 400 to 1000 without any concern to cost this decision. The head of IT explained this in terms of the CE's concern to communicate to as many members of staff as possible the importance of Loanco remaining a mutual organization, and the intranet was clearly an effective means of enabling speedy communications. Indeed, remaining mutual had been a cornerstone of the CE's corporate vision and strategy. Here we can see how money can be available without costing the benefits providing that those in power deem that the issue is of sufficient importance.[7] In the haste to extend coverage of OTIS to as many staff as possible, the preoccupation with monitoring benefits was sidelined. Remaining mutual was more important than the costs involved – unfortunately sharing information and knowledge was not.

Discussion and summary

We have examined the changes to Loanco without engaging heavily in the academic debates about the relationship between 'technology' and 'the social'. Nonetheless, we have intimated a position that we would argue is different in its rejection of technological determinism than either the sociology of knowledge of science or the social constructionists and social shaping theorists. The latter avoids technological determinism only to replace it with social determinism. This fails to recognise the socially embeddedness of technology. The former, Grint and Woolgar (1997: 376), argue that the technological is a function of the effort required to show that it is social. In effect, they are arguing that everything is social since we have no access to the physical world except through our interpretations of it, and these are inescapably socially mediated. With the eye-catching appeal of linking this debate to a famous rock group, the "guns" and "roses" argument aroused a great deal of heat recently. It began with the claim on the part of those wishing to preserve some independence for 'the techno-logical' as against 'the social' arguing that roses, in contrast to guns, would not be much use in war. Is it not 'much harder to kill a platoon of soldiers with a dozen roses than with well-placed, high speed bullets?', Kling (1992: 362) asked.

Like earlier polarized debates between realism and relativism, there is a dan-ger here of degenerating into academic 'points scoring' over increasingly more obscure intellectual arguments as to what is technological and what is social.[8] We have refrained from adding to this esoteric debate and concentrated more on the way that ideas about technology appear to be reproduced in management practice. Nor have we sought to denigrate the way in which managerial common sense persistently returns to some variant of technological determinism.

Rather, our intent has been to question the practical consequences of a managerial faith in technology and a new-found instrumental design on know-ledge represented by KM. Of course, the IT promoted by Loanco was embed-ded in 'the social' since it was to be seen as both the content and consequence of everyone working as 'one team'. The technology – the intranet – was seen to be the vehicle if not the stimulant for sharing knowledge in the company. As companies grow, they are increasingly dependent on 'managing at a distance'. Those responsible for direction and development in an organization require more information and knowledge to increase the 'efficiency of their representa-tions' (Cooper 1992: 266) of the 'sharp end' of the business from which senior managers are necessarily remote. That is to say, when not involved in an activity directly, as is the case with senior management, they have to rely on generic descriptions or representations of the activity on which to base policy decisions designed to facilitate or improve it. Without knowledge and information-rich representations of how the organization works, executive decisions could be entirely inconsistent or incompatible with routine practices. This becomes even more important if staff are to assume greater autonomy and authority (empowerment). But the political character of organizations make neither the construction of appropriate representations of what is happening in the workplace or beyond, nor the effective use of them, straightforward let alone a guaranteed matter.

In the pilot of OTIS, opportunities arose for staff to use the intranet in ways that saved time, for example, but there was little evidence that middle management were prepared to support this. One reason was that to cost these savings would require that not only staff but also line and middle management become more accountable and open to the gaze of surveillance. Such accountability was necessary in order to make use of the slack left in the system following improvements in knowledge sharing and communication. A number of uncertainties arose over whether such improvements would lead to redundancies or different ways of working. Moreover, it was not at all clear that management would allow sufficient time for staff to make use of OTIS, taking into account the daily operational pressures of work. It would, therefore, seem that managers and their engagement in organizational politics are an obstacle to management by distance and, of course, KM. The inactivity was reinforced by an unwillingness among senior management to commit to OTIS when the savings were seemingly so intangible and the need to save costs was so imperative. Thus, although it was possible to *enable* knowledge creation through OTIS, management seemed unwilling to support such an endeavour. OTIS was also unpredictable in that it offered staff new ways to escape control either by not using or by misusing the information system. This supports Von Krogh *et al.*'s (2000: 4) view that the processes of KM 'may be inherently uncontrollable' although we suspect that they would not envisage resistance as being a problem let alone a solution. The emphasis on performativity in the corporate vision and strategy created the conditions, then, for both managers and staff to thwart the intentions behind OTIS.

The reason why OTIS was discontinued was partly the failure of the IT manager to persuade other managers to change their practices. This was necessary if the time saved by staff adopting new technology was to be redirected into productive channels. Clearly it is more difficult to change the behaviour of managers who have an equal or perhaps even more senior ranking than the person (i.e. the head of IT) who is seeking to transform their practices. While this was not directly put to us in this form, the head of IT did argue that a major obstacle for OTIS was the failure to secure middle management support. We suspect that this was partly a rationalization, however, since pressure could have been brought to bear on line and middle managers from the executive team. It seems to us that other developments had run ahead of this 'management' obstacle and that these were seen to be of greater priority.

A number of companies (e.g. Scottish Equitable, NPI) had recently lost their mutual status as a result of being at the receiving end of takeovers. The CE of Loanco and his board seemed to feel the need to demonstrate not only cost cutting rationalizations but also 'progressive' developments that would support their case for remaining mutual. Rather than continue with a strategy that might be extremely beneficial internally but could not be guaranteed to reduce costs, the company abandoned its previous commitment to OTIS and embarked on the use of e-commerce.

It would seem then that the managers at Loanco were unaware of, or unprepared to enact Nonaka's (1991: 96) prescription that 'successful com-panies are those that consistently create new knowledge, disseminate it widely throughout the organisation, and quickly embody it in new technologies and products'. Indeed, a curious paradox arises from the case for although manage-ment pursued KM, they remained wedded to the notion that 'the key metric for measuring the values of new knowledge is . . . quantifiable – increased efficiency, lower costs, improved return on investment'. Yet, as indicated at the beginning of this chapter, we should not be surprised by such a paradox for it is central to KM itself. In a way that is reminiscent of Mintzberg's 'emergent' strategic approach, discussed in Chapter 5, Nonaka appears to want both to have his cake and to eat it. Thus, on the one hand, he points towards knowledge that is 'tacit and often highly subjective'; that relies on 'insights, intuitions, and hunches' and 'recognises the serendipitous quality of innovation' (p. 97). Yet, on the other, he suggests that executives 'are managing that serendipity' by 'making those insights available for testing and use by the company as a whole'. Nonaka suggests that 'in most companies, the ultimate test for measuring the value of new knowledge is economic' (p. 103). By contrast, in the knowledge-creating company 'other more qualitative factors are [deemed] . . . equally important'. Yet these include whether the idea is 'an expression of top management's aspirations and strategic goals'. This indicates a shift from the strictly short-term economic but only to the long-term economic and, as such, KM is saturated in hierarchical thinking: 'an expression of top management's aspirations'.

One does not have to scratch the surface to uncover KM's preoccupation with control for just as with Taylorism 'making personal knowledge available to others is the central activity of the knowledge creating company' (Nonaka 1991: 98). If organizations were not embedded in relations of power, control and inequality, then such knowledge *sharing* may not be a problem, but, as they are, then knowledge is also bound up with the kinds of political issues that we have seen in our case study. Management were preoccupied with controlling and costing the savings associated with the knowledge generated by staff. This is not inconsistent with Nonaka's prescriptions for once 'tacit' knowledge is ren-dered 'explicit', it is to be controlled. 'Sharing' knowledge clearly sounds like a positive development but one needs to ask who is giving up knowledge and at what cost? Moreover, who is the recipient and the beneficiary? The concern to seize 'tacit' knowledge and render it 'explicit', and then to 'incorporate it into new technologies and products' (p. 104) underlines the sense in which some-thing is appropriated from subordinates by superordinates. However, we believe that the obstacles to doing so have barely been considered by the followers of

KM. These obstacles are not just concerned with subordinates resisting the sharing of knowledge but also with managers being anxious about how such a development could be exploited by staff.

In our case study, management were loath to allow staff the benefits of knowledge sharing. Any savings generated in terms of time had to be ploughed back into the company. Any slack had to be quickly taken out and yet it is precisely such slack that would be needed for staff to develop 'insights, intuitions, and hunches'. Indeed, despite its association with 'unnecessary duplication, waste, or information overload' (Nonaka and Takeuchi 1995: 80), space or spare time to think is an important condition of knowledge creation. Individuals may be required to share knowledge that is not of any immediate practical use to them for it 'brings about "learning by intrusion"' (1995: 81) into spheres that are outside one's own specific practices. Explicit knowledge may well enable staff 'to broaden, extend, and reframe their own tacit knowledge' (1995: 99) but, as we saw in Chapter 5 in the case of Qualbank, rarely are staff allowed the time and resources to develop ideas and solve the problems they face.

The problem then is that Nonaka and Takeuchi (1995) divorce knowledge from the social context through which it is produced. As we saw in the case of Inco Insurance in Chapter 3, employees frequently hoard what is tacit knowledge or 'tacit secrets' so as to evade the pressures of work intensification. Such tensions do not feature in Nonaka's schema. Indeed, while in our case, management sought to restrict access to the internet, Nonaka and Takeuchi argued that the Kao Corporation 'does not allow any discrimination in access to information among employees', for 'no one dept. or group of experts has the exclusive responsibility for creating new knowledge in the knowledge-creating company' (1995: 102).

To conclude, it would seem, as we discussed in Chapter 2, that KM, like the other innovations we have considered, offers a Utopian vision that rarely seems to match everyday organizational reality. Despite emerging in Japan, the message behind KM is curiously similar to the promise of the American Dream. For, in discussing the role of management, Nonaka and Takeuchi (1995: 104) quote the words of Hiroshi Honma, senior researcher at Honda who says 'senior managers are romantics who go in quest of the ideal'. Knowledge Management seeks to reconstruct the world so that everyone believes that they can be winners. To underline this point we will close with the words of Nonaka and Takeuchi (1995: 97):

> The essence of innovation is to re-create the world according to a particular vision or ideal. To create new knowledge means quite literally to re-evaluate the company and everyone in it in a nonstop process of personal and organizational self-renewal . . . It is a way of behaving, indeed a way of being, in which everyone is a knowledge worker – that is to say, an entrepreneur.

In Part 3 we revisit the American Dream and consider the contribution and limitations of our research to dialogue and debate around 'new' management ideas and practices in contemporary Britain.

PART THREE

Conclusion

The American Dream is to be better off than you are. How much money is 'enough money'? 'Enough money' is always a little bit more than you have. There's never enough of anything. This is why people go on. If there was enough, everybody would stop. You always go for the brass ring that's always out there about a hundred yards farther. It's like a mirage in the desert: it always stays about a hundred yards ahead of you.

(Jay Slabough, corporate executive in an
interview with Studs Terkel, 1980)

In order to dream it is necessary to suspend disbelief or our scepticism of the changes promised by Utopian visions. Despite this, our capacity for dreaming shows few limits whether it is about an ideal house, an ideal partner or the unbelievable riches that would come from winning the lottery. Dreaming of Utopian futures seems to make bearable living within somewhat more limited, drab and mundane realities. The American Dream reflects and reproduces the myths that add spice to the mundane and provides a vision of future security and wealth to conceal the reality of the precarious and uncertain present. As dreamers we can regain the innocence of childhood, believing that anything is possible and that our potential is unbounded. Upon waking, however, we find our nose pressed up against what Fitzgerald referred to as the 'indiscernible barbed wire' of inequality and limitation that stops us in our tracks. This is not to deny alternative realities but merely to recognize that we cannot easily side-step the economic, social and cultural barriers to realizing our dreams.

The gurus of management appeal to the child within us to embrace their disparate dreams and given that they promise so much, it must be a puzzle to them that anyone should doubt or question their prescriptions. For the world that they offer where everyone is free to fulfil their human potential and maximize their rewards is truly seductive. Such dreams rely on what Scott

(1996) refers to as the 'innocence theory', which is central to films such as *Mr Smith Goes to Washington*, *E.T.*, and *Field of Dreams*, where all Hollywood requires of us is that we believe. Such films present us with individuals who are innocent, who 'crusade to do good' and believe in the American way. Yet, 'just as importantly, the audience must also believe in the dark and corrupt forces which are trying to subvert the process of freedom and righteousness' (Scott 1996: 234). The juxtaposition is between good and evil or, for example, the contrast between Luke Skywalker and Darth Vader in *Star Wars*. Such films present an individual, an institution or a way of life as 'always needing saving' and we are required to identify with the cause or 'the force'. The villain is 'as critical to the story as the redeeming heroes, because they compose the embodiment of an institution that has abandoned its principles and lost its way' (Scott: 235). The parallel with the management gurus is that they also present corporate America as having lost its way and in need of salvation. Certain management practices (e.g. bureaucracy, inflexibility) or competitors such as Japan are cast as the villain while the heroes are those managers and employees who adapt to change by answering the clarion call of reform. Indeed, the weakness of both the UK and US economies, especially in the 1970s, may help to explain the popularity and proliferation of guru texts over the past 20 years. Both the US and the UK economies had seemingly lost their way for a diversity of reasons and were in need of salvation:

> a recent *New York Times Magazine* cover story noted that just a decade ago the world feared being bowled over by American management technique, not just our labs, our factories, or even our sheer size. 'These American invaders were superior, in [French editor Jean-Jacques] Servan Schreiber's view, not because of their money resources, or technology but because of their corporate organizational ability – and the genius behind it all was the American Corporate Manager.'
>
> But something has happened in the thirteen years since Servan-Schreiber first published *The American Challenge*. American business has gotten mired in a swamp of economic and political woes . . . In truth, however, these problems are shared by many other countries, some of which are islands of good news. The performance of many Japanese and West German companies is oft-cited evidence that 'it can be done' . . . Within the space of a few weeks in late 1980, *Newsweek*, *Time*, *The Atlantic Monthly*, *Dun's Review* (twice), and even *Esquire* carried stories on the general theme that the managers were to blame for the sad state of American business.
>
> (Peters and Waterman [1982] 1995: 33–4)

Over ten years later, the message that America is in need of saving and has lost its way continued to be reiterated:

> So, if managements want companies that are lean, nimble, flexible, responsive, competitive, innovative, efficient, customer-focused, and profitable, why are so many American companies bloated, clumsy, rigid, sluggish,

noncompetitive, uncreative, inefficient, disdainful of customer needs, and losing money? Corporations do not perform badly because – as some critics have claimed – American workers are lazy and American manage- ments are inept . . . it is because the world in which they operate has changed beyond the limits of their capacity to adjust or evolve.

(Hammer and Champy 1993: 7–11)

Implicit in such prescriptions is that the homestead is under threat, and the appeal is for everyone to unite to fight off the foreign invaders or older ways of managing that seemingly threaten everyone in equal measure. The appeal to innocence is evident in the childlike need to embrace yet another panacea and the necessity of suspending our belief in the past as a way of rendering our experience congruent with the gurus' prescriptions. It is also apparent in the sense of naïveté that is required of us to believe that seven- or eight-step plans can solve all of our woes. Like Dorothy in the Hollywood musical, it seems that we have only to click our ruby slippers in order to go 'Somewhere over the rainbow'. In 1893, Frederick Jackson Turner argued that the defining feature of American political culture and of the American character is the frontier experi- ence. It is the pushing across the continent and the promise of freedom that awaits people. His summing up of the characteristics of the frontier mentality has its parallels in the individual subject that guru narratives appeal to and seek to constitute:

That coarseness and strength combined with acuteness and inquisitive- ness, that practical, inventive turn of mind, quick to find expedients, that masterful grasp of material things, lacking in the artistic but powerful to effect great ends, that restless, nervous energy, that dominant individual- ism, working for good and for evil, and within that buoyancy and exuber- ance which comes with freedom – these are the traits of the frontier.

(Turner 1893)

Yet, as we have seen, the promise of freedom or that we all can be winners is not an everyday experience for many staff and managers in the companies we have visited. Nor is it a realistic vision for those who are in low-paid jobs or excluded from employment altogether. This discrepancy between dream and reality is multiplied and intensified for those who live outside of the prosperous economies of the West. While the US gurus continue to export their panaceas worldwide, the frontier mentality that supposedly partly shaped the American Dream is now recognized as largely a myth. For as Munslow (1996) notes, in locating the essence of American history in the frontier thesis Turner denied the social problems he found in contemporary America. These included issues surrounding class, industrialism, poverty, racism 'and the perversion of the American free-market ideal in the shape of monopoly capitalism' (Munslow 1996: 20). The frontier thesis neglects the role of urban life in defining Ameri- can culture. Moreover, the mythos surrounding the individualism of the frontier conveniently forgets the concurrent necessity for cooperation/community. One has only to recall the image of the wagon train replete with families and trade persons to underline the necessity for mutual protection. Not, however, as Hollywood would have it from marauding Indians but from hunger, accidents, disease and geography/terrain. It should not surprise us then, that the promises of the gurus fail to find much relevance in the UK, for the frontier thesis refers to a way of being that is a myth even in its country of origin. In seeking to suppress class and cultural conflicts it at once offers a potent legitimizing ideology and sows the seeds of its own demise. For as Guest (1992: 12) notes in his critique of *In Search of Excellence*, 'notions of pluralism and of collective representation of sectional interests, perhaps through a trade union, are almost absent'. This critique could equally be applied to many of the gurus for just as their prescriptions are unitary in design and content so are the descriptions of organizational life that form the basis of their interventions. Invariably they demonize corporations as beasts of bureaucracy and institutionalized inertia. The irony of their unitary accounts of organizational life is that were they true, there would be little scope for gurus past, present or future to have much impact, for change would either be impossible or already have been enacted or at least underway.

In this book, through extensive empirical research, we have criticized the account of a unitary past as well as the Utopian vision of a unitary future. We characterized the latter in terms of the American Dream – a bizarre promise of riches for all, but one that survives, like the desert mirage, only on the basis of our perpetual striving for what becomes an ever-receding ideal. But the support for a society based on maximizing the opportunities of individual citizens is strong not only in private industry but also within modern governments. Whether it takes the form of the *New Right* philosophy of Reagan and Thatcher or the *Third Way* of Blair, the neo-liberal economics that has been on the ascendancy in recent years within the West subscribes to this ideology of the 'opportunity society'. It promotes an individual rather than a collective relationship to well-being, economic growth rather than a redistribution solution to social problems, a market rather than a state allocation of scarce resources, a tinkering around the margins rather than radical change. What we have found is that the values based around enterprise, individualism, the free market and the gospels of wealth and success for everyone fail to deliver that which is promised in the workplaces we have visited. We are not arguing that all such innovations are a failure or without impact. Nor are we suggesting that the message of hope and the promise of a better tomorrow should be rejected out of hand. But from our observations and interviews, it seems that few are unequivocally willing to suspend their experiences of everyday life sufficiently to embrace this 'dream'. For many, the prevailing inequalities of opportunity and rewards challenges the view that everyone is rendered equal through innovations such as BPR and teamworking, especially when redundancies preceded, accompanied or followed their introduction. Likewise, continuing hierarchical structures and preoccupations with control and cost cutting undermine the innocence that is necessary to believe in the message of unity.

Nonetheless, we came across more than a few individuals who either sought to promote the dream for others, or lived their own lives according to its precepts and who appeared to live the dream. For example, think of those staff in Loanco, in Chapter 4, who thrived on the dream of equality that the CE held out to them — before, that is, the call centre in which they worked was closed. Prior to the redundancies many of the staff at Loanco appeared to embrace the individualistic subjectivity promoted by management and were seemingly seduced by the American Dream. Had they been American, they might well have endorsed the following:

> Business is the very soul of an American; he pursues it, not as a means of procuring for himself and his family the necessary comforts of life, but as the fountain of all human felicity . . . An American carries the spirit of invention even to the counting-room . . . He is an inventor, not an imitator; he creates new sources of wealth . . . An American mechanic does not exercise his trade as he has learned it: he is constantly making improvements.
>
> (Grund 1837)

The above extract suggests that the ideals of empowerment, innovation and continuous improvement, that are so much a part of the modern guru's sales kit, were shared by the early Americans as much as they were a part of life at Loanco before the closure. For other workers such as those at Intermotors (Chapter 6) who took industrial action, the dream of teamworking did not begin to address the inequalities they experienced and they did not support the individualistic subjectivity that teamworking held out to them. Similarly, there are Americans who question the unitary message of work that imbues guru publications, yet they often hold onto the hope that their children may be able to achieve the American Dream, even if they cannot. Sennett and Cobb (1977) exemplified how many of their respondents who had in their own eyes failed to succeed, lived their lives vicariously through the expected or realized success of their children. Similarly, in 1974, Studs Terkel recorded the words of Mike Lefevre, a steel-mill worker, as follows:

> I got chewed out by my foreman once. He said, 'Mike, you're a good worker but you have a bad attitude'. My attitude is that I don't get excited about my job. I do my work but I don't say whoopee-doo. The day I get excited about my job is the day I go to a head shrinker. How are you gonna get excited about pullin' steel? How are you gonna get excited when you are tired and want to sit down? . . . I want my kid to be an effete snob. Yeah, mm-hmm. [Laughs.] I want him to be able to quote Walt Whitman, to be proud of it . . . Every time I see a young guy walk by with a shirt and tie and dressed up real sharp, I'm lookin' at my kid, you know?

This points to the seductive qualities of the American Dream as a goal to aspire to or strive for, at least for one's kids if not for oneself. It can serve as a powerful medium of control in enabling some workers to more readily tolerate the present. The antagonism or conflict of interests that Mike and many Intermotors' employees identified between management and employees is something about which the gurus of management have curiously little to say. Yet as we have seen in the preceding chapters, this polarization of interests appears to be an obstacle to the realization of the dreams that are proffered.

Intriguingly, there are other American Dreams than the individualistic one we discussed in Chapter 2, but they are a far cry from those that the management gurus expound. A diverse number of American Dreams have railed against the inequalities that characterize American life – most especially racial, but also material inequality:

> There are those who are asking the devotees of civil rights, 'When will you be satisfied?' . . . We cannot be satisfied as long as the Negro's basic mobility is from a smaller ghetto to a larger one . . . I say to you today, my friends, that in spite of the difficulties and frustrations of the moment I still have a dream. It is a dream deeply rooted in the American Dream. I have a dream that one day this nation will rise up and live out the true meaning of its creed: 'we hold these truths to be self-evident; that all men are created equal'. . . . With this faith we will be able to transform the jangling discords of our nation into a beautiful symphony of brotherhood.
>
> (Luther King 1963)

A year later President Lyndon B. Johnson in a special message to Congress also evoked the American Dream in launching his 'War on Poverty'. The message he conveyed demonstrates an awareness of inequality to which the current wave of management gurus and indeed Republican politicians seem oblivious:

> With the growth of our country has come opportunities for our people – opportunity to educate our children, to use our energies in productive work, to increase our leisure – opportunity for almost every American to hope that through work and talent he could create a better life for himself and his family.
>
> The path forward has not been an easy one. But we have never lost sight of our goal – an America in which every citizen shares all of the opportunities of his society, in which every man has a chance to advance his welfare to the limit of his capacities. We have come a long way toward this goal. We still have a long way to go . . .
>
> There are millions of Americans – one-fifth of our people – who have not shared in the abundance which has been granted to most of us, and on whom the gates of opportunity have been closed.
>
> (Johnson 1964: 223)

A particularly famous American Dream is present in the novel by Edward Bellamy published in 1888 entitled *Looking Backwards*. In this novel, Julian West, a Bostonian, awakes from a sleep or trance that has lasted for over a century to find America in the year 2000 transformed. The world he finds (Bellamy's dream) only shares superficial similarities with that evoked by management gurus for not only has fear and strife been eliminated but also wider structural inequalities including class struggle, industrial disputes and disparities in wealth and poverty. In their stead full employment, material abundance and social harmony prevail. Julian West articulated to those who awakened him the nature of Boston society in the nineteenth century:

> By way of giving the reader some general impression of the way people lived together in those days, and especially the relations of the rich and poor to one another, perhaps I cannot do better than to compare society as it then was to a prodigious coach which the masses of humanity were harnessed to and dragged toilsomely along a very hilly and sandy road. The driver was hunger, and permitted no lagging, though the pace was necessarily very slow. Despite the difficulty of drawing the coach at all along so hard a road, the top was covered with passengers who never got down, even at the steepest ascents. These seats at the top were very breezy and comfortable . . . Naturally such places were in great demand and the competition for them was keen, every one seeking as the first end in life to secure a seat on the coach.
>
> (Bellamy [1888] 1986: 38–9)

Envisaging society in this way as fundamentally unequal is not too dissimilar from the way in which some employees at Intermotors experienced work following the introduction of teamworking (Chapter 6). It also shares similarities with the closure of the call centre at Loanco (Chapter 4) and the imposition of change at Carco in Chapter 3. As with the early Americans that Grund (1837) identified, many staff in our case study were capable of being an 'inventor' or 'constantly making improvements' but doing so raises the possibility of further redundancies. At Carco, however, it is not only employees who shared this concern, for managers expressed similar dilemmas (see McCabe 1999). Bellamy ([1888] 1986: 39–40) is critical of the self-interested 'age of individualism' of the nineteenth century, but it resonates with many contemporary anxieties. For as Julian West continues (emphasis added):

> But did they think only of themselves? You ask. Was not their very luxury rendered intolerable to them by comparison with the lot of their brothers and sisters in the harness, and the knowledge that their own weight added to their toil? Had they no compassion for their fellow beings from whom fortune only distinguished them? Oh yes, commiseration was frequently expressed by those who rode for those who had to pull the coach, especially when the vehicle came to a bad place in the road . . . At such times, the desperate straining of the *team*, their agonized leaping and plunging under the pitiless lashing of hunger . . . made a very distressing spectacle, which often called forth highly creditable displays of feeling on the top of the coach. At such times the passengers would call down encouragingly to the toilers of the rope, exorting them to patience, and holding out hopes of possible compensation in another world.

These encouraging calls from the passengers and appeals for patience for a better tomorrow are curiously reminiscent of the strategic appeals that we have discussed throughout this book. Hence, the MD of Carco, in Chapter 3, appealed to employees to support a new programme of change in the face of economic difficulties:

> Whilst all of you know that there has been a general improvement in our results through the actions we have taken, part of the success story during the last 18 months has been due to the buoyancy in the marketplace and our order book. Without this our results would show a very different picture, which in turn tells us, we still have a long way to go.

And in Chapter 7, the CE of Loanco warned of the dangers of failing to embrace change: 'Growth equals opportunities and by the way no growth leads down a much less attractive path and no efficiency leads down a much less attractive path. In fact it leads down a path that means that we haven't got a future. So not only is it the best thing for them it's the only thing for us'.

Bellamy believed that his dream of America could be attained through social solidarity – a sentiment shared by many management gurus who believe that employees need to unite under the banner of quality or re-engineering so as to fulfil their potential. The difference, however, is that Bellamy does not believe that such solidarity is possible within the existing capitalist order. For as Doctor Leete, the physician who attends Julian West, when he is revived 113 years after he went to sleep, explains, the key factor in establishing the New World order was that: 'At last, strangely late in the world's history, the obvious fact was perceived that no business is so essentially the public business as the industry and commerce on which the people's livelihood depends, and that to entrust it to private persons to be managed for private profit is a folly' (Bellamy [1888] 1986: 66). Doctor Leete could have been talking about the twenty-first as much as he was referring to the late nineteenth century when he commented that 'the excessive individualism which then prevailed was inconsistent with much public spirit' (p. 57). Although the extremes of poverty have been ameliorated in western economies, and the masses are now often wealthier than their parents, the gap between the rich and the poor has been widening in the past 20 years. Moreover, racial, gendered and global inequalities have largely gone unchecked despite the elegant words of JFK in his inauguration speech over 40 years ago:

> To those peoples in the huts and villages of half the globe struggling to break the bonds of mass misery, we pledge our best efforts to help them help themselves, for whatever period is required . . . because it is right. If a free society cannot help the many who are poor, it cannot save the few who are rich.
>
> (Kennedy 1961)

What can we as researchers, academics and human beings do to help lighten the load for those who are forced to pull the coach? As critical theorists, we do not believe that it is our role to help the passengers develop a better coach, or a more efficient means of communicating their encouraging messages of hope and patience. But rather it is to raise a critical voice about the coach and the inequalities it reproduces on its journey. We can, of course, disseminate these alternative stories about working life to those we teach and to our research students. Through publishing our findings and offering critical insights we can appeal to a wider audience. We also believe that merely by researching the workplace and asking searching questions, our respondents may be led to assume more reflective positions about their situation and that of their colleagues or subordinates/superordinates. Yet the opposition that is often confronted when presenting alternative interpretations and perspectives to management practitioners arrests our optimism. Even with our captured audiences of students it is difficult enough to challenge their taken for granted individualistic assumptions that reflect a lifetime of reinforcement. How much more difficult is it then to affect the more deeply embedded values and assumptions of those we research, except indirectly through an incitement to self-reflection?

The obstacles to changing the mindset or worldview of others cannot be overstated, as we have indicated elsewhere (Knights and McCabe 2003). Not least in this context is the problem of the 'other' being a mere vehicle for sustaining our own sense of a secure self or identity. It can be argued that radicals use the demand for change as a crutch for self or a source of meaning in an insecure and uncertain world. That is to say, being critical enables us to assuage our guilt and feel better about ourselves, despite enjoying the relative privileges of academia in a world characterized by immense inequality. Consequently, there is often a battle between academics on the basis of who is the most radical. Who is to be the hero or heroine of the oppressed? Acknowledging this possibility leaves us always sceptical about our own motives but it does not preclude us from attempting to disrupt the taken for granted or indeed from questioning the inequalities we observe.

It is important to note that regardless of whether people are content with their dreams, they may not be willing to countenance ours. This does not mean that, as indicated at the beginning of this book, we subscribe to Goffman's (1975: 14) approach of 'sneaking in' merely to 'watch the way the people snore'. We agree with Goffman that the sleep can be 'very deep' and that to 'combat' it is often beyond us. However, we do not agree with his view about 'false consciousness' deflecting people from their 'true interests'. Indeed we reject both of these concepts in the sense that they are part of the problem rather than the solution to our sedation to, or complacency about, the individualization of society.[1] They are part of the problem because they not only reflect and reinforce an individualism that we would want to challenge, but also they rest upon a belief that intellectuals/observers have a privileged access to the 'true' conditions of society and, hence, can claim to know better than people do themselves what are their 'real interests'. That we, as the alarm clocks of society, are truly conscious and are capable of seeing what others cannot – so much so that we have the right to preach to or speak on behalf of others.

It is partly for this reason that we have been influenced by Foucault (1980, 1982) who recognized that our interests are not independent of our social relations and the power in which they are embedded. Thus we are fabricated through power and cannot stand outside of it like a referee, judge or sage. For

Foucault, our subjectivity and hence our interests are constituted as an effect of power rather than its principal resource.[2] Since all social relations can be seen to involve some exercise of power even if it is simply that of impressing the other of the importance of your views (Goffman 1959), everything is political. However, politics can work not only to support but also to disrupt and resist conventional exercises of power and how they reflect and reproduce what is often taken for granted. We want, therefore, to go beyond Goffman's (1975: 14) mere refusal to 'provide a lullaby' that is soporific; we need at least to make sufficient noise that could waken us all to the recognition that our dreams are rarely realized. This is not a matter of waking people up to their 'true interests' so much as asking them to question and reflect upon how they came to acquire their interests in the first place. In short, it is an incitement to reflect on power and the seductive ways in which it transforms us into subjects that secure our sense of identity, meaning and reality as we engage in the practices that it generates and sustains. If we have been successful, it is up to others to decide how or whether to act, not for us to tell them as if we know best. For following Foucault, we recognize, and indeed much of our empirical research supports the view, that the outcomes of power are uncertain. While we believe, for instance, that a better society would be one that has greater global, gender and racial equality, the road to hell is often paved with good intentions.[3]

Importantly, senior managers and investors have considerable vested interests and much to lose from challenges to their dreams. For through criticizing dreams we question the identity and material conditions of those who hold them and challenge the power relations they support and reproduce. Consequently, different dreams reflect different ways of seeing and understanding the world that may simply pass each other by. One has to be cognizant of the fact that even if we are successful in persuading others to our cause, they, in turn, face immense institutional barriers to enacting change and in the process face the real possibility of losing their employment. This is not a 'get out' clause but it is to recognize that while our jobs may be comparatively secure and, indeed, our career prospects may be enhanced through publications such as these, our prescriptions may harm the lives of others. We need to be cautious therefore about the exercise of power, not least because with the best intentions we cannot be certain about the outcomes. For regardless of whether it is prevailing dreams or alternative visions, enrolling people and mobilizing resources and networks (Latour 1987) in their support is a necessary condition of their realization. This involves exercising power and no one, including ourselves, can be exempt from this charge.

The power relations that can prevent change are akin to those that can grant or deny access to companies for the purposes of research. For without management's blessing we would not be able to conduct research and so challenging dreams of innovation presents a prickly problem. The difficulties cannot be overstated for if we tread too lightly they may not hear us and if we tread too heavily the door will be closed before we can have any impact or gain any understanding of the lives of others.

The following extract is from a feedback session with Gordon Dee, a director at Intermotors, conducted in January 1997, and it is indicative of how different dreams can be blind to one another. This director's individualistic way of looking at the world is seemingly blind to the dreams of others and/or denies their legitimacy. For the director simply reiterated his dream when confronted with an alternative one and this underlines the difficulties involved in endeavours to encourage discussion let alone to secure change. As we shall see, Gordon is frustrated that employees will not accept his dream or definition of events. Yet this did not give rise to sustained reflection as to the legitimacy of his dream or the relative merits of the employees' position or concerns. At a practical level, we would argue that such deafness to the concerns of others is destructive of dialogue or progress for one's own dreams. Here Gordon is confronted with the feelings of insecurity/uncertainty among the workforce at Intermotors:

> *Darren:* There is still resentment about the way the redundancies were handled . . . that issue constantly came up.
>
> *Gordon:* The thing about the selection rather than last in first out?
>
> *Darren:* I think it was the first wave of redundancies when couriers went out to people's homes . . . that's an issue that still haunts a lot of people and they are not going to forget that.
>
> *Gordon:* Even though they were not affected by it?
>
> *Darren:* But some people emphasized that they sat at home thinking they would be. It's that general uncertainty . . .
>
> *Gordon:* Scratch the surface and those issues come flooding back . . . there is a feeling of betrayal that results in a real lack of trust even though there is not a single member of the board who was here in 1991 . . . it's a difficult issue . . . No matter how often you say it and no matter how emotionally you say it, it makes no difference. Because the underlying feelings are so great that you have to be able to prove to those people who have those concerns that you are not going to behave like that and you cannot do that. I don't know any management that can promise jobs for life, you can never do that. And when you turn round and say 'It's up to you. If we could actually perform better, perform more efficiently, and make more margins out of every car and improve the quality of the cars and deliver on time more often. Help us do that and that starts to guarantee the future' people don't often want to play that or see that – 'Well why should I do that? What's in it for me?' That's what you get thrown back at you. So it's this difficult issue of constant communication, where the key communication down through the local management, the local team leader, has got to play a crucial role.

This extract is intriguing for a number of reasons, for when confronted with the emotional anxieties and insecurities of the workforce, Gordon asked a technical question concerning the way in which the redundancies were handled. Then when the point was reiterated he attempted to deflect or dismiss it by stating that the workers who remained had not been made redundant and so should not feel anxious or bear any animosity. Here we see him denying the legitimacy of their concerns but eventually, after a third prompting, he acknowledged that such issues are only just beneath the surface. Unfortunately, rather than tackling the issue raised he quickly reverted to his individualistic dream of the world. Unable or unwilling to acknowledge any fundamental inequity or conflict between management and workers, he justified job insecurity on the basis that other companies do not offer jobs for life. Finally he began to chant the dream that the management gurus offer – everyone is equal and as such they can equally contribute to the success of the company. Yet, when he argues that the future of the company rests upon the willingness and ability of employees to produce quality vehicles efficiently, it seems to him that it falls upon deaf ears. For 'people don't often want to play that or see that'. Such a line of argument is difficult to accept for employees who are paid to produce vehicles and do not gain in equal measure from improvements in productivity or quality. As we saw in Chapter 6, they also find it difficult to reconcile their ability to manufacture vehicles with their inability to control sales. Once settled in the comfort of his 'dream', however, Gordon was able to explain away any problems as due to a failure of communication rather than any shortcomings with the dream itself.

Here then is a problem that has pervaded this book. Despite flaws in the dreams that the gurus peddle, each new guru or manager finds a way to expound the same unitary dream. Such dreams provide some managers with much needed solace from the difficulties in which they find themselves. Thus rather than acknowledging contradictions or questioning the inequalities they reproduce, the dream of innovation allows managers to alleviate their anxieties and uncertainties. They can simply fall back on rational/economic explanations of the 'way things are'. The problem is perceived or explained as a lack of understanding or a need to improve communication, so as to resolve the difficulties faced. Gordon's belief that employees should simply concentrate on the task at hand and accept the inevitable shares some resonance with the philosophy of Andrew Carnegie, the Scottish-born steel tycoon, who became an American business mogul:

> The problem of our age is the proper administration of wealth, so that the ties of brotherhood may still bind together the rich and poor in harmonious relationship. The conditions of human life have not only been changed, but revolutionized, within the past few hundred years . . . But whether the change be for good or ill, it is upon us, beyond our power to alter, and therefore to be accepted and made the best of it. It is a waste of time to criticize the inevitable.
>
> The price which society pays for the law of competition, like the price it pays for cheap comforts and luxuries, is also great; but the advantages of this law are also greater still . . . while the law may be sometimes hard for the individual, it is best for the race, because it ensures the survival of the fittest in every department. We accept and welcome, therefore, as conditions to which we must accommodate ourselves, great inequality of

environment, the concentration of business, industrial and commercial, in the hands of a few, and the law of competition between these, as being not only beneficial, but essential for the future progress of the race.

(Carnegie 1900: 192)

Here Carnegie reveals his own American Dream and it is one in which the 'poor' do not question the superiority of the 'rich' but rather defer to their greater wisdom. It is informed by a 'social evolutionism' that had not yet been discredited.[4] It is curious that the idealized world according to Carnegie, Gordon and other managers we have represented, shares considerable overlaps with that outlined in Bellamy's dream of a post-capitalist scenario; for as Dr Leete informs Julian West:

If I were to give you, in one sentence, a key to the mysteries of our civilization as compared with that of your age, I should say that it is the fact that the solidarity of the race and the brotherhood of man, which to you were fine phrases, are, to our thinking and feeling, ties as real and as vital as physical fraternity.

(Bellamy [1888] 1986: 111)

The gurus of management and their disciples preach and promote precisely this unity without, however, tackling or confronting the social inequality reflected in, and reproduced by, the organizations that they seek to improve. Yet, at least according to Bellamy, redressing such inequality is central to promoting unity. For as Dr Leete continued:

The equal wealth and equal opportunities of culture which all persons now enjoy have simply made us all members of one class, which corresponds to the most fortunate class with you. Until this equality of condition had come to pass, the idea of the solidarity of humanity, the brotherhood of all men, could never have become the real conviction and practical principle of action it is nowadays. In your day the same phrases were indeed used, but they were phrases merely.

(Bellamy [1888] 1986: 125)

There is then a critical limitation within the guru literature and in the discourse of the managers who imbibe it, in that it seeks to promote unity and equality in a world that is frequently divided and undoubtedly unequal. Dr Leete contrasts the nineteenth century with the year 2000 by arguing that 'The producers of the 19th Century were not, like ours, working together for the maintenance of the community, but each solely for his own maintenance at the expense of the community' (p. 170). We would not go so far as Dr Leete, for while we recognize that individualism, competition and antagonism are features of capitalist societies, so are cooperation, community and interdependence, but the latter are severely constrained by the former. For us then, the contemporary American Dream as enshrined in a host of recent innovations is fundamentally flawed, and our aim in this book has been to stimulate critical reflection upon its limitations.

Notes

Introduction

1   We elaborate this point in the conclusion to this book.

2   We acknowledge funding from the ESRC on grant numbers R000234403 (Quality in UK financial services); L125251061 (The implementation of BPR in financial services); RO22250042 (Past, present and future 'innovations' in UK management control); RO22250186 (Managing call centres: knowledge, learning and subjectivity at work in consumer products and financial services).

3   We recognize that the Japanese Sun began to set following its economic crisis in the late 1980s but ideas about working practices associated with Japan had already impacted upon the West and continue to do so.

Chapter 1

1   In this chapter, we seek to contextualize our discussion of recent management innovations. Those not interested in the history or would like to go directly to the heart of our text may wish to skip this chapter.

2   Kondratieff economic cycles refer to the 50-year economic long waves from 'boom' to 'bust' as opposed to the much shorter cycles between less dramatic periods of economic growth and recession.

3   The increase in credit or debt has been dramatic in recent years. It has grown by around 1300 per cent over the past ten years (see www.statistics.gov.uk/statbase/TSDtimezone.asp).

4   'Here is one of the most remarkable aspects of the still-unfolding financial scandals swirling around WorldCom, Xerox, Global Crossing, Enron, Arthur Andersen, Tyco and a growing number of other companies: the

fraud occurred in the most heavily regulated and monitored area of corporate activity. If an epidemic of corporate malfeasance could occur in the financial arena, how serious is the more general problem of corporate crime?' (Mokhiber and Weissman 2002: 9).

5   'Unlike financial investors, [employees] have no legal rights to a voice in corporate governance, their employment status is at will, meaning they can be fired or laid off for any or no reason' (Kochan 2002).

6   We are aware of the gender insensitivity of using the term 'man' as a universal but this is principally how the literature has described these various approaches and there are no perfect literary devices to achieve political correctness here. It is also our view that being political is more important than is so-called political correctness.

7   Moreover, it is perhaps to exaggerate the importance of scientific management, as distinct from other factors such as the technical substitution of capital for labour, in explaining the historical development of management control.

8   This can be seen as an embryonic version of 'time and motion studies' where management could determine the exact amount of time it should take to carry out a task. Rates of pay were adjusted to a standard that left no room for employees to 'steal' time from the employer.

9   Psychologists have invariably referred to the concept of 'need' unproblematically and often as if it were an essential condition of human life, whereas we want to argue that needs are socially created, changed or sustained. Even so-called basic needs for food have been shown by anthropologists to be culturally mediated such that in some societies adults will sacrifice their own sustenance for the sake of their children whereas in others the opposite might be the case (see Turnbull 1984).

Chapter 2

1   For example, it was included as one of the 50 best books of all kinds in a recent *Observer* newspaper collection.

2   For more information on our research, we suggest you consult the following: Knights and McCabe (1998c) Dreams and designs on strategy – a critical analysis of TQM and management control, *Work, Employment and Society*, 12(3): 433–56; Knights and McCabe (1998d) When 'life is but a dream' – obliterating politics through business process re-engineering? *Human Relations*, 51(6): 761–98; McCabe (2000) The team dream: the meaning and experience of teamworking for employees in an automobile manufacturing company, in S. Proctor and F. Mueller (eds) *Teamworking* (London: Macmillan); McCabe and Knights (2000) Such stuff as dreams are made on – BPR against the wall of functionalism, hierarchy and specialization, in D. Knights and H. Willmott (eds) *The Reengineering Revolution?* (London: Sage).

3   The connection with the American Dream has been made in relation

to HRM (Guest 1990) and what Dunn (1990) refers to as the new industrial relations. Our theme shares a resonance with these early literatures but also with Jackson (2001), who speaks about guru innovations as a vehicle for various fantasies. For example, BPR is seen as having an underlying narrative of the self – its preservation, redemption and representation.

4   There is a considerable literature on Utopia from the sixteenth century to the present day that can be accessed through the New York Public Library website at http://www.nypl.org/utopia/primarysources.html. Visit, for example, the Utopia Pathway Association at http://www.angelfire.com/co/harmony/utopiapa.html, the Utopian Studies Society at http://www.utopianstudies.org/ and the Society for Utopian Studies website at http://www.utoronto.ca/utopia/. A comprehensive gateway to information on Utopia is at http://users.erols.com/jonwill/utopialist.htm. For a contemporary mainstream study of Utopia, see Carey (1999) and for a critical analysis, see Parker (2002).

5   After his father had emigrated to Pittsburgh from Dunfermline in Scotland because of the decline of hand loom work due to the introduction of steam power, Andrew Carnegie began work in 1848 at the age of 13. His first job was as a bobbin boy in a textile mill, earning $1.20 per week. Fifty-three years later in 1901, Carnegie allowed J.P. Morgan to buy his steel business for $480 million, a move which allowed Morgan to create US Steel, and made Carnegie the richest man in the world. As one of the biggest US philanthropists, Carnegie gave away 90 per cent of his fortune. In 1889, he published *The Gospel of Wealth*, claiming that there was a moral obligation on the part of the wealthy to serve as stewards for society.

6   In 1879, John D. Rockefeller and a handful of associates created what became known as Standard Oil of New Jersey. Rockefeller made Standard Oil an amazing example of consolidation and efficiency. In fact, he was so successful *that* at his death his personal fortune was estimated at $815,647,796.89.

7   While this is not the place to critique the reduction of human potential or social relations to a form of capital, the origin of the discourse in economics (Becker 1964) quickly sensitizes us to the strong instrumental dimension to the analysis. Whether it is economic, human or social capital in question, their development is primarily for purposes respectively of advancing economic, individual or social interests. Underlying each is a consensual view about what these interests are and so it is just a matter of developing the most efficient and effective tools for their achievement. As is clear from this book, we think that the consensus on any of these issues cannot be presumed.

8   The amnesia concerning the indigenous Indians and African slaves is reflected in much writing on America.

9   This was apparent in Bush's position on the environment in 2001 when he refused to sign the Kyoto international agreement on reducing the release of fossil fuel gases under the ozone layer. He was willing to sacrifice

this to ensure the continuing health and wealth of the American economy threatened by economic recession.

10   Humanistic values do not necessarily reflect the full-blown philosophy of humanism. The latter revolves around treating human beings as at the centre of the universe and elevated above everything else, including God. The former have become almost synonymous with common sense, following a view not dissimilar from a Christian ethic or a Kantian categorical imperative of treating others as you would like to be treated yourself.

11   Our concern here is not to attempt a comprehensive review of the innovation literature even if that were possible, but merely to provide sufficient context for our case studies to be comprehensible. We specifically set out our theoretical approach in relation to TQM in Chapter 3.

12   The steady erosion of salaries in academia is a further stimulation for management academics to pursue such outside income.

13   Success is not defined at this point but there is no doubting it means profits, growth and competitive advantage. The very fact that success can be taken for granted in this way reveals the managerial outlook of the authors since terms like profit, growth and competitive advantage that are frequently mentioned throughout the book are never the subject of critical examination, as is innovation.

14   There are very few heroines in the field of guru management but Dorothy Parker Follett and Rosebeth Moss Kanter may lay that claim. Interestingly, their work is more substantive and less flamboyant than the work of their male counterparts but less successful, probably as a result.

15   Munro also uses the same language to demonstrate the superficiality of much change management. He argues that the 'notion of changing culture with its emphasis on empowerment and trust, hardly begins to get off the ground as anything other than the latest of a series of devices to extract profit . . . The more it changes, the more it remains the same' (1998: 224).

16   We are not suggesting here that change is absent. The competitive aspects of capitalism clearly stimulate change or, as Marx claimed, there is a constant revolution in the forces of production if only to meet the demands of profit in competitive conditions. But there are not only countervailing pressures (e.g. mergers, branding etc.) that ameliorate the effects of competition, change itself only makes sense against a background of stability and which of these we choose to emphasize is not an innocent or neutral political event.

Chapter 3

1   The substitution of the term 'management' for 'control' in TQM does not mean the demise of control, as the critics make clear.

2   Among Deming's 14 points are 'create constancy of purpose', 'drive out

fear', 'break down barriers between departments', 'eliminate slogans' and 'eliminate work quotas'. It is argued that adopting all 14 will provide the means for transforming American industry into a world leader in quality.

3   It should be noted that despite Delbridge *et al.*'s (1992) emphasis upon the intensive opportunities for control within TQM/JIT regimes they recognized that opportunities for resistance would remain.

4   The case of Carco is drawn from D. McCabe's PhD research that has formed the basis of a number of publications, one of which deals with the period of time discussed here (McCabe 1996).

5   As with all systems of classification, whether we are speaking about influences or content there is a degree of artificiality and arbitrariness about what is included or excluded and where the boundaries are drawn. For this reason, our three approaches should not be treated too literally but simply as a heuristic device for assisting us in seeking to understand the 'progress' of TQM.

6   There are currently computerized expert systems available to carry out the bulk of underwriting that falls into the normal rating category. Clerical Medical, for example, has used them in life insurance underwriting for some time.

7   There is not space here to develop the argument but backlogs create a major problem for most individuals in the sense of making them feel out of control. If they cannot be 'shifted', then for some staff, backlogs represent a threat to identity (Sturdy 1992). See also earlier reference to backlogs in relation to Kim.

8   Mars studied how cashiers were able to cheat their employers and/or customers when collecting and/or accounting for their payments.

9   It should be noted that these staff, because of their enthusiasm and willingness to do so, have been specially selected to be involved in a number of special projects, such as developing a telephone skills package, in which the bulk of staff have not been involved.

10   We are partially indebted to our colleague Deborah Kerfoot for directing us to a view of disparate or disconnected instances of individual resistance having an aggregated effect through transformations of the culture.

Chapter 4

1   A building society is a mutual organization that uses its members' savings to lend money primarily to customers for the purpose of buying their homes. Of late, many of these building societies have demutualized to become fully-fledged banks.

2   'Hand-offs' are where one member of staff passes a customer to another member of staff who specializes in the particular query or request. Frequently, hand-offs would involve delays generating a great deal of customer and staff irritation.

Chapter 5

1   We are, of course, using the device to draw a distinction between 'rhetoric' and 'reality' in a rhetorical fashion to give symbolic credence to what we say. While clearly there is a distinction between words and actions or prescription and practices, we only have words to describe them and behind every discourse is an intent and an inevitable inten(t)sion as it seeks to mobilize support for and enrol others in its rhetoric.

2   During a period of six years studying innovations, we came across several companies switching their allegiances or priorities from one type of intervention to another without conducting an investigation or monitoring outcomes.

3   We might also be accused of jumping on the 'fads' and 'fashions' bandwagon but it is largely to criticize and understand them. Moreover, rather than seeking to prescribe or criticize the latest management idea to appear the focus has emerged out of our empirical investigations.

4   One might have expected the merger or rationalization activity to have been more concentrated in the life insurance sector which was the most deeply affected by the new regulations. Although merger mania has recently begun to affect this sector, it is not on the scale of banking.

5   This, of course, should not be exaggerated because consumer inertia remains prevalent within financial services due partly to the relative low priority verging on complete indifference that financial products hold for a majority of people and partly due to the continued complexity involved in switching from one supplier to another.

6   This is a highly dubious explanation for what is essentially an exercise in cherry-picking the more profitable customers on the internet and squeezing the lemons dry (i.e. shedding the unprofitable customers) in rural areas (Noble *et al.* 2000).

Chapter 6

1   Contingency theory seems simply to reinforce or even magnify the tendency for academics to qualify any statement with 'it all depends'. This is not attractive to politicians, management practitioners and the media. The Advanced Institute for Management (AIM) has been awarded £19m partly to seek to reverse the 'it all depends' conditionality of research conclusions.

2   Empiricism is a philosophy of science that is committed to studying the world through human sense perceptions independently of analytical preconceptions. It is contrasted with cognitive or constructionist philosophies of science that examine the world through theoretical models. We perceive these as misleading binaries since the two approaches can be mutually interdependent in practice.

3   In particular, the auto industry in Japan had acquired a reputation for

being dirty, hard and dangerous. Also, a US survey found few employees prepared to recommend the industry to their children because of the low pay, long hours and the hard and intensive nature of the work (Berggren 1993: 183).

4   Given that management selected those who were to be interviewed, it would be expected that respondents would be the more conformist or the least resistant of employees.

5   The following is a one paragraph synopsis of a journal paper (Knights and McCabe 2000a) and a book Chapter (McCabe 2000a).

6   Foucault was extremely ambivalent about humanistic beliefs such as 'human rights', recognizing that while they confined us within our individualized preoccupations and interests, they were one of the few vehicles for resisting and protesting about the conditions of human subjugation under power/knowledge regimes.

Chapter 7

1   Data consist of a collection of facts, pictures and numbers presented without context (Brooking 1999: 4).

2   Nonaka and Takeuchi (1995) and Von Krogh et al. (2000) claim to be constructionists but they seem not to recognize the political implications of such a position and slip readily into an episteme of representation in which reality is not seen as problematic.

3   Nonaka and Takeuchi (1995) do recognize Polanyi's contribution to the distinction between tacit and explicit knowledge but justify not focusing on his work in their philosophical Chapter 2 because 'he is still considered minor in Western philosophy' (p. 91 n. 5). They nonetheless limit their discussion of his notion of tacit knowledge because it is discussed in a philosophical context whereas they wish to 'expand his idea in a more practical direction' (p. 60). We suggest that further exploration of his ideas might have led to rather more scepticism about their faith in converting tacit into explicit knowledge, which is the foundation of their whole thesis.

4   This could be related to the Gestalt notion in psychology that the whole is greater than the sum of its parts. Or it could relate to the distinction in physics between the Newtonian classical world that we can describe as a singular reality and the quantum world that cannot be spoken about. The latter because it defies Kantian logic where a 'thing' has to be either *what it is* or its negation but not both at one and the same time. The Schroedinger equation in quantum mechanics suggests a superposition of objects that are precisely in a state of being and non-being simultaneously (See Wilson 2000).

5   Is it ironic that through the growth of KM as a new panacea Nonaka and Takeuchi have been turned into academic gurus? It is only through a selective interpretation and usage of their work that this can be sustained.

For apart from their contradicting a central premise of the new panacea that knowledge can be managed, their faith in the special expertise of the Japanese in this area has hardly been verified by economic results. Take, for example, their prediction that because 'Japanese companies have traditionally turned to organizational knowledge creation as a way of breaking from the past and moving them into new and untried territories of opportunity', . . . 'they will emerge stronger from the current recession'. Yet no economy in the twentieth century had been in recession for as long as Japan since the mid-1980s. Nonaka and Takeuchi must be wrong either in their assertions that Japanese companies have a competitive edge in their knowledge creating capacities or that knowledge creation alone can be instrumental to economic success. It is perhaps not surprising that the literature is blind to this discrepancy in the rhetoric of KM.

6   Following the line of approach adopted in other chapters, it is the use of the terminology of KM by the practitioners and not any external criteria of judgement that leads us to study this case as an example of KM.

7   This is not unlike the situation when governments go to war. Billions of dollars or pounds can be expended in a matter of days whereas during peacetime money is seemingly unavailable for a host of worthy causes.

8   The heated debate between 'realists' and 'constructionists' (sometimes denigrated as relativists) in relation to technology can readily run into an intellectual cul-de-sac: 'Self declared "realists" dream up a formulation which turns, so to speak, the "world upside down". They then challenge self-described "constructivists" to show how it can stay that way. This sets off an endless circle in which increasingly preposterous propositions are constructed (by realists) only to be "de-constructed" (by constructivists) so the whole thing can start all over again – until both sides lose interest' (Knights *et al.* 2002: 12). While, for example, the dispute over whether guns are as effective in warfare as roses is not uninteresting, few of the protagonists provide narratives of the conditions and contexts in which social enactments might favour one or the other.

Chapter 8

1   This may seem contradictory given that the notion of false consciousness derives largely from Marx (1973) whose preoccupation was with transforming society through a proletarian collective revolution. However, his humanistic phase, where false consciousness was introduced, is entirely compatible with an individualistic view that begins with human interests as if they were an essential part of human nature. This regards people in capitalist societies as being corrupted by power as if a radical analysis and account of life could be sufficient in and of itself to awaken them to their real consciousness and interests. At such time, following revolutionary action, they would seemingly be free of power, which we reject. For even if such a society was more equal in our view, individuals would still be

constituted through power relations, albeit relations that express different values and beliefs.

2   When confronted with such views, many (e.g. Benhabib 1992; McNay 1992; Mouzelis 1995; Newton 1998) are inclined to accuse Foucault of a deterministic stance that neglects or marginalizes agency. Since this is a book largely for students, we have avoided becoming embroiled in esoteric scholarly debates such as these but that is not to dismiss them as of minor importance. Suffice it to say here that, as we have seen in the empirical case studies, it is precisely because individuals are *active* agents that extensive resources have to be directed towards controlling them or persuading them to be self-disciplined (Knights and McCabe 2003). For the exercise of power is 'always a way of acting upon an acting subject or acting subjects by virtue of their acting or being capable of action' (Foucault 1982: 220). Our approach and handling of the empirical material does not follow a strictly Foucauldian line for we are also influenced by labour process theory and interpretive approaches. In our case studies we tend to present subject 'voices' in a way that Foucault never did. Nevertheless we remain cognisant of his concerns, for Foucault continually strove to break down dualistic representations that distinguish between agency and structure. Both are implicit in his accounts of discipline and punishment (Foucault 1977), for example, where we find people rioting, protesting and setting prisoners free. Yet Foucault does not separate these people (agents) from the (con)text (structure) of their practices and so his critics tend to charge him with a neglect of agency. The problem is that such a critique emanates from a dualistic understanding of the world where structures are seen as separate and distinct from agents – an epistemological position that Foucault eschewed. Those following a dualistic line of thinking believe that a focus on subjectivity is tantamount to a neglect of the wider structures of power and inequality and a concentration on structured power relations leaves the academic open to the charge that the subject has been forgotten. In order to avoid such dualistic thinking, our concern in this book has been to follow Foucault by incorporating a theoretical awareness of how structures/agents constitute and reproduce one another in routine discursive practices (see Knights and McCabe 1999) .

3   It was the hell of the Gulag with its salt mines and torture that made Foucault, though strongly influenced by Marx, sceptical about Marxism or the way in which ideas can be taken up and corrupted.

4   It is important to note that Carnegie was a self-made mogul and philanthropist, who gave away 90% of his fortune. Such philanthropy could do much to relieve present day suffering.

References

Abrahamson, E. (1991) Managerial fads and fashions: the diffusion and rejection of innovation, *Academy of Management Review*, 16(3): 586–612.

Abrahamson, E. (1996) Management fashion, *Academy of Management Review*, 21(1): 254–85.

Abrahamson, E. (1997) The emergence and prevalence of employee management rhetorics: the effects of long waves, labour unions, and turnover, 1875 to 1992, *Academy of Management Journal*, 40(3): 491–533.

Academy of Management Review (1994) Special issue, 19(3).

Ackers, P., Smith, C. and Smith, P. (1996) *The New Workplace and Trade Unionism*. London: Routledge.

Allee, V. (1997). *The Knowledge Evolution: Expanding Organisational Intelligence*. London: Butterworth-Heinemann.

Anderson, J.C., Rungtusanatham, ? and Schroeder, ? (1994) A theory of quality management underlying the Deming management method, *Academy of Management Review*, 19(3): 472–510.

Andrews, K.R. (1971) *The Concept of Corporate Change*. Homewood, IL: Irwin.

Ansoff, H. (1965) *Corporate Strategy*. New York: McGraw-Hill.

Ansoff, H. (1991) Critique of Henry Mintzberg's 'The design school: reconsidering the basic premises of strategic management', *Strategic Management Journal*, 12: 449–61.

Armstrong, P. (2000) The politics of management science, an inaugural lecture. Keele University Westminster Theatre, 18 May.

Bain & Co. (1994) *A Survey of Management Innovations: Private Consultants Report*. London: Bain & Co.

Bain, G.S. (1970) *The Growth of White Collar Unionism*. Oxford: Clarendon Press.

Bain, P. and Taylor, P. (2000) Entapped by the 'electronic panopticon'? Worker resistance in the call centre, *New Technology, Work and Employment*, 15(1): 2–18.

Baldry, C., Bain, P. and Taylor, P. (1998) 'Bright satanic offices': intensification, control and team Taylorism, in P. Thompson and C. Warhurst (eds) *Workplaces of the Future*, pp. 163–83. London: Macmillan Business.

Barker, J.R. (1993) Tightening the iron cage: concertive control in self-managing teams, *Administrative Science Quarterly*, 38: 408–37.

Barker, J.R. (1999) *The Discipline of Teamwork*. London: Sage.

Barley, S. and Kunda, G. (1992) Design and devotion: surges of rational and normative ideologies of control in managerial discourse, *Administrative Science Quarterly*, 37: 363–99.

Barnard, C.I. (1938) *The Functions of the Executive*. Cambridge, MA: Harvard University Press.

Batt, R. (1999) Work organization, technology and performance in customer service and sales, *Industrial and Labour Relations Review*, 52(4): 539–64.

Becker, G. (1964) *Human Capital*. New York: National Bureau of Investigative Research.

Bell, V. (1999) *Feminist Imagination*. London: Sage.

Bellamy, E. ([1888] 1986) London: *Looking Backwards*. London: Penguin.

Belt, V. (1999) Are call centres the new sweatshops?, the *Independent*, 14 January: 4.

Bensman, J. and Gerver, I. (1963) Crime and punishment in the factory: the function of deviancy in maintaining the social system, *American Sociological Review*, 28: 588–98.

Benhabib, S. (1992) *Situating the Subject*. London: Sage.

Berger, P. (1963) *Invitation to Sociology*. Harmondsworth: Penguin.

Berger, P. and Luckmann, T. (1966) *The Social Construction of Reality*. London: Penguin.

Berggren, C. (1993) Lean production – the end of history, *Work, Employment and Society*, 7(2): 163–88.

Berry, L.L., Zeithaml, V.A. and Parasuraman, A. (1985) Quality counts in services too, *Business Horizons*, 28(3): 44–52.

Berry, L.L., Parasuraman, A. and Zeithaml, V.A. (1988) The service-quality puzzle, *Business Horizons*, July–August: 35–43.

Benyon, H. (1973) *Working For Ford*. Harmondsworth: Penguin.

Blair, H., Grey Taylor, S. and Randle, K. (1998) A pernicious panancea – a critical evaluation of BPR, *New Technology, Work and Employment*, 13(2): 116–28.

Blauner, R. (1964) *Alienation*. Chicago, IL: University of Chicago Press.

Blumer, H (1969) *Symbolic Interactionism: Perspective and Method*. Englewood Cliffs, NJ: Prentice Hall.

Boaden, R.J. and Dale, B.G. (1993) Managing quality improvement in financial services: a framework and case study, *Service Industry Journal*, 13(1): 13–39.

Boje, D.M. and Winsor, R.D. (1993) The resurrection of Taylorism: TQM's hidden agenda, *Journal of Organizational Change Management*, 6(4): 57–70.

Boudon, R. (1981) *The Logic of Social Action*. London: Routledge & Kegan Paul.

Braverman, H. (1974) *Labor and Monopoly Capital*. New York: Monthly Review Press.

Brooking, A. (1999) *Corporate Memory: Strategies for knowledge management*. London: Thomson Business Press.

Brown, J.S. (1998) Research that reinvents the corporation, *Harvard Business Review On Knowledge Management*, Harvard Business School Press, originally published 1987.

Brown, J.S. (2002) Managing knowledge in a new century, in S. Little, P. Quintas and T. Ray (eds) *Managing Knowledge: An Essential Reader*. London: Sage.

Bukowitz, W.R. and Williams, R.L. (1999) *The Knowledge Management Fieldbook*. London: Prentice Hall.

Burawoy, M. (1979) *The Manufacture of Consent*. Chicago, IL: Chicago University Press.

Burrell, G. and Morgan, G. (1979) *Sociological Paradigms and Organisational Analysis*. London: Heinemann.

Butler, J. (1990) *Gender Trouble*. New York: Routledge.

Callon, M. (1986) Some elements of a sociology of translation: domestication of the scallops and fishermen of St Brieuc's Bay, in J. Law (ed.) *Power, Action and Belief: A New Sociology of Knowledge* (*Sociological Review* monograph no. 32). London: Routledge & Kegan Paul.

Carey, A. (1965) The Hawthorne studies: a radical criticism, *American Sociological Review*, 32: 403–16.

Carey, J. (ed.) (1999) *The Faber Book of Utopias*. London: Faber & Faber.

Carnegie, A. (1900) The gospel of wealth, in A. Breidlid *et al.* (eds) *American Culture: An Anthology of Civilization Texts*, pp. 192–3. London: Routledge.

Carter, C. and Scarborough, H. (2000) Regimes of knowledge, stories of power: a treatise of knowledge management, paper presented to the 'Working Together? Knowledge and Management in the Information Society' conference. Department of Management, University of Keele, 16–17 June.

Champy, J. (1995) Reengineering's revolutionary sticks to his guns, interview by Mick James, *Management Consultancy*, 27–8 May.

Chumer, M., Hull, R. and Prichard, C. (2000) Introduction: situating discussions about 'knowledge' in C. Prichard, R. Hull, M. Chumer and H. Willmott (eds) *Managing Knowledge: Critical Investigations of Work and Learning*, London: Macmillan.

Clark, T. and Salaman, G. (1996) The management guru as organizational witchdoctor, *Organization*, 3(1): 85–107.

Clark, T. and Salaman, G. (1998) Telling tales: management gurus' narratives and the construction of managerial identity, *Journal of Management Studies*, 35(2): 138–61.

Clegg, S.R. (1979) *The Theory of Power and Organization*. London: Routledge & Kegan Paul.

Clifford, J. (1986) Introduction: partial truths, in J. Clifford and G.E. Marcus (eds) *Writing Culture*. London: University of California Press.

Collinson, D. (1992) *Managing the Shopfloor: Subjectivity, Masculinity and Workplace Culture*. Berlin: de Gruyter.

Collinson, D. (1994) Strategies of resistance: power, knowledge and subjectivity in the workplace, in J.M. Jermier, D. Knights and W.R. Nord (eds) (1994) *Resistance and Power in Organization*. London: Routledge.

Coombs, R. and Hull, R. (1998) 'Knowledge management practices' and path dependency in innovation, *Research Policy*, 27(3): 239–55.

Cooper, R. (1992) Formal organization as representation: remote control, displacement and abbreviation, in M. Reed and M. Hughes (eds) *Rethinking Organization*. London: Sage.

Cottrell, J. (1992) Favourable recipes, *The TQM Magazine*, February: 17–29.

Crainer, S. (1998) *The Ultimate Book of Business Gurus: 110 Thinkers Who Really Made a Difference*. New York: American Management Association.

Cressey, P. and MacInnes, J. (1980) Voting for Ford: industrial democracy and the control of labour, *Capital and Class*, 11: 5–37.

Cressey, P. and Scott, P. (1992) Employment, technology and industrial relations in the UK clearing banks: is the honeymoon over? *New Technology, Work and Employment*, 7(2): 83–96.

Crosby, P.B. (1979) *Quality is Free*. London: McGraw-Hill.

Davenport, T., De Long, D.W. and Beers, M.C. (1998) Successful knowledge management projects, *Sloan Management Review*, winter: 43–57.

Davenport, T.H. (1993) *Process Innovation: Reengineering Work through Information Technology*. Boston, MA: Harvard Business School Press.

Davenport, T.H. and Short, J.E. (1990) The new industrial engineering information technology and business process redesign, *Sloan Management Review*, winter: 11–27.

Dawson, P. (1994) *Organizational Change – A Processual Approach*. London: Paul Chapman.

Dawson, P. and Webb, J. (1989) New production arrangements, the totally flexible cage, *Work, Employment and Society*, 3(2): 221–38.

De Certeau, M. (1988) *The Practice of Everyday Life*. Berkeley, CA: University of California Press.

Deal, T. and Kennedy, A. (1982) *Corporate Cultures: The Rites and Rituals of Corporate Life*. Harmondsworth: Penguin.

Dean, J.W. and Bowen, D.E. (1994) Management theory and total quality: improving research and practice through theory development, *Academy of Management Review*, 19(3): 392–419.

Deetz, S. (1992) *Democracy in an Age of Corporate Colonialization*. New York: State University of New York Press.

Delbridge, R. (1995) Surviving JIT: control and resistance in Japanese transplant, *Journal of Management Studies*, 32: 803–17.

Delbridge, R., Turnbull, P. and Wilkinson, B. (1992) Pushing back the frontiers: management control and work intensification under JIT/TQM regimes, *New Technology, Work and Employment*, 7: 97–106.

Deming, W.E. (1986) *Out of the Crisis*. Cambridge, MA: MIT Centre for Advanced Engineering Study.

Derrida, J. (1982) *Margins of Philosophy*, trans. A. Bass. Chicago, IL: University of Chicago Press.

Dohse, K., Jurgens, U. and Malsch, T. (1985) From Fordism to Toyotaism? The social organisation of the labour process in the Japanese automobile industry, *Politics and Society*, 14(2): 115–46.

Douglas, J.D. (1970) *Understanding Everyday Life*. London: Routledge & Kegan Paul.

Drew, S.A.W. (1996) Accelerating change: financial industry experiences with BPR, *International Journal of Bank Marketing*, 14(6): 23–35.

Drory, A. and Romm, T. (1990) The definition of organizational politics: a review, *Human Relations*, 43(11): 1133–54.

Drucker, P. (1969) *The Age of Discontinuity: Guidelines in our Changing Society*. London: Heinemann.

Drucker, P.F. (1988) The coming of the new organization, *Harvard Business Review*, Jan–Feb: 45–53.

Drucker, P.F. (1992) The new society of organizations, *Harvard Business Review*, Sept–Oct: 95–104.

Dubin, R. (1956) Industrial workers' worlds: a study of the central life interests of industrial workers, *Social Problems*, 3: 1312.

du Gay, P. (1996). *Consumption and Identity at Work*. London: Sage.

du Gay, P. (2000) *In Praise of Bureaucracy*. London: Sage.

du Gay, P. and Salaman, G. (1992) The Cult[ure] of the customer, *Journal of Management Studies*, 29(5): 615–33.

Dunn, S. (1990) Root metaphor in the old and new industrial relations, *British Journal of Industrial Relations*, 28(1): 1–31.

Durkheim, E. ([1933] 1947) *The Division of Labour in Society*, trans. G. Simpson. Glencoe, IL: Free Press.

Economic Intelligence Unit (1996) *The Learning Organization: Managing Knowledge for Business Success*. London: EIU.

Eldridge, J.E.T. (1971) *Sociology and Industrial Life*. London: Michael Joseph.

Elger, T. and Smith, C. (2000) *Global Japanization*. London: Macmillan.

Emery, R.E. and Trist, E.K. (1960) Socio-technical systems, in C.W. Churchaman and M. Verhulst (eds) *Management Science, Models and Techniques*, Vol. 2, pp. 83–97. London: Pergamon Press.

Ezzamel, M., Willmott, M. and Worthington, F. (2001) Accounting, organizational transformation and shareholder value creation. Paper presented at Keele University.

Fairhurst, G.T. (1993) Echoes of the vision when the rest of the organization talks total quality, *Management Communication Quarterly*, 6(4): 331–71.

Fairhurst, G.T. and Wendt, R.F. (1993) The gap in total quality: a commentary, *Management Communication Quarterly*, 6(4): 441–51.

Fayol, H. ([1916] 1949) *General and Industrial Administration*, trans. C. Storrs. London: Pitman.

Fernie, S. and Metcalf, D. (1998) *(Not Hanging on the Telephone): Payment Systems in the New Sweatshops*. London: Centre for Economic Performance, LSE.

Fincham, R. (2000) Management as magic: reengineering and the search for business salvation, in D. Knights and H. Willmott (eds) *The Reengineering Revolution*. London: Sage.

Fitzgerald, F.S. ([1925] 1986) *The Great Gatsby*. New York: Macmillan.

Flanders, A. (ed.) (1969) *Collective Bargaining*. Harmondsworth: Penguin.

Foucault, M. (1977) *Discipline and Punish*. Harmondsworth: Peregrine.

Foucault, M. (1979) *The History of Sexuality*, vol. 1. Harmondsworth: Penguin.

Foucault, M. (1980) *Power/Knowledge: Selected Interviews and Other Writings 1972–1977*, ed. and trans. C. Gordon. London: Harvester Wheatsheaf.

Foucault, M. (1982) The subject and power, in H. Dreyfus and P. Rabinow (eds) *Michel Foucault: Beyond Structure and Hermeneutics*, pp. 208–26. Brighton: Harvester Press.

Foucault, M. (1984) 'What is enlightenment? in P. Rabinow (ed.) *A Foucault Reader*. Harmondsworth: Penguin.

Fox, A. and Flanders, A. (1969) The reform of collective bargaining: from Donovan to Durkheim, *British Journal of Industrial Relations*, 7: 151–80.

Freeman, C. (1982) *Economics and Industrial Innovation*. London: Frances Pinter.

Frenkel, S., Tam, M., Korczynski, M. and Shire, K. (1998) Beyond bureaucracy? Work organization in call centres, *The International Journal of Human Resource Management*, 9(6): 957–79.

Friedman, A. (1977) *Industry and Labour*. London: Macmillan.

Fuller, S. (2002) *Knowledge Management Foundations*. Boston, MA: Butterworth- Heinemann.

Garrahan, P. and Stewart, P. (1992) *The Nissan Enigma: Flexibility at Work in a Local Economy*. London: Mansell.

Goffman, E. (1959) *The Presentation of Self in Everyday Life*. New York: Doubleday Anchor.

Goffman, E. (1961) *Role-Distance*. New York: Bobbs Merrill.

Goffman, E. (1975) *Frame Analysis: An Essay of the Organization of Experience*. Harmondsworth: Penguin.

Goldthorpe, J.H., Lockwood, D., Bechhofer, F. and Platt, J. (1968) *The Affluent Worker: Industrial Attitudes and Behaviour*. Cambridge: Cambridge University Press.

Gouldner, A.W. (1954) *Wildcat Strike*. New York: Atioch Press.

Grant, R.M., Shani, R. and Krishnan, R. (1994) TQM's challenge to management theory and practice, *Sloan Management Review*, winter: 25–33.

Grey, C. (2000a) The fetish of change. Unpublished paper, Judge Institute of Management Change, University of Cambridge.

Grey, C.J. (2000b) The myth of change. Unpublished presentation, Department of Management, University of Keele, 15 March.

Grey, C. and Mitev, N. (1995) Reengineering organization: a critical appraisal, *Personnel Review*, 24(1): 6–18.

Grint, K. (1994) Reengineering history: social resonances and business process re-engineering, *Organization*, 1: 179–201.

Grint, K. and Case, P. (2000) Now where were we?': BPR lotus-eaters and corporate amnesia, in D. Knights and H. Willmott (eds) *The Reengineering Revolution*. London: Sage.

Grint, K. and Woolgar, S. (1997) *The Machine at Work; Technology, Work and Organization*. Oxford: Polity Press.

Gronroos, C. (1984) *Strategic Management and Marketing in the Service Sector.* London: Chart Bratwell.

Grover, V., Rynl Jeong, S. and Teng, J.T.C. (1998) Survey of reengineering challenges, *Information Systems Management,* spring: 53–9.

Grund, F. (1837) To Americans, business is everything, in A. Breidlid *et al.* (eds) *American Culture: An Anthology of Civilization Texts,* pp. 190–2 (1996). London: Routledge.

Guest, D. (1990) HRM and the American Dream, *Journal of Management Studies,* 27(4): 377–97.

Guest, D. (1992) Right enough to be dangerously wrong: an analysis of the in search of excellence phenomenon, in G. Salaman (ed.) *Human Resource Strategies.* London: Sage.

Hackman, J.R. and Wageman, R. (1995) TQM: empirical, conceptual and practical issues, *Administrative Science Quarterly,* June: 309–42.

Hall, G., Rosenthal, J. and Wake, J. (1993) How to make reengineering really work, *Harvard Business Review,* Nov–Dec.: 119–31.

Hall, S. (1985) Authoritarian populism: a reply, *New Left Review.* 151: 115–24.

Hammer, M. (1990) Reengineering work: don't automate, obliterate, *Harvard Business Review,* July/August: 104–12.

Hammer, M. and Champy, J. (1993) *Reengineering the Corporation: A Manifesto for Business Revolution.* London: Nicholas Brealey Publishing.

Hammer, M. and Stanton, S. (1995) *The Reengineering Revolution Handbook.* London: HarperCollins Business.

Hertzberg, F., Mausner, B. and Snyderman, B. (1959) *The Motivation to Work.* New York: John Wiley.

Hickson, D., Pugh, D.S. and Pheysey, D.C. (1969) Operations technology and organizational structure: an empirical appraisal, *Administrative Science Quarterly,* 14: 216–29.

Hofer, C.W. and Schendel, D. (1978) *Strategy Formation: Analytical Concepts,* St Paul, MN: West.

Holmberg, I. and Strannegård, L. (2002) The ideology of the 'new economy', in I. Holmberg, M. Salzer-Mörling and L. Strannegård (eds) *Stuck in the Future? Tracing the 'New Economy'.* Stockholm: Bookhouse Publishing.

Howcroft, B. (1992) Customer service in selected branches of a UK clearing bank, *The Service Industries Journal,* 2(1): 125–42.

Huczynski, A. (1993a) Explaining the succession of management fads, *International Journal of Human Resource Management,* 4(2): 443–63.

Huczynski, A. (1993b) *Management Gurus.* London: Routledge.

Huczynski, A. and Buchanan, D. (2001) *Organizational Behaviour: an Introductory Text,* 4th edn. London: *Financial Times* & Prentice Hall.

Hughes, E.C (1958) *Men and their Work.* New York: Free Press.

Hunter, L. and Beaumont, P.B. (1993) Implementing TQM: top down or bottom up?, *Industrial Relations Journal,* 24(4): 318–27.

Hutchinson, S., Purcell, J. and Kinnie, N. (2000) Evolving high commitment management and the experience of the RAC call centre, *Human Resource Management Journal,* 10(1): 63–78.

IRJ (Industrial Relations Journal) (1988) Special issue: *Japanization,* 10(1).

Ishikawa, K. (1985) *What is Total Quality Control? The Japanese Way.* London: Prentice Hall.

Jackson, B. (2001) *Management Gurus and Management Fashions.* London: Routledge.

Jackson, B.G. (1996) Re-engineering the sense of self: the management and the management guru, *Journal of Management Studies,* 33(5): 571–90.

Jacques, R. (1996) *Manufacturing the Employee: Management Knowledge from the 19th to the 21st centuries.* London: Sage.

Jacques, R.J. (2002) What is a crypto-utopia and why does it matter? in M. Parker (ed.) *Utopia and Organization.* Oxford: Blackwell.

Jermier, J.M., Knights, D. and Nord, W.R. (eds) (1994) *Resistance and Power in Organization.* London: Routledge.

Johnson, L.B. (1964) The war on poverty, in A. Breidlid *et al.* (eds) (1996) *An Anthology of Civilization Texts,* p. 223. London: Routledge.

Jessop, B., Bonnet, K., Bromley, S. and Ling, T. (1984) Authoritarian populism, two nations and Thatcherism, *New Left Review,* 147: 32–60.

Juran, J. (1988) *Juran on Planning for Quality.* Basingstoke: Macmillan.

Kamata, S. (1983) *Japan in the Passing Lane.* London: Allen & Unwin.

Kanter, R.M. (1989) The new managerial work, *Harvard Business Review,* Nov–Dec: 85–92.

Karr, A. (1849) *Les Guêpes,* quoted in R.T. Tripp (ed.) *The International Thesaurus of Quotations* (1979). Harmondsworth: Penguin.

Keiser, A. (1997) Rhetoric and myth in management fashion, *Organization,* 4(1): 49–74.

Kennedy, J.F. (1961) First inaugural address, in A. Breidlid *et al.* (eds) (1996) *An Anthology of Civilization Texts,* p. 346. London: Routledge.

Kerfoot, D., and Knights, D. (1992) Planning for personnel? HRM reconsidered, *Journal of Management Studies,* 29(5): 651–68.

Kessler, S. and Bayliss, F. (1992) *Contemporary British Industrial Relations.* London: Macmillan.

Klimoski, R. (1994) A 'total quality' special issue, *Academy of Management Review,* 19: 390–1.

Kling, R. (1992) Audiences, narratives and human values in the social studies of technology, *Science, Technology and Human Values,* 17: 349–65.

Knights, D. (2002) Reflecting on authoritative representations of reality. Paper presented at the Judge Institute of Management, University of Cambridge, 23 January.

Knights, D. and Collinson, D. (1987) Disciplining the shopfloor: a comparison of the disciplinary effects of managerial psychology and financial accounting, *Accounting, Organisations and Society,* 12(5): 457–77.

Knights, D. and McCabe, D. (1997) How would you measure something like that?: quality in a retail bank, *Journal of Management Studies,* 34(3): 371–88.

Knights, D. and McCabe, D. (1998a) The times they are a changin'?: transformative organisational innovations in UK financial services, *The International Journal of Human Resource Management,* 9(1): 168–84.

Knights, D. and McCabe, D. (1998b) What happens when the phone goes wild? BPR, stress and the worker, *Journal of Management Studies,* 35(2): 163–94.

Knights, D. and McCabe, D. (1998c) Dreams and designs on strategy: a critical analysis of TQM and management control, *Work, Employment and Society,* 12(3): 433–56.

Knights, D. and McCabe, D. (1998d) When 'life is but a dream': Obliterating politics through business re-engineering, *Human Relations,* 51(6): 761–98.

Knights, D. and McCabe, D. (1999) 'Are there no limits to authority?': TQM and organizational power, *Organization Studies,* 20(2): 197–224.

Knights, D. and McCabe, D. (2000a) Bewitched, bothered and bewildered: the meaning and experience of teamworking for employees in an automobile company, *Human Relations,* 53(11): 1481–517.

Knights, D. and McCabe, D. (2000b) A'int misbehavin'?: opportunities for resistance within bureaucratic and quality management innovations, *Sociology,* 34(3): 421–36.

Knights, D. and McCabe, D. (2001) 'A Different World': shifting masculinities in the transition to call centres, *Organization,* 8(4): 619–45.

Knights, D. and McCabe, D. (2003) Governing through teamwork: reconstituting subjectivity in a call centre, *Journal of Management Studies,* 40(6).

Knights, D. and Murray, F. (1994) *Managers Divided: Organizational Politics and IT Management.* London: Wiley.

Knights, D. and Willmott, H. (1989) Power and subjectivity at work: from degradation to subjugation in social relations, *Sociology*, 23(4): 535–58.

Knights, D. and Vurdubakis, T. (1994) Foucault, power, resistance and all that, in J.M. Jermier, D. Knights and W.R. Nord (eds), *Resistance and Power in Organizations*, pp. 167–98. London: Routledge.

Knights, D., Noble, F., Vurdubakis, T. and Willmott, H. (2002) Allegories of creative destruction: technology and organisation in narratives of the e-economy, in S. Woolgar (ed.) *Virtual Society? Technology, Cyberbole, Reality.* Oxford: Oxford University Press.

Kochan, T.A. (2002) Addressing workers' interests in corporate reform, c-m-workshop @hscmail.ac.uk, 27 July.

Kondo, D. (1990) *Crafting Selves: Power, Gender and Discourses of Identity in a Japanese Workplace.* Chicago, IL: University of Chicago Press.

Korczynski, M., Shire, K., Frenkel, S. and Tam, M. (1996) Front line work in the 'new model service firm': Australian and Japanese comparisons, *Human Resource Management Journal*, 6(2): 72–87.

Kunda, G. (1992) *Engineering Culture.* Philadelphia, PA: Temple University Press.

Landsberger, H.A. (1958) *Hawthorne Revisited.* Ithaca, NY: Cornell University Press.

LaNuez, D. and Jermier, J. (1994) Sabotage by managers and technocrats: neglected patterns of resistance at work, in J. Jermier, D. Knights and W.R. Nord (eds) *Resistance and Power in Organization.* London: Routledge.

Latour, B. (1987) *Science in Action.* Milton Keynes: Open University Press.

Lawrence, P.R. and Lorsch, J.W. (1967) *Organization and Environment.* Boston, MA: Harvard University Press.

Lawson, H. (2001) *Closure: A Story of Everything.* London: Routledge.

Leonard-Barton, D. (1995) *Wellsprings of Knowledge: Building and Sustaining the Sources of Innovation.* Boston, MA: Harvard Business School Press.

Lewis, B.R. (1989) Quality in the service sector: a review, *International Journal of Bank Marketing*, 17(5): 4–12.

Lightfoot, G. and Lilley, S. (2002) Writing Utopia, in M. Parker (ed.) *Organisational Utopias: Sociological Review Monograph.* Oxford: Blackwell.

Likert, R. (1961) *New Patterns of Management.* New York: McGraw-Hill.

Likert, R. (1967) *The Human Organization.* New York: McGraw-Hill.

Little, S., Quintas, P. and Ray, T. (eds) (2002) *Managing Knowledge: An Essential Reader.* London: Sage.

Littler, C. (1986) Taylorism, Fordism and job design, in D. Knights and D. Collinson (eds) *Job Redesign.* Aldershot: Gower.

Luckmann, T. and Berger, P. (1964) Social mobility and personal identity, *Archives of the European Journal of Sociology*, V: 331–48.

Luther King jr, M. (1963) I have a dream, in A. Breidlid *et al.* (eds) *American Culture: An Anthology of Civilization Texts*, pp. 86–7 (1996) London: Routledge.

Lyotard, J-F. (1984) *The Postmodern Condition*, Minneapolis, MN: University of Minnesota Press.

MacInnes, J. (1987) *Thatcherism at Work.* Milton Keynes: Open University Press.

MacKenzie, D. and Wajman, J. (eds) (1985) 'Introduction', in *The Social Shaping of Technology.* Milton Keynes: Open University Press.

Marchington, M. (1995) Fairy tales and magic wands: new employment practices in perspective, *Employee Relations*, 17(1): 51–66.

Marchington, M., Wilkinson, A., Ackers, P. and Goodman, J. (1993) The influence of managerial relations on waves of employee involvement, *British Journal of Industrial Relations*, 31(4): 553–76.

Marglin, S.A. (1974) What do bosses do? The origins and functions of hierarchy in capitalist production, in A. Gorz (ed.) *The Division of Labour: The Labour Process and Class Struggle in Modern Capitalism*. Brighton: Harvester Press.

Marglin, S.A. (1979) Catching flies with honey: an inquiry into management initiatives to humanize work, *Economic Analysis and Workers Management*, 13: 473–85.

Mars, G. (1982) *Cheats at Work: An Introduction of Workplace Crime*. London: Counterpoint, Unwin Books.

Martinez, L.M. and Stewart, P. (1997) The paradox of contemporary labour process theory: the rediscovery of the 'employee' and the disappearance of 'collectivism', *Capital and Class*, (62): 49–78.

Marx, K. ([1867] 1976) *Capital*, vol. 1. Harmondsworth: Penguin.

Marx, K. (1973) *Economic and Philosophical Manuscripts*. London: Lawrence & Wishart.

Maslow, A. (1954) *Motivation and Personality*. New York: Harper & Row.

May, T. (1999) From banana time to just-in-time: power and resistance at work, *Sociology*, 33(4): 767–83.

Mayo, E. (1933) *The Human Problems of an Industrial Civilization*. New York: Macmillan.

Mayo, E. (1949) *The Social Problems of an Industrial Civilization*. London: Routledge & Kegan Paul.

McArdle, L., Rowlinson, M., Proctor, S., Hassard, J. and Forrester, P. (1995) Employee empowerment or the enhancement of exploitation, in A. Wilkinson and H. Willmott (eds) *Making Quality Critical*. London: Routledge.

McCabe, D. (1996) The best laid schemes o' TQM: strategy, politics and power, *New Technology, Work and Employment*, 11(1): 28–38.

McCabe, D. (1999) TQM: anti union Trojan horse or management albatross? *Work, Employment and Society*, 13(4): 665–91.

McCabe, D. (2000) Factory innovations and management machinations: the productive and repressive relations of power, *Journal of Management Studies*, 37(7): 931–53.

McCabe, D. (2000a) 'The Team Dream: the meaning and experience of teamworking for employees in an automobile manufacturing company' In Procter, S. and Mueller, F. (eds) *Teamworking*. London: Macmillan Press.

McCabe, D. and Knights, D. (1998) Wooing factory workers through profit schemes: industrial action in an automobile manufacturing company. Paper presented at the 16th International Labour Process Conference, 7–9 April, Manchester School of Management, UMIST.

McCabe, D. and Wilkinson, A. (1998) The rise and fall of TQM: the vision, meaning and operation of change, *Industrial Relations Journal*, 29(1): 13–29.

McCabe, D. Knights, D. and Wilkinson, A. (1997) Financial services – every which way but quality? *Journal of General Management*, 22(3): 53–73.

McCabe, D., Knights, D. and Wilkinson, A. (1998a) The politics of IT-enabled restructuring and the restructuring of politics through total quality management, *Accounting, Management and Information Technology*, 8: 107–26.

McCabe, D., Knights, D., Kerfoot, D., Morgan, G. and Willmott, H. (1998b) 'Making sense of quality – towards a review and critique of quality initiatives in financial services, *Human Relations*, 51(3): 389–411.

McGregor, D. (1960) *The Human Side of Enterprise*. New York: McGraw-Hill.

McInerney, C. and LeFevre, D. (2000) Knowledge managers: history and challenges, in C. Prichard, R. Hull, M. Chumer and H. Willmott (eds) *Managing Knowledge: Critical Investigations of Work and Learning*, London: Macmillan.

McLynn, F. (2002) *Wagons West: The Epic Story of America's Overland Trails*. London: Jonathan Cape.

McNay, L. (1992) *Foucault and Feminism*. Oxford: Polity Press.

Mead, G.H. (1934) *Mind, Self and Society*. Chicago, IL: University of Chicago Press.

Micklethwait, J. and Wooldridge, A. (1996) *The Witch Doctors: Making Sense of the Management Gurus*. New York: Times Books.

Miller, E.J. and Rice, A.K. (1967) *Systems of Organization*. London: Tavistock.

Mintzberg, H. (1983) *Power in and around Organizations*. Englewood Cliffs, NJ: Prentice Hall.

Mintzberg, H. (1987) Patterns in strategy formation, *Management Science*, 24(9): 934–48.

Mintzberg, H. (1990) The design school: reconsidering the basic premises of strategic management, *Strategic Management Journal*, 11: 171–95.

Mintzberg, H. (1991) Learning 1, planning 0: reply to Igor Ansoff, *Strategic Management Journal*, 12: 463–6.

Mintzberg, H. (1994) *The Rise and Fall of Strategic Planning*. New York: Prentice Hall.

Mintzberg, H. and Waters, A. (1985) Of strategies, deliberate and emergent, *Strategic Management Journal*, 26: 257–72.

Mokhiber, R. and Weissman, R. (2002) Cracking down on corporate crime, really, corp-focus@lists.essential.org.

Moore, W. (1969) Climbers, riders, treaders, in B. Rosen, H. Crockett and C. Nunn (eds) *Achievement in American Society*. Cambridge, MA: Schenkmann Publishing.

Mouzelis, N. (1995) *Sociological Theory: What went wrong?* London: Routledge.

Munro, R. (1998) Belonging on the move: market rhetoric and the future as obligatory passage, *Sociological Review*, 46(2): 208–24.

Munslow, A. (1996) Imaging the nation: the frontier thesis and the creating of America, in P.J. Davis (ed.) *Representing and Imagining America*. Keele: Keele University Press.

Myers, C.S. (1924) *Industrial Psychology in Great Britain*. London: Cape.

Newell, S., Scarbrough, H., Swan, J. and Hislop, D. (2000) Intranets and knowledge management: de-centred technologies and the limits of technological discourse, in C. Prichard, R. Hull, M. Chumer and H. Willmott (eds) *Managing Knowledge: Critical Investigations of Work and Learning*, London: Macmillan.

Newell, S., Robertson, M. and Swan, J. (2001) Special issue on management fads and fashions, *Organization*, 8(1): 1–144.

Newton, T. (1998) Theorizing subjectivity in organizations: the failure of Foucauldian studies, *Organization Studies*, 19(3): 415–47.

Noble, F., Knights, D., Willmott, H. and Vurdubakis, T. (2000) Faceless finance – the unkindest cut, *Consumer Policy Review: Journal of the Consumers' Association*, 10(3) May/June, 92–9.

Nonaka, I. (1991) The knowledge-creating company, *Harvard Business Review*, Nov–Dec: 96–104.

Nonaka, I. and Takeuchi, H. (1995) *The Knowledge Creating Company*. Oxford: Oxford University Press.

Oliver, N. and Wilkinson, B. (1988) *The Japanization of British Industry*. Oxford: Blackwell.

Palm, G. (1970) *The Flight from Work*. Cambridge: Cambridge University Press.

Parker, M. (ed.) (2002) *Utopia and Organisation*. London: Sage.

Parker, M. and Slaughter, J. (1988) *Choosing Sides: Unions and the Team Concept*. Boston, MA: South End Press.

Parker, M. and Slaughter, J. (1993) Should the labour movement buy TQM? *Journal of Organizational Change Management*, 6(4): 43–56.

Parrington, V.L. jnr ([1947] 1964) *American Dreams: A Study of American Utopias*. New York: Russell & Russell Inc.

Parsons, T. (1951) *The Social System*. London: Tavistock.

Peters, T. (1987) *Thriving on Chaos: Handbook for a Management Revolution*. New York: Knopf.

Peters, T. (1992) *Liberation Management*. New York: Knopf.

Peters, T. and Waterman, R. (1995) *In Search of Excellence*, 2nd edn. London: HarperCollins Business.

Pettigrew, A. (1973) *The Politics of Organisational Decision Making*, London: Tavistock.

Pettigrew, A. (1979) On studying organisational cultures, *Administrative Science Quarterly*, 24: 570–81.

Pettigrew, A. (1985) *The Awakening Giant*. Oxford: Blackwell.

Pfeffer, J. (1981) *Power in Organisations*. London: HarperCollins.

Pine II, B.J., Victor, B. and Boynton, C. (1993) Making mass customization work, *Harvard Business Review*, Sept–Oct: 108–19.

Piore, M.J. and Sabel, C.F. (1984) *The Second Industrial Divide: Possibilities for Prosperity*, New York: Basic Books.

Polanyi, M. (1958) *Personal Knowledge*. Chicago, IL: Chicago University Press.

Polanyi, M. (1962) *Personal Knowledge: Towards a Post-critical Philosophy*. London: Routledge & Kegan Paul.

Polanyi, M. (1966) *The Tacit Dimension*. London: Routledge & Kegan Paul.

Pollert, A. (1996) 'Teamwork' on the assembly line: contradiction and the dynamics of union resilience, in P. Ackers, C. Smith and P. Smith (eds) *The New Workplace and Trade Unionism*. London: Routledge.

Porter, M. (1980) *Competitive Strategy*. New York: Free Press.

Porter, M. (1985) *Competitive Advantage*. London: Collier Macmillan.

Procter, S. and Mueller, F. (2000) *Teamworking*. London: Macmillan.

Pugh, D.S. and Hickson, D.J. (1976) *Organizational Structure and its Context*. London: Saxon House.

Putnam, R.D. (1995) Bowling alone: America's declining capital, *Journal of Democracy*, 6: 65–78.

Putnam, R.D. (2000) *Bowling Alone: The Collapse and Revival of American Community*. New York: Simon & Schuster.

Quintas, P. (2002) Managing knowledge in a new century, in S. Little, P. Quintas and T. Ray (eds) *Managing Knowledge: An Essential Reader*. London: Sage.

Ramsey, H. (1977) Cycles of control: worker participation in sociological and historical perspective, *Sociology*, 11(3): 481–506.

Ramsey, H. (1985) What is participation for? A critical evaluation of 'labour process' analysis of job reform, in D. Knights and D. Collinson (eds) *Job Redesign*. London: Routledge.

Ray, A. (1985) Corporate culture: the last frontier of control? *Journal of Management Studies*, 23(3): 287–97.

Reich, R.B (1983) *The Next American Frontier*. New York: Penguin.

Reich, R.B. (1987) Entrepreneurship reconsidered: the team as hero, *Harvard Business Review*, May–June: 77–83.

Roethlisberger, F.J. and Dickson, W.J. (1939) *Management and the Worker*. Cambridge, MA: Harvard University Press.

Rogers, E.M. (1962) *Diffusion of Innovations*. New York: Free Press.

Rogers, E.M. (1995) *Diffusion of Innovations* (4th edn). New York: Free Press.

Rogers, E.M. and Shoemaker, F.F. (1971) *Communication of Innovations*. New York: Free Press.

Rose, M. (1975) *Industrial Behaviour: Theoretical Developments Since Taylor*. Harmondsworth: Penguin.

Rose, N. and Miller, P. (1992) Political power beyond the state: problematics of government, *British Journal of Sociology*, 43(2): 173–205.

Roy, D. (1952) Quota restriction and goldbricking in a machine shop, *American Journal of Sociology*, 57: 427–42.

Runciman, W.G. (1966) *Relative Deprivation and Social Justice*. London: Routledge.

Sayer, A. (1986) New developments in manufacturing: the JIT system, *Capital and Class*, 40–73.

Sayles, L.R. (1958) *Behaviour of Industrial Work Groups*. New York: Wiley.

Scarborough, H. and Corbett, J.M. (1992) *Technology and Organization: Power, Meaning and Design*. London: Routledge.

Scher, M. (1997) *Japanese Interfirm Networks and their Main Banks*. New York: St Martin's Press.

Scott, I. (1996) Mr Innocence goes to Washington: Hollywood and the mythology of American politics, in P.J. David (ed.) *Representing and Imagining America*. Keele: Keele University Press.

Senge, P. (1990) *The Fifth Discipline: The Art of Practice of the Learning Organization*. New York: Doubleday.

Sennett, R. and Cobb, J. (1977) *The Hidden Injuries of Class*. Cambridge: Cambridge University Press.

Sewell, G. (1998) The discipline of teams: the control of team-based industrial work through electronic and peer surveillance, *Administrative Science Quarterly*, 43: 397–427.

Sewell, G. and Wilkinson, B. (1992) Someone to watch over me: surveillance, discipline and the JIT labour process, *Sociology*, 26(2): 271–89.

Silverman, D. (1970) *The Theory of Organizations*. London: Heinemann.

Silverman, D. (1986) *Qualitative Methodology and Sociology: Describing the Social World*. Aldershot: Gower.

Silverman, D. (1993) *Interpreting Qualitative Data Methods for Analysing Talk, Text and Interaction*. London: Sage.

Skeldon, P. and Johnson, T. (1998) *Call Centre Recruitment and Training*. London: FT Finance.

Skinner, B.F. (1953) *Science and Human Behaviour*. New York: Macmillan.

Smart, B. (1983) *Foucault, Marxism and Critique*. London: Routledge & Kegan Paul.

Smircich, L. (1983) Concept of culture and organizational analysis, *Administrative Science Quarterly*, 28: 339–58.

Smith, A. ([1776] 1970) *The Wealth of Nations*. Harmondsworth: Penguin.

Spencer, B.A. (1994) Models of organization and total quality management: a comparison and critical evaluation, *Academy of Management Review*, 19(3): 446–71.

Steingard, D.S. and Fitzgibbons, D.E. (1993) A postmodern deconstruction of total quality management (TQM), *Journal of Organizational Change Management*, 6(5): 27–42.

Stewart, P. and Garrahan, P. (1995) 'Employee responses to new management techniques in the auto industry, *Work, Employment and Society*, 9(3): 517–36.

Stewart, T.A. (1993) Reengineering: the hot new managing tool, *Fortune*, 128(4): 32–7.

Sturdy, A. (1992) Clerical consent: shifting work in the insurance office, in A. Sturdy, D. Knights and H. Willmott (eds), *Skill and Consent*. London: Routledge.

Sturdy, A. (1997) The consultancy process – an insecure business? *Journal of Management Studies*, 34(3): 389–413.

Taylor, F.W. (1911) *The Principles of Scientific Management*. New York: Harper.

Taylor, P. and Bain, P. (1999) An assembly line in the head: work and employee relations in the call centre, *Industrial Relations Journal*, 30(2): 101–17.

Terry, M. (1983) Shop steward development and management strategies, in G.S. Bain (ed.) *Industrial Relations in Britain*. London: Blackwell.

Thomas, W.I. (1971) The definition of the situation, in L.A. Coser and B. Rosenberg (eds) *Sociological Theory*, 3rd edn, New York: Macmillan.

Thompson, P. (1990) Crawling from the wreckage: the labour process and the politics of production, in D. Knights and H. Willmott (eds) *Labour Process Theory*. London: Macmillan.

Thompson, P. and Ackroyd, S. (1995) All quiet on the workplace front? A critique of recent trends in British industrial sociology, *Sociology*, 29(4): 615–33.

Thompson, P. and Wallace, T. (1996) Redesigning production through teamworking case studies from the Volvo Truck Corporation, *International Journal of Operations and Production Management*, 16(2): 103–18.

Thompson, P. and Warhurst, C. (eds) (1998) *Workplaces of the Future*. London: Macmillan.

Tidd, J., Bessant, J. and Pavitt, K. (1997) *Managing Innovation: Integrating Technological Market and Organizational Change*. London: Wiley.

Tilston, D. (1989) *Making Progress in Quality in Financial Services: European Retail Finance for the 1990s – Special Report No. 1199*, London: PA Consulting Group, The Economist Publications.

Toffler, A. (1981) *The Third Wave*, London: Pan.

Trist, E.L. and Bamforth, K.W. (1951) Some social psychological consequences of the longwall method of coal getting, *Human Relations*, 4(1): 3–38.

Trist, E.L., Higgin, G.W., Murray, H. and Pollock, A.B. (1963) *Organizational Choice*. London: Tavistock.

Tuckman, A. (1994) The Yellow Brick Road: total quality management and the restructuring of organizational culture, *Organization Studies*, 15(5): 727–51.

Tuckman, A. (1995) Ideology, quality and TQM, in A. Wilkinson and H.C. Willmott (eds) *Making Quality Critical*. London: Routledge.

Turkel, S. (1974) Interview with a steel mill worker, in A. Breidlid *et al.* (eds) *American Culture: An Anthology of Civilization Texts*, pp. 221–3. London: Routledge, 1996.

Turkel, S. (1980) Interview with a corporate executive, in A. Breidlid *et al.* (eds) *American Culture: An Anthology of Civilization Texts*, p. 379. London: Routledge, 1996.

Turnbull, C. (1984) *The IK*. Harmondsworth: Penguin.

Turner, F.J. (1893) The significance of the frontier in American history, in A. Breidlid *et al.* (eds) *American Culture: An Anthology of Civilization Texts*, p. 377. London; Routledge, 1996.

Turner, H.A. (1969) *Is Britain Really Strike Prone?* Cambridge: Cambridge University Press.

Van Maanen, J. (1979) Reclaiming qualitative methods for organizational research: a preface, *Administrative Science Quarterly*, 24: 520–6.

Vogel, E.F. (1979) *Japan as Number One: Lessons for America*. London: Harvard University Press.

Von Krogh, G., Ichijo, K. and Nonaka, I. (2000) *Enabling Knowledge Creation: How to Unlock the Mystery of Tacit Knowledge and Release the Power of Innovation*. Oxford: Oxford University Press.

Vroom, V.H. (1964) *Work and Motivation*, New York: Wiley.

Walker, C.R and Guest, R.H. (1952) *The Man on the Assembly Line*. Cambridge, MA: Harvard University Press.

Watson, T.J. (1980) *Sociology, Work and Industry*. London: Routledge & Kegan Paul.

Watson, T.J. (1994) *In Search of Management*. London: Routledge.

Webb, J. and Cleary, D. (1994) *Organisational Change and the Management of Expertise*. London: Routledge.

Weber, M. (1947) *The Theory of Social and Economic Organization*, trans. A. Henderson and T. Parsons, Glencoe, IL: Free Press.

Weber, M. (1978) *Economy and Society*, trans G. Roth and C. Wittich (2 vols). Berkeley, CA: University of California Press.

Wendt, R.F. (1994) Learning to 'Walk the Talk': a critical tale of the micropolitics at a total quality university, *Management Communication Quarterly*, 8(1): 5–45.

Which? The Independent Consumer Guide (1993) Can you bank on your account? December: 8–13.

Which? The Independent Consumer Guide (1994) Don't bank on a good service, December: 14–17.

Whitehead, T.N. (1936) *Leadership in Free Society*. Cambridge, MA: Harvard University Press.

Wickens, P. (1992) Lean production and beyond: the system, its critics and the future, *Human Resource Management Journal*, 4(3): 1–21.

Wilkinson, A. and Willmott, H.C. (eds) (1995) *Making Quality Critical*. London: Routledge.

Wilkinson, A., Allen, P. and Snape, E. (1991) TQM and the management of labour, *Employee Relations*, 13(1): 24–31.

Wilkinson, A., Marchington, M., Goodman, J. and Ackers, P. (1992) TQM and employee involvement, *Human Resource Management*, 2(4): 1–20.

Willis, P.E. (1977) *Learning to Labour*. London: Saxon House.

Willmott, H. (1993) Strength is ignorance: slavery is freedom: managing culture in modern organizations, *Journal of Management Studies*, 30(4): 515–53.

Willmott, H. (1994) Business process reengineering and human resource management, *Personnel Review*, 23(3): 34–46.

Willmott, H. (1995a) The odd couple? Re-engineering business processes, managing human resources, *New Technology, Work and Employment*, 10(2): 89–98.

Willmott, H. (1995b) Will the turkeys vote for Christmas? The re-engineering of human resources, in G. Burke and J. Peppard (eds) *Examining BPR: Current Perspectives and Research Directions*. London: Kogan Page.

Wilson, P. (2000) *Managing for Knowledge, Dossier 05*. Margate: Scitech Educational.

Womack, J., Jones, D. and Roos, D. (1990) *The Machine that Changed the World*. London: Macmillan.

Woodward, J. (1958) *Management and Technology*. London: HMSO.

Woodward, J. (1965) *Industrial Organization*. Oxford: Oxford University Press.

Woodward, J. (ed.) (1970) *Industrial Organization: Behaviour and Control*. Oxford: Oxford University Press.

Wrong, D. (1970) *From Max Weber: An Intellectual Approach*. New York: Wiley.

Zairi, M., Letza, S.R. and Oakland, J.S. (1993) *Does TQM Impact on Bottom Line Results?* Bradford: University of Bradford Management Centre.

Zeithaml, V.A., Parasuraman, A. and Berry, L.L. (1990) *Delivering Quality Service: Balancing Customer Perceptions and Expectations*. New York: The Free Press.

Zinn, H. (2002) A History of the United States (Session IV, optional reading 2). www.wilpf.org/corp/VI/VI-option1.pdf.

Index

Abrahamson, E., 2, 10, 40
accessibility, 148
accountability, 122
advertising, 11
agency, 173–4, 186
Alger, H., 30, 32
Allee, V., 146
American Dream, 1, 2, 4, 36, 83, 161,
    167–77
  flawed nature of, 28, 177
  frontier thesis, 31, 34, 167–8
  and inequality, 28, 31–2, 170–3
  innocence theory, 165–7
  and management guru literature, 29–33,
    34–6, 38–9
  success ethic, 9, 38
  teamworking and, 121–3
  unitary future, 168–9
Anderson, J.C., 50
Ansoff, H., 102
anti-discrimination laws, 63
Armstrong, P., 46
assembly-line production, 15
assignment work, 66
authoritarian control, 14
auto-component manufacturer case study,
    53–7, 171–2
auto industry, 120–3, 182
  Intermotors case study, 5, 124–39,
    139–42, 169, 171, 175–7
automatic call distribution (ACD), 80

autonomy, 5, 77–96
  call centre work, 79–81
  constituting the autonomous self, 83–6
  job insecurity and, 93–4, 95
  Loanco case study, 5, 81–96, 171, 172
  manufacturing, 86–90
  restricting, 90–2

backlogs, 66, 182
Bain, P., 72
Bamforth, K.W., 119
bank wiring room experiments *see*
    Hawthorne studies
banks, 103–4
  case studies, 105–10
Barclays Bank, 104
Barings Bank, 102
Barker, J.R., 91
Barley, S., 10, 19
Batt, R., 92
Bensman, J., 72
behaviourism, 58
Bellamy, E., *Looking Backwards*, 170–2,
    177
benefits and costs *see* cost/benefit analysis
Berger, P., 27, 146
Berggren, C., 118, 121
best practice, 41
Blair, H., 96
Blair, T., 168
Boje, D.M., 52

bonus payments, 123–4, 124, 131–4, 136–7, 138
boredom, 16–17
Boudon, R., 50, 102
BPR *see* re-engineering
Braverman, H., 52, 63
breadmaking, 148–9
Brooking, A., 146
Brown, J.S., 146, 154
Buchanan, D., 119
building societies, 4, 23–4, 24–5, 102, 182
  case study *see* Loanco case study
Bukowitz, W.R., 146
Burawoy, M., 52, 90, 91
bureaucracy, 43–5
Burrell, G., 17, 116
business performance reward scheme (BPRS), 131–4
  see also bonus payments
business schools, 28
business process re-engineering (BPR) *see* re-engineering

call centres, 4, 79–81
  building society case study, 4, 81–96, 169, 171
Calvinism, 29
capitalism, 11–12, 47
  autonomy and, 90–1, 95–6
  global, 47
Carco case study, 53–7, 171–2
Carey, A., 16
Carey, J., 29
Carnegie, A., 30, 176–7, 180
Case, P., 10
causal analysis, 141
celebrity, cult of, 9, 28
Champy, J., 30, 32, 35, 37, 38, 47, 50, 77, 81, 82, 104, 108, 110, 166–7
change
  gurus, change and remaining the same, 43–8
  unprecedented, 47, 98
checking, 91–2
child labour, 48
choice, 89–90
Chumer, M., 143
Clark, T., 38
Clegg, S.R., 14
Clifford, J., 81

Clinton administration, 30
closures
  bank branches, 103–4
  call centre, 92, 96
Cobb, J., 31, 169
collaboration, 12
collective bargaining, 13, 20–2
collectivism, 12–13
  American Dream and, 124
  postwar, 21, 22
  spontaneous and wildcat strike, 134–5, 138–9
  unintended consequence of Thatcherism, 25–6
commitment, 130
communication, 83–4
  conflict as failure of, 135
  functionalism, 59
  and job insecurity, 95, 176
competition, 12, 177
  masculine discourses and, 35–6
  Thatcherism, 24–5
compliance, 140
computerized work tracking systems, 70–1
consent, 91–2
constructionism, social, 147
constructivists, 185
consultation, 83–4, 85
consumption, 11
contingency theory, 116–17, 183
control
  authoritarian, 14
  and autonomy, 80, 90–1, 92–3
  critical, 52–4, 56, 57, 60
  knowledge management and, 161
  normative, 78, 118, 121
  tightening through technology, 69–70
Cooper, R., 159
core workers, 154
corporate strategy, 130
cost/benefit analysis, 145, 158–9
  unnecessary and important issues, 160, 185
costs, 11
  cost savings, 46, 92–3
Crainer, S., 36
creativity, 99–100
credit, 11, 179
Cressey, P., 23, 90
critical control, 52–3, 57, 58, 60

Crosby, P.B., 39, 41, 105
cult of celebrity, 9, 28
culture change, 5, 12, 77–96, 129
    call centre work, 79–81
    knowledge management and, 155–8
    Loanco case study, 5, 81–96, 168, 170

Davenport, T., 77, 83, 145
Dawson, P., 58
De Certeau, M., 43
Deal, T., 77
Declaration of Independence, 27
delayering, 128–9
Delbridge, R., 42, 51, 72
Deming, W.E., 32, 40, 47, 50, 107, 121, 181
Denton, D., 29
deregulation, economic, 22–3, 24–5
Derrida, J., 147
design, 98–9, 113
    strategic planning and innovation,
      99–103
Design School, 101–2
determinism, 140–1
Dickson, W.J., 17, 145
diffusion, 40
direct savings service, 81–96
disciplinary power, 24
discipline, 141–2
discourse, 44
Donovan Commission, 21
Douglas, J.D., 146
dreams, 1–2, 165–77
    American Dream *see* American Dream
    blindness between different dreams,
      175–6
    innocence theory, 165–7
Drew, S.A.W., 95
Drucker, P.F., 5, 146
du Gay, P., 22, 24, 71, 78, 85
Dunn, S., 29
Durkheim, E., 31

E&M Insurance case study, 105, 110–13
E.T., 165
economic deregulation, 22–3, 24–5
Economic Intelligence Unit, 143
electronic media, 145–6
e-mail system, 153–4
emergent strategies, 99–100, 101, 108, 116
Emery, R.E., 117

empiricism, 117, 184
employee involvement, 52–3, 55, 91
empowerment, 87–8, 96
    management discourses, 77–8
    rational managerialism, 51–2
    see also autonomy; power
Enron, 12
enterprise culture, 4, 22, 24
entrepreneurs, 2
environment, 100–1
equal opportunities legislation, 63
equality, 54–5, 177–8
    see also inequality
error rates, 66, 70
examination, 130
excellence, 36
excess capacity, 11
expectancy theory, 116
explicit knowledge, 146, 147–9, 161
Ezzamel, E., 47

Fairhurst, G.T., 58
false consciousness, 173, 185
Fernie, S., 79
Field of Dreams, 166
films, 166–7
financial scandals, 12, 178
financial services, 79–80, 103, 104–6
    banks, 105, 106, 107–8
    building societies *see* building societies
    case studies, 105–14
    insurance companies *see* insurance
      companies
Fitzgerald, F.S., *The Great Gatsby*, 27, 33–9
Fitzgibbons, D.E., 51
Flanders, A., 42
flexibility, 36, 112
Follett, D.P., 181
Ford, 120
Fordism, 14
Foucault, M., 24, 43, 49, 61, 73, 94, 115, 129,
    130, 131, 138, 139, 140, 141, 142, 150,
    173–4
Fox, A., 43
freedom, 80–1
Freeman, C., 40
Frenkel, S., 94
Friedman, A., 87, 129
frontier thesis, 31, 35, 167–8
Fuller, S., 148

functional structure, 14, 113–14, 116
functionalism, 59
functionalist sociology, 153

Garrahan, P., 121, 122, 123
General Motors, 120
Gerver, I., 71
global social movements, 64, 73
goals, key, 129–30
Goffman, E., 2, 78, 174
Gouldner, A.W., 135
governance, 122
Great Gatsby, The (Fitzgerald), 27, 33–9
Grey, C., 47, 78, 98
Grint, K., 10, 79, 151, 158
Grover, V., 96
growth, efficiency and managing
    effectiveness (GEM), 150
Grund, F., 169, 171
Guest, D., 30, 34, 38, 168
guns and roses argument, 158, 185
gurus, 1–2, 165–77
    change and remaining the same, 43–8
    literature and American Dream, 30–4,
        35–40, 41–8
Gypsum, 135

Hackman, J.R., 46
Hall, S., 22
Hammer, M., 29, 30, 33, 35, 37, 38, 40,
    41, 47, 77, 82, 83, 104, 108, 111,
    166–7
hand-offs, 82, 182
Hawthorne studies, 14–15, 16–17, 18–19,
    116, 119, 145
Heath, E., 20
hero, 37–8
Hertzberg, F., 17, 18, 119
Hickson, D., 120
historical perspective, 4, 9–26
    human relations, 10, 12, 17–18, 18–20
    neo-human relations, 12, 17–19, 20
    post-war consensus, 12, 19–22
    scientific management, 12, 12–15,
        18–19
    Thatcherism, 12, 22–5, 25–6
Holmberg, I., 1, 2
Honma, H., 161
Howcroft, B., 98
Huczynski, A., 36, 46, 47, 122

human relations, 10, 12, 15–17, 18,
    18–20
    and teamworking, 119, 120–1, 122
humanistic values, 35, 181
Hutchinson, S., 92

identity, 56–8, 63
    see also self; subjectivity
implementation, 1, 93–4, 113–14
incentives, economic, 14
Inco insurance case study, 64–73
income restraint, 21
individualism, 4, 15–16, 124–5, 172
    frontier thesis, 167–8
    neo-human relations, 17–18, 20
    Thatcherism, 24, 25
individualization, 10, 12
    autonomy and, 90–1
    Intermotors case study, 131–2
    scientific management, 14, 15
industrial action, 19
    Intermotors case study, 124, 134–9, 140,
        141, 142
    1970s, 20, 21
Industrial Relations Act 1971, 20
inequality, 169–73, 176–8
    American Dream, 28, 31–2, 170–3
    labour process theory, 43–4
    processual approach, 58–9
inflation, 21
informal norms, 78, 120, 122
information, 146
information technology (IT)
    IT-based work tracking system, 69–71
    knowledge management and, 146–7, 151,
        153–60, 161–2, 163
    Loanco case study, 149, 150–7, 158–9,
        160
    system review for insurance company,
        111–14
innocence theory, 165–6
innovation, meaning of, 39–43
insecurity, 88–9, 91, 98, 176–7
instrumentalism, 14–15
insurance companies, 104
    E&M case study, 105, 110–13
    Inco case study, 64–71, 71–3
interactionism, symbolic, 58–9
inter-branch league tables, 106
interests, true, 173–4

Intermotors case study, 4, 124–39,
    139–42, 169, 171, 174–6
International Monetary Fund (IMF),
    21
internet, 157
intranet, 152–4, 159–60
involvement, employee, 54–7, 58, 92
Ishikawa, K., 38, 50
IT *see* information technology

Jackson, B., 47
Jacques, R., 9, 29, 30, 31, 32, 38, 46
Japan, 123
Japanese management, 4, 23, 121–2
Japanization of British industry, 23
Jermier, J.M., 52
Jessop, B., 22
JIT (just in time), 23, 54, 55
job insecurity, 93–4, 96, 102, 175–6
job performance, 18
job satisfaction, 17, 18, 116
Johnson, L.B., 170
Johnson, T., 79
Joint Stock Company Act 1844, 46
just in time (JIT), 23, 54, 55

Kanter, R.M., 32, 37, 38, 39, 181
Kao Corporation, 161
Karr, A., 46, 47
Kennedy, A., 77
Kennedy, J.F., 29, 172
Kerfoot, D., 103
key goals, 129
Klimoski, R., 49
Kling, R., 158
Knights, D., 35, 40, 63, 64, 71, 73, 102,
    103, 117, 140, 151, 157, 173
knowledge
    explicit, 145, 145–8, 160
    power/knowledge and subjectivity,
        61–4, 173–4
    tacit, 145, 146, 147–9, 160–1
    teamworking and, 117–24, 139
knowledge hierarchy, 148
knowledge management (KM), 4,
    143–61
    Loanco case study, 5, 149–58, 159–60,
        161, 172
    in perspective, 145–9
knowledge sharing, 161

knowledge workers, 153
Kondratieff cycles, 9, 178
Kunda, G., 10, 19, 78

Labour governments
    New Labour, 25
    1970s, 22
labour markets, tight, 20
labour process theory, 42–3, 54, 65
    teamworking, 125, 129–30
Landsberger, H.A., 16
language, 46–7
Latour, B., 174
Lawrence, P.R., 17
Lawson, H., 147
leadership, 37–9
league tables, 106
lean production, 120, 122
    critics of, 121, 122
Leeson, N., 102
LeFevre, D., 146, 150
Lefevre, M., 169
Leonard-Barton, D., 143
Lewis, B.R., 104
Likert, R., 116
Little, S., 143
Lloyds TSB, 104
Loanco case study
    knowledge management, 5, 149–58, 159,
        160, 172
    re-engineering of call centre, 5, 79–96,
        169, 171
longwall production methods study,
    119–20
Looking Backwards (Bellamy), 170–2, 177
Lorsch, J.W., 17
L-shaped layout, 55
Luckmann, T., 27, 146
Luther King, M., 170
Lyotard, J.-F., 144

MacInnes, J., 23, 88
management style, 78–82, 86
managerialism, 120, 121, 124–5, 126–7
    rational managerialism, 50–1, 58, 62
Mandela, N., 62
manufacturing, 23, 24
    Carco case study, 53–7, 170–1
    Intermotors case study, 5, 124–39,
        139–42, 169, 171, 175–6

Marchington, M., 45, 46
Mars, G., 72
Marshall, A., 145
Marx, K., 47, 50
Marxism, 42
masculinity, 35
Maslow, A.H., 18
mass customization, 39
May, T., 44
Mayo, E., 11, 16
McCabe, D., 23, 32, 35, 40, 60, 61, 62, 63,
    71, 73, 95, 102, 117, 151, 157, 171,
    173
McGregor, D., 14
McInerney, C., 146, 150
McLynn, F., 31
Mead, G.H., 57
mechanistic stance, 40
Medbank case study, 108–10
mergers, 103, 183
Metcalf, D., 80
Micklethwait, J., 46
middle managers, 134–5, 136, 137–8
Miller, P., 25
miners' strike, 20
mining, study of, 119–20
Mintzberg, H., 57, 98, 99, 112, 113
Mitev, N., 78
monetarism, 22
Moore, W., 34
morality, 37–8
Morgan, G., 17, 116
motivation, 116
    theory, 13, 18–20
Mr Smith Goes to Washington, 165
Mulholland Drive, 9
Munslow, A., 167
mutual status, 156, 157–8

NatWest Bank, 103
needs, 17–18
neo-human relations, 13, 17–19, 20
neo-liberal economics, 22–3, 168
    see also Thatcherism
neurotic incompetence, 88
New Deal, 29
New Labour, 25
new labour agreement (NLA), 125
New Right, 23, 168
Newell, S., 40–1

Nonaka, I., 146, 147–8, 149, 160–1
normative control, 78, 119, 121

oil price shock, 21
oligopolies, 19
Oliver, N., 120
one-team information services (OTIS),
    151–6, 157–8
    post-pilot scheme review, 155–7
    shelved, 158
'one team' vision and strategy, 149–51,
    156–7
open management style, 83–6, 88–9
opportunity society, 168
Organization of Petroleum Exporting
    Countries (OPEC), 21
organizational politics (OP), 42
organizational structure, 14, 110–11, 112
output restriction, 15
ownership, property, 63

Parker, M., 51
Parrington, V.L., 29, 31, 34, 35
peer pressure, 119
pension products, 112
performance
    guru interventions and corporate
        performance, 45
    job performance, 18
performativity, 144, 156–8
Peters, T., 32, 35, 36, 38, 39, 40, 41, 45, 48, 78,
    114, 121, 166
Pettigrew, A., 58
piece-work, 14
Pine, B.J., 35, 37, 38
Piore, M.J., 23
plan, do and review (PDR) meetings,
    126
pluralism, 43, 140
Polanyi, M., 145, 146, 149
politically charged organizations, 114
positivism, 147
post-war consensus, 13, 19–22
poverty, 31
power, 24, 44
    call centres, 79, 80–1
    fragility of management power, 56,
        139–40
    power/knowledge and subjectivity,
        61–4, 176–9

processual approach, 60
resistance and, 140–2
teamworking, 116–24, 140
wildcat strike, 134–6, 137
see also empowerment
prescription, 40, 41
price of non-conformance (PONC), 40
privatization, 23
problem solving, 126
process-based structure, 110–11, 112
processes, new and simplified, 82–3
processual approach, 57–60, 60
production, 11
production flow, 54
productivity
post-war industrial conflict, 20
scientific management, 13–14, 15–16
tightening control through IT and,
69–70
productivity measures, 109–10
professional managers, 46
profitability, 45
bonus payments scheme linked to,
131–2
financial services restructuring,
103–4
progression, 9
property ownership, 62–3
Pugh, D.S., 117
Putnam, R.D., 31

Qualbank case study, 105–7
quality, 35, 37
quality circles, 121
quality management, 4, 49–50
Intermotors case study, 124
TQM *see* total quality management
quality meetings, 104–5, 106
Quintas, P., 143, 145

'rags to riches', 30
Ramsey, H., 20, 42
rational managerialism, 50–1, 56, 60
rational/technical approaches, 40
rationality, 100–1, 147
Reagan, R., 23, 168
Reaganism, 29
realists, 185
recession, global, 124–5
redundancies, 193–4, 95, 103–4, 175–6

re-engineering, 5, 10, 77–96
failures, 38
financial services, 108, 110–11, 112
Loanco case study, 5, 81–96, 169, 171
masculinity and, 35
unintended outcomes, 100, 108, 110–11,
112, 113–14
regulation
economic deregulation, 22–3, 24
financial services, 103–4
Reich, R.B., 31, 123
relational approach, 63
research framework, 4, 49–73
alternative perspective, 60–3
Carco case study, 53–7
critical control, 51–3, 57, 58, 61
Inco case study, 64–71, 71–3
processual approach, 57–61, 61
rational managerialism, 50–1, 57, 61
resistance, 10, 16–17
autonomy and, 89–90, 97
escaping into work, 61
Inco case study, 65, 68–9, 70
individual strategies, 61, 65, 68–9, 70,
72–3
Intermotors case study, 124–39
relational approach, 63
subversive forms, 61
teamworking and, 5, 115–42
responses to change, 128
restrictions on autonomy, 90–4
restructuring, 131
financial services, 104–5
revolution, 47
rewards, 131
roadshows, 83
Rockefeller, J.D., 30, 180
Roethlisberger, F.J., 17, 145
Rogers, E.M., 40
Rose, M., 13, 14, 16, 18
Rose, N., 25
rules, 32
Runciman, W.G., 31

Sabel, C.F., 23
Salaman, G., 24, 25, 37, 38, 68, 77
salvation, need for, 166
Scher, M., 123
scientific management, 13, 13–15, 18–19,
147

Scott, I., 166
Scott, P., 23
self, 64
    constituting the autonomous self, 83–6
    symbolic interactionist concept of, 58
    see also identity; subjectivity
self-interest, 14, 23, 31–2
    see also individualism
self-regulated time pressures, 65–6
Senge, P., 38
Sennett, R., 31, 169
sequence, historical, 9
service quality, 103, 114
    autonomy and, 90–1
    productivity measures and, 110–11
    restructuring of financial services,
        104–5
Sewell, G., 157
share prices, 12
shifting work, 63
Shoemaker, F.F., 40
short-termism, 11
Silverman, D., 14, 105
Skeldon, P., 78
skill demarcations, 125
Skinner, B.F., 58
Slabough, J., 166
Slaughter, J., 51–2
slavery, 63
Smart, B., 44
Smircich, L., 105
social, the, vs the technological, 158
social capital, 31
social constructionism, 147
social contract, 21
social movements, 64, 73–4
social problems, 167–8
social relations, meaning in, 17
social solidarity, 172–3, 176–7
sociotechnical systems approach, 119,
        120–1, 122–3
solidarity, social, 172–3, 176–7
Spartacus, 63
Spencer, B.A., 50
spirituality, 44–5
spontaneous collective action, 135–6,
        140–1
standards, quality, 70–2
Stanton, S., 29, 35, 37, 39
Star Wars, 168

state, under Thatcherism, 23
Steingard, D.S., 50
Stewart, P., 121, 124, 125, 126
stock levels, reducing, 56
stock markets, 12
Strannegård, L., 2
strategic management, 5, 97–114
    case studies, 105–12
    financial services context, 103–4
    strategic planning and innovation,
        97–99
Strategic Management Journal, 100
strategy
    corporate strategy, 130
    emergent, 100–1, 101, 108, 112
    'one team' vision and strategy, 149–51,
        155–6
    strategies and tactics, 44
strikes *see* industrial action
striving, 39
structure
    and agency, 186
    organizational structure, 13, 109–10,
        111
Sturdy, A., 67
subjectivity, 44, 95
    insurance company case study, 70, 73,
        74–5
    power/knowledge and, 61–4, 173–4
    teamworking and, 116–24, 140, 141
subjugation, 44, 128–31
success ethic, 9, 38
surplus value, 43–4
surveillance, 140–1
    delayering and, 128–9
    and resistance, 87
    technological, 80
Swedish auto industry, 121
symbolic changes, 84
symbolic interactionism, 57
systems theory, 17, 122

tacit knowledge, 147, 148, 149–52,
        163–5
tactics, 44
Takeuchi, H., 145–6, 148, 149–52, 164–5
Taylor, F.W., 10, 12–15, 46, 147
Taylor, P., 74
team leaders, 136–9
team meetings, 108

teamworking, 5, 97, 115–42
  American Dream, 123–4
  approaches to, 116–24
  Intermotors case study, 5, 124–39,
    139–42, 171, 173, 177–9
  Loanco case study, 81–85, 151–61
  unintended consequences of using
    mature women returnees, 100
  wildcat strike, 125, 134–9, 140, 141,
    142
technical division of labour, 123–4
technological determinism, 145, 146, 155,
  160
technological surveillance, 80
technological trajectories, 9
technology, 145
  IT *see* information technology
  sociotechnical systems approach, 117,
    118–19, 120–1
  the technological and the social, 158–9
  tightening control through, 72–4
Terry, M., 21
Thatcher, M., 4, 21, 23, 24, 25, 168
Thatcherism, 13, 22–5, 25–6
Theory X, 15
'Thinkers, 50' survey, 43
Third Way, 168
Thomas, W.I., 74
Thompson, P., 42, 119, 122, 127
Tidd, J., 41
tight labour markets, 19
time savings, 154
Toffler, A., 47
total quality management (TQM), 4,
  49–73
  Carco case study, 53–7
  critical control, 51–3, 57, 58, 61
  Inco case study, 64–71, 71–3
  power/knowledge and subjectivity,
    61–4
  processual approach, 57–60, 60
  rational managerialism, 50–1, 57, 60
  unintended outcomes, 102–3, 106–10,
    113–14
Trade Dispute Act 1906, 20
trade unions, 122
  Carco case study, 53, 55, 56–7
  growing under New Labour, 25
  Intermotors case study, 124–5, 135–6,
    138–9, 140, 141

  marginalization of, 129
  post-war collective bargaining, 20,
    21
  Thatcherism and, 22, 23
Transport and General Workers Union
  (TGWU), 53
travelling, 28
trim shop, 136–40
Trist, E.K., 118
Trist, E.L., 119, 120–1
true interests, 173–4
Tuckman, A., 53, 123
turbulent environments, 101–2
Turner, F.J., 167–8

unattainable, 33–4
uncertainty, 114
underwriting, 66–7, 182
unemployment, 22
unintended consequences, 5, 99–114
  case studies, 105–13
  financial services context, 103–5
  strategic planning and innovation,
    99–103
United Kingdom (UK), 168
  New Labour, 25–6
  post-war consensus, 20–2
  Thatcherism, 22–5
United States of America (USA), 123–4,
  166–7
  American Dream *see* American
    Dream
unity, 168–9, 172–3, 176–8
unprecedented change, 99
Utopia, 29, 165, 180–1

value, knowledge and, 149
values, 77–8, 131
  humanistic, 34, 181
  see also culture change
Van Mannen, J., 105
variation, 53
video, 83
video surveillance, 130
vision, 131
  Loanco case study, 149–51, 158–9
Vogel, E.F., 120–1, 123–4
Von Krogh, G., 147, 148, 150, 160
Vroom, V.H., 18, 119
Vurdubakis, T., 140

Wageman, R., 46
Wallace, T., 120, 124, 129
waste elimination, 53
Waterman, R., 32, 36, 38, 39, 43, 77, 120, 168
Watson, T.J., 17, 43
Webb, J., 59
Weber, M., 10, 44–5, 58, 102
Whitehead, T.N., 16
Whitley Consultation Committees, 20
Wickens, P., 121, 122, 123
wildcat strike, 124, 134–40, 141, 142, 143
Wilde, O., 29
Wilkinson, A., 59, 103, 104
Wilkinson, B., 120, 158
Williams, R.L., 148
Willmott, H., 77, 78, 87, 102
Wilson, P., 149

Winsor, R.D., 53
Winter of Discontent, 21
Womack, J., 23, 120, 122, 123, 124, 125
women returnees, 103
Woodward, J., 119
Wooldridge, A., 46, 47
Woolgar, S., 152, 158
work dissatisfaction, 17
work study, 14, 65–7
work tracking system, 70–2
World War II, 20, 22
WorldCom, 12

Xerox Corporation Palo Alto Research Centre (PARC), 148

zero defects, 129
Zinn, H., 30

RISK, ENVIRONMENT AND SOCIETY
ONGOING DEBATES, CURRENT ISSUES AND FUTURE PROSPECTS

Piet Strydom

- How and why have the closed expert debates of past decades become an open public discourse about nuclear, environmental and biotechnological risks?
- What can a cultural and institutional analysis reveal about risks and their social construction?
- Is it possible to develop a new critical theory of the risk society?

This book offers an overview and analysis of nuclear, global environmental and biotechnological dangers, threats and hazards in the context of public debates about risk from the 1950s to the present. It considers what impact these risks and debates are having on society, transforming underlying cultural assumptions (for example about nature) but also public communication, social institutions, and even the way society is organized. Piet Strydom reconstructs public debates and social scientific theories to provide a fresh approach to the risk society. From this comes a new theoretical perspective for studying the emerging social conditions of the twenty-first century. The result is a penetrating and essential text for students and researchers across a range of areas including sociology, environmental studies, politics, and cultural and communications studies.

Contents
Series editor's foreword – Preface & acknowledgements – Introduction – Part one: problems, debates, frameworks and theories – The risk discourse: the contemporary concern with risk – Background theories and frameworks of understanding – Major theoretical directions – Part two: cultural and institutional analysis – Risk: what is it? – Societal production of risk: society as laboratory – Discursive construction of risk: the new public sphere – Consensus and conflict in the risk society – Part three: rethinking the risk society – Towards a new critical theory – Conclusion – References – Index.

208pp   0 335 20783 9 (Paperback)   0 335 20784 7 (Hardback)

GOVERNING SOCIETIES
DILEMMAS, DIAGNOSES, DEPARTURES

Mitchell Dean

- Given that governance is supposed to have displaced government, how do we proceed to govern societies and individuals today?
- What modalities of power are involved in governing societies and how are they connected?
- How is the liberal idea of governing through freedom linked to the increasing control of marginalized populations and of those who are non-citizens?

Many people in academia, as in politics and business, today question the idea of being able to govern society. Theories of globalization and individualization, and ideas of governance and governmentality, present a story of the displacement of the nation state and sovereign government by the polycentric networks of governance. Social scientists urged us to dispense with the 'container view of society' and contemplate the 'death of the social'. But should we? Is it really possible to discard such notions if we wish to analyse how to attain security, prosperity and welfare? Have we reached the end of history in which governing largely concerns self-governing individuals, networks and communities? This book radically re-examines these ideas. It provides an overview of current perspectives and theories, and examines recent transformations in techniques and rationalities of rule. It presents a new argument for the importance and transformation of sovereignty and powers of life and death and how they are integral to governing liberal-democratic societies.

Contents

Series editor's foreword – Part one: Dilemmas – Government, governance, and governmentality – Culture, governance and individualization – Part two: Diagnoses – Powers of freedom, powers of life and death – Authoritarian practices and liberal democracies – Part three: Departures – Changing problematics of security – Politics and the meaning of life – World order and international government – References – Index.

160pp   0 335 20897 5 (Paperback)   0 335 20898 3 (Hardback)